Creating
Integrated
Curriculum

**CORWIN
PRESS**

The Corwin Press logo—a raven striding across an open book—
represents the happy union of courage and learning. We are a
professional-level publisher of books and journals for K–12 educators, and we are committed to creating and providing resources
that embody these qualities. Corwin's motto is "Success for All
Learners."

Creating Integrated Curriculum

Proven Ways to Increase Student Learning

Susan M. Drake

CORWIN PRESS, INC.
A Sage Publications Company
Thousand Oaks, California

For information:

Corwin Press, Inc.
A Sage Publications Company
2455 Teller Road
Thousand Oaks, California 91320
E-mail: order@corwinpress.com

SAGE Publications Ltd.
6 Bonhill Street
London EC2A 4PU
United Kingdom

SAGE Publications India Pvt. Ltd.
M-32 Market
Greater Kailash I
New Delhi 110 048 India

Printed in the United States of America

Library of Congress Cataloging-in-Publication Data

Drake, Susan M., 1944-
  Creating integrated curriculum: Proven ways to increase
student learning/by Susan M. Drake.
    p. cm.
  Includes bibliographical references and index.
    ISBN 0-8039-6716-0 (cloth: acid-free paper)
    ISBN 0-8039-6717-9 (pbk.: acid-free paper)
    1. Interdisciplinary approach in education—United States. 2.
Interdisciplinary approach in education—Canada. 3.
Education—United States—Curricula. 4.
Education—Canada—Curricula. 5. Education—Standards—United
States. 6. Education—Standards—Canada. I. Title.
    LBI570 .D73 1998
    374' .000973—dc21   98-9034

This book is printed on acid-free paper.

98 99 00 01 02 03 10 9 8 7 6 5 4 3 2 1

Production Editor: Sherrise Purdum/Diana Axelsen
Corwin Editorial Assistant: Kristen L. Gibson
Editorial Assistant: Denise Santoyo
Designer/Typesetter: Danielle Dillahunt
Indexer: Teri Greenberg

CONTENTS

✳ ✳ ✳

PREFACE   ix
    An Overview of the Contents   xii

ACKNOWLEDGMENTS   xvii

ABOUT THE AUTHOR   xix

1. WHAT IS INTEGRATED CURRICULUM
   AND WHY IS IT IMPORTANT?   1
    Why Is Curriculum Integration Important?   2
    Why Should Integrated Curriculum
      Be a Part of the New Story?   11
    What Is Integrated Curriculum?   18
    Summary   23

2. DOES INTEGRATED
   CURRICULUM WORK?   25
    What Type of Research Counts?   26
    What Is the Background of Integrated Studies?   27
    The 8-Year Study   28
    How Do Interdisciplinary Studies Relate to
      Postsecondary Destinations?   30

When Doesn't Integration Work?   32
Student Benefits   33
Effect on Teachers   40
Summary   42

3. CREATING MULTIDISCIPLINARY
   PROGRAMS   43
   Fusion   44
   Integrating the Subdisciplines   46
   Parallel or Multidisciplinary?   47
   Standards-Based
        Multidisciplinary Curriculum   50
   Summary   56

4. USING INTERDISCIPLINARY
   APPROACHES   60
   A Theme Approach   61
   The Human Connections Model   68
   The Interdisciplinary Concept Model
        With Essential Questions   71
   Concept-Based Integrated Units
        With Essential Questions   76
   Summary   91

5. EXPLORING TRANSDISCIPLINARY APPROACHES   92
   Problem-Based Learning   93
   Story as an Organizing Center   97
   Negotiating the Curriculum   113
   Collaborative Planning Process   116
   A Study of Reality: A Supradisciplinary Approach   120
   Summary   123

6. CONNECTING STANDARDS
   TO CURRICULUM   124
   What Is Worth Knowing?   126
   What Is a Standards-Based Approach?   127
   The Problems With Standards   128
   Defining Standards   128
   The Story of Developing This Model   143
   Assessing a Curriculum Model   147

Summary   148

7. ALIGNING TEACHING,
   LEARNING, AND ASSESSMENT   150
   What Does Alignment Mean?   152
   Constructivism   153
   Using Story to Determine Teaching,
       Learning, and Assessment Principles   154
   Proven Strategies to Integrate the Curriculum   156
   Multiple Intelligences   162
   Brain-Based Education   164
   Teaching Across the Curriculum   169
   Assessment   172
   Dealing With Diversity   173
   Summary   175

8. OVERCOMING THE OBSTACLES
   AND FINDING SUCCESS   177
   Overcoming Obstacles   177
   On Being a Change Agent   189
   Leadership   191
   Summary   197

RESOURCES   198

RESOURCE A: BOOKS   199

RESOURCE B: JOURNALS   208

RESOURCE C: VIDEOS   210

RESOURCE D: NEWSLETTERS   211

RESOURCE E: PROGRAMS   212

REFERENCES   213

INDEX   225

PREFACE

✳ ✳ ✳

It was the early seventies. Thirty-six grade 9 tech boys sat in rows in front of me. I was a new teacher and my department head was inspecting me. The scheduled lesson was grammar. I had dreaded this day. At the best of times, I had a difficult time holding these boys' attention. Unlike some of the other teachers in the school, I had no luck with discipline by threat. If I yelled at anyone, my shouts were greeted with peals of laughter. And now I was faced with teaching grammar—a disaster waiting to happen!

The lesson commenced. The boys were not uproariously bad. There were no spitballs, no curses, no outright rebellions. Instead, they sat quietly for the 45 minutes. I was relieved. As a class, we were parsing the sentences that I had put on the board. There was only one thing not quite right. I shifted between more difficult and easy questions. The boys dutifully answered but, regardless of the question that I asked, the answer was always wrong.

I sensed the conspiracy, but hoped that my department head could not. The lesson passed uneventfully, even if I had to correct each answer. Finally it was over, and the boys filed silently out of the room. I breathed a sigh of relief, thinking that the ordeal was over.

My department head met with me to discuss the lesson. He didn't begin with pleasantries. His words cut to the core. In short, he told me that I should quit teaching. "You can't spend a lifetime facing young people who treat you like that." No word on how the young men had learned nothing about grammar.

As soon as he was finished, I rushed to the ladies room and let the tears flow. I wasn't going to be a teacher. What was I going to do? I had a young child to support. I couldn't imagine any other job. The department head was quite right, however. I didn't want to spend the rest of my life trying to teach students that I assumed weren't willing to learn.

I clearly did not have the classroom management skills to discipline students. I had no brute force behind me, no authority in my voice. I could think of only one recourse. I would have to make the lessons so interesting that the students would want to learn. They would be good in my classes because they were so engaged in the learning that they wouldn't think of spending their time trying to upset me.

Thus began my personal quest.

I scoured existing books on teaching, and finally found one that offered lessons on body language and voice for English classes. It was a departure from what was I was expected to teach, but it sounded like fun. The lessons involved dancing and mime. This was a natural direction for a teacher who spent the rest of her teaching schedule in the gym. My classes soon gained a reputation for being quite unconventional. Students who were not in the class would peep in the window to see what they were missing. And I rarely had another class like the one with the grade 9 tech boys.

As I learned how to hold students' attention, I discovered several rules of thumb. The most important one was that the students felt the lesson was relevant to them. Eventually I developed a full-credit health course that the students labeled *psychology*. It was a very popular course that students from grade 10 to grade 13 enrolled in. The class included students who had been identified on both ends of the scale from gifted to at-risk. In hindsight, this was a multiage inclusive classroom. It worked because the text was the students' lives. Students learned life skills as we covered the content on wellness from many perspectives.

I have spent the rest of my educational career trying to unlock the secrets of learning and teaching. This has led me directly to integrated approaches to education. Today, I am joined by many kindred spirits. Few of them are like I was, searching desperately for a classroom management tool. The quest is the same, however. What is important for students to know? How do students learn best? How can we teach so that we are capitalizing on the most effective ways to learn?

Today, the assumptions underlying education are being challenged in almost every conceivable way. There is no clear picture of a universal model of education that will work under all circumstances. Rather, many different groups are trying different approaches in an attempt to revamp classroom learning in ways that enable students to learn best.

Integrating the curriculum is one of the most popular explorations that is ongoing at all levels of educational reform. There is no common definition for curriculum integration, however. As a result, many versions of integration are being adapted for classroom use. As well, there is a lack of a common language to discuss these different approaches, and therefore there is much confusion around potentially fruitful discussions.

This book offers detailed descriptions of different approaches to integration. The key ideas of the model are explored, and examples are given to illustrate how these approaches could be applied in a classroom. Some examples were created by practicing teachers enrolled in my integrated curriculum graduate education course at Brock University and Ontario Institute for Studies in Education, University of Toronto. Others were created by teachers in the field.

Most books on integration discuss only one framework. This book is unique in that it illustrates the work of a range of curriculum theorists rather than presenting applications from only one author's repertoire. The examples of the frameworks of popular authors include elementary, middle, and high school settings. All approaches are intended to be generic, however, and can be adapted for use at any level.

An underlying theme of this book and all the approaches explored is a new vision of teaching and learning. In this vision, standards, assessment, teaching strategies, content, and reporting are aligned with how people learn best. Students are active learners involved in meaningful tasks that are often set in real-life contexts. Integrated approaches facilitate this type of learning.

This book is intended to clarify some of the mysteries surrounding curriculum integration. Educators can make more informed curricular choices when they are aware of the range of approaches and the unique aspects inherent in them. This book is written for educators, curriculum specialists, and classroom teachers who are curriculum planners and interested in designing more integrated approaches. Any discipline area can successfully become more integrated. There are examples of successful projects at all levels of education. By offering an overview, this book enables educators to make informed choices and choose which approaches they would like to explore in more depth.

An Overview of the Contents

Chapter 1, "What Is Integrated Curriculum and Why Is It Important?" sets the current context. Education in the United States and Canada is undergoing radical and fundamental change. In this sense, educational reform parallels the changes happening in the world in which we live. As other professions, businesses, organizations, and governments redefine how they operate, education must too. The media have acted as a catalyst for loud criticism of education as educators try to negotiate this change. The public is demanding more accountability, demonstrated primarily by higher scores on standardized tests.

Some explorations with innovative ways of teaching are just beginning to show results, yet many people despair that we are simply going back to the traditional model of education. This chapter applies the story model as a framework for understanding some of the seeming chaos. According to the story model, we are not going backwards but are rapidly moving toward a new vision in education. This vision is guided by how people learn best.

This chapter offers a range of degrees of integration, moving from a multidisciplinary to a fully integrated level. None of the approaches is presented as superior to another. Rather, different types fit different purposes. In almost all the types explored, the disciplines are very present.

The chapter also offers a rationale for why integrated approaches offer an ideal teaching approach for our times.

Chapter 2, "Does Integrated Curriculum Work?" reviews the available research on integrated approaches to curriculum. This research comes from a wide range of applications and levels of integration. It reflects an upward trend in increased standardized test scores for students who are in integrated programs. The measurement of the success of these programs by increases in standardized test scores is challenged. Most teachers who teach this way are teaching for understanding and transference of learning—criteria not addressed by such tests.

The evidence clearly supports the fact that school is much more inviting when these types of programs are put in place. Students find learning more relevant. Absenteeism drops and discipline problems decrease. Teachers also benefit by experiencing a renewal of personal energy through collaboration with others and taking on the role of teacher as leader.

Concerns that students will not do well in college are addressed by the success of students involved in the 8-Year Study. Examples are also given of how universities and colleges are redefining themselves and the programs they offer.

Multidisciplinary approaches are featured in Chapter 3, "Creating Multidisciplinary Programs." In these examples, the disciplines are stressed. The content is parallel or connected to other subject areas, however. A program using visiting artist educators is described as an example of fusion. A 3-year overview of a successful integrated science program is offered as an example of integration within a discipline itself. This program from the University of Alabama, with over 170,000 students, has many of the elements common to interdisciplinary approaches. Finally, a fully developed standards-based curriculum is presented based on the work of Harris and Carr (1996). This example will be useful to planners who want a sound but basic way to begin curriculum planning with standards.

Chapter 4, "Using Interdisciplinary Approaches," offers four interdisciplinary approaches in detail. The disciplines are easily discernible in these examples; activity planning is still focused on individual subject areas. Each one has a common theme around which to organize content. Each one also emphasizes different aspects of curriculum as key to ensuring a level of connection across disciplines. Robin Fogarty's (1991) 10 curriculum models are shown, and the webbed model is explored further. This particular model is a good example of how many successful first efforts at integration started. Activities, goals, and assessment all revolve around a "fertile" theme. The web is used as the graphic for brainstorming content and activities.

Roger Taylor's (1996) human connection model goes one step further with themes. He begins with a universal theme and then adds 10 human activity categories that can be applied to the universal theme. He also adds critical thinking, moral reasoning, and creative thinking to the mix. Rather than a free-wheeling process of brainstorming to determine content and activities, this model requires filling in a large number of categories to determine the curriculum.

Heidi Hayes Jacobs's (1989) interdisciplinary model is also well-known. Teachers see an instant logic to this approach and how they can apply it to their classrooms. Jacobs stresses guiding questions as a way to connect content beyond the common theme. She also ensures depth in the curriculum by setting out a detailed approach to generating activities and assessment using Bloom's (1956) taxonomy.

The final approach, from Lyn Erickson (1995, in press), is a concept-based one. Curriculum planners spend time deciding what is worth knowing and applying the structure of knowledge. Working with concepts requires students to use higher-order thinking. One level higher than concepts are essential understandings or generalizations. For Erickson, the essential understandings are how the curriculum is connected at its highest level. This is a thoughtful approach that asks teachers to rethink some of the basics of education.

Chapter 5, "Exploring Transdisciplinary Approaches," presents a variety of transdisciplinary models. *Transdisciplinary* refers to transcending or working beyond the disciplines. The disciplines are not necessarily in the planning stage. Rather, the real-life context is of utmost importance. The chapter begins with the principles behind problem-based learning and offers several examples from real classrooms. This approach holds great promise. It can be applied in one discipline and actively involves the student in problem solving. Apart from the real-life context, problem-based learning is familiar enough to be accepted by parents and the public. What is exciting about problem-based learning is that students respond to solving real-life problems and it demands that the classroom look very different than a traditional one.

Two narrative approaches are offered. These models have much in common. The basic premise is that we make meaning through stories. Hence, if we are to create meaningful curriculum, story should play a part in it. The first approach is the narrative curriculum developed by Carol Lauritzen and Michael Jaegar (1997). They use stories to connect knowledge. The second approach is the story model (Drake et al., 1992), and it is both a transdisciplinary model and the framework used in this book to explain the current situation in education. As a curriculum model, it has been used from K-12 and beyond. It develops a personal, cultural, and global story as the context for any topic being studied.

The next examples of transdisciplinary approaches move into more radical territory. Negotiating the curriculum (Boomer, 1992) can occur in any existing classroom, but negotiation does not begin with a set curriculum. The teacher selects a topic, and he or she and the students are all a part of the negotiations. The lessons are generated from four questions.

- What do we know about the topic?
- What do we need to know?
- How will we learn it?
- How will we know that we know it?

James Beane's (1997) collaborative planning model is more radical than the negotiation of the curriculum. The lessons begin from the students' questions, not some predetermined topic. There are two questions from which the curriculum is generated:

- What questions or concerns do you have about yourself?
- What questions or concerns do you have about your world?

Finally Marion Brady's (1989) conceptual framework of reality is presented. Brady, unlike any of the other models on this book, totally rejects the disciplines. He believes that they should be replaced by a holistic curriculum where all knowledge is integrated into one conceptual framework. Hence, he provides a master conceptual framework.

Chapter 6, "Connecting Standards to Curriculum," explores how to connect standards to integrated curriculum. This chapter uses a framework of content (information and procedural) and lifelong and character standards—know, do, be. Typical content standards are analyzed. The issue of how students will "be" with the knowledge and skills they obtain is addressed. Multidisciplinary approaches are linked with content standards; interdisciplinary standards include lifelong standards, whereas transdisciplinary approaches address character standards. Measurement of the achievement of these standards becomes progressively more difficult as one moves from content standards to lifelong and character ones. This is one of the problems with implementation.

An interdisciplinary standards-based curriculum is presented in detail. It is accompanied by a story of how this curriculum was developed and describes some of the shifts in beliefs that occurred during the process.

The principles of learning are the dominant feature of Chapter 7, "Aligning Teaching, Learning, and Assessment." These principles are embedded in the descriptions of curriculum innovations in the previous chapters. It is from the principles of learning that all other aspects of curriculum are rationalized. Teaching and assessment must align with the learning principles. An exploration of what this alignment of the curriculum means follows.

Stories of educators' good and bad educational experiences are culled for learning principles and compared to constructivist theory. Frameworks for integrating the curriculum are offered in some detail. Renate and Geoffry Caine's (1997) brain-based education approach is presented along with Jim Curry and John Samara's (1990) matrix for curriculum development using Bloom's (1956) taxonomy. Multiple intelligences are described, and Robin Fogarty and Judy Stoehr's (1995) view of how to apply these to integrated curricula is offered.

Strategies for teaching across the curriculum are also described, including storytelling, graphic organizers, and the student as researcher. Assessment aligned with learning principles is also discussed.

Implementing integrated curriculum can be a struggle until one begins to think in an interdisciplinary way. There are many obstacles to overcome. Some of these are personal ones. Others come from external roadblocks. Chapter 8, "Overcoming the Obstacles and Finding Success," identifies potential obstacles and offers solutions from people who have managed to navigate them. Finally, there is a section on how to be a change agent. Although there are countless good reasons to implement an integrated model, it still seems to be true that those who take the plunge find themselves in the position of being a change agent. This part of the chapter describes the nature of change and how it has been successfully managed.

ACKNOWLEDGMENTS

✳ ✳ ✳

There are so many people that have made this book possible that it is impossible to name them all. First I must acknowledge the generous support of the Social Sciences and Humanities Research Council of Canada, who funded the researching of this project. Second, I am deeply grateful to all the students in my masters of education classes, who learned along with me the intricacies of different approaches. Some of their work is highlighted in this book, but there were many more excellent examples that I could have selected.

The people who helped with the technical end of this book were indispensable. Barbara Drewette, who kick-started the process, and Rachel Basaraba and Trevor Shears, who jumped in when I reached crisis state, are all appreciated for their contributions. A special thanks goes to Daphne Zuliani for her excellent comments on the manuscript and to Tony DiPetta for always being there when I needed him.

To my colleagues in the field, I thank you for the endless hours of dialogue and experimentation in our search for better ways to reach students. At Merritton High School, Bruce Hemphill, Joan Sturch, and Ron Chappell all added to a deep understanding of integrated approaches. Thanks to Betty Tieche and the Lincoln County School Board, who gave me the opportunity to work with these and other dedicated teachers. Jan Basaraba, Marg Jarvis, and Lenke Tucci collaboratively explored the story model in their classrooms with me. Thank you.

I also am very grateful to the many different groups and organizations that have entrusted me with inservicing and consulting. I have learned so much through working with educators across the United States and Canada. This is an exhilarating time to be in education, and I have been lucky to have worked with many exciting and positive people. Their spirits and vision have inspired me to continue the search.

Thanks also goes to Corwin Press and Alice Foster for their belief in this project from the beginning.

And finally, to my family and friends who supported me through all the ups and downs of writing this book, I thank you all very much.

This research was funded in part by the Social Sciences and Humanities Research Council of Canada (Grant #410-94-1120).

ABOUT THE AUTHOR

✳ ✳ ✳

Susan M. Drake has taught at all levels of education, spending 20 years at the high school and elementary level. Now she works in the Department of Graduate Studies, Faculty of Education, Brock University, St. Catharines, Ontario. She coordinates the Integrated Studies program for the Masters of Education Program. She is coauthor of *Holistic Learning: A Teachers' Guide to Integrated Learning* (1990). She was funded by the Curriculum Superintendents of Ontario to head a provincial team to refine her ideas on interdisciplinary curriculum, resulting in *Developing Integrated Curriculum Using the Story Model* (1992). She has written numerous articles on integration and authored *Planning for Integrated Curriculum: The Call to Adventure* (1993). In 1997, she wrote a research paper for the Ministry of Ontario Education and Training, providing background

on interdisciplinary studies for high school reform policy. She has
been involved with extensive inservicing for teachers in the United
States, Canada, South Africa, Thailand, and Japan. She taught integrated curriculum courses at the graduate level at Brock University,
Ontario Institute for Studies in Education, University of Toronto, the
University of Colorado at Denver, and Goddard College in Vermont.
Her expertise comes from practice rather than theory. Through a
research grant provided by the Social Sciences and Humanities Research Council of Canada (SSHRC), she attended workshops given
by most of the developers of the models in this book. She also was
involved in a 3-year research project funded by SSHRC that explored
how teachers create new models of education in real-life contexts.

1

XXXXXX

WHAT IS INTEGRATED CURRICULUM AND WHY IS IT IMPORTANT?

✳ ✳ ✳

Grade 9 students are presenting their work to other grade 9 classes in a workshop format. They are armed with a standard research report and a variety of artwork, models, and other innovative ways to teach the knowledge that they have gleaned from their own research on their own environmental question. Many different skills have been learned in their quest. They have had to use information management, computer skills, reading, writing, creativity, analysis, synthesis, and evaluation. They have also had to learn presentation skills.

In a similar grade 9 class, the teacher wanted to integrate language skills into the science class. He worked hard to connect knowledge bases and create an interesting and integrated curriculum. This curriculum was then presented to the students through the teacher's usual lecture format and evaluated by a written exam. The teacher was disappointed when the students did not respond much differently than they had to his discipline-based curriculum.

This book examines curriculum integration. It is not about connecting knowledge bases and going about business as usual, however. Knowledge can be very integrated, but students may not be motivated to learn. This book explores a range of curriculum integration approaches that motivate students. It is not so much about curriculum integration as it is about a radically different way of thinking about the teaching and learning process. Curriculum integration involves shifting all aspects of curriculum design to align with what we know about the learning process.

Why Is Curriculum Integration Important?

Exploring what is happening in education from a larger context helps one understand where we are going and how curriculum integration fits into this bigger picture.

Educational Reform in a Personal Context

As I listen to educators across North America, I am troubled by their distress. Similar conversations echo similar concerns everywhere. I cannot accept educators' laments that we are moving backward after efforts at innovation have just begun to meet with success. Rather, I believe that we are continuing to move forward. These seeming steps backward are, in reality, the steps necessary to move forward to create a "new story" in education.

My situation is not much different from that of my colleagues across North America. I live in Ontario, where educational change has been escalating at an unprecedented rate. It seems as if we are stuck—or worse than stuck. After some valiant struggles by many teachers to make authentic changes with holistic, integrated approaches, teachers are now being mandated to turn "back to the basics." Document after document has appeared clearly defining the outcomes, expectations, or competencies expected of students in each subject area, and there is an increasing emphasis on standardized testing.

At the same time, the government is mandating new expectations of teachers that range from cutting preparation time and professional development days to creating a College of Teachers intended to monitor the quality of teachers in the province and to ensure lifelong learning. In the classroom, teachers' roles are changing. Mainstreaming means that many teachers feel ill-prepared to teach students with severe disabilities. Teachers often find themselves acting as social workers. In addition, they feel undervalued when the press criticizes them for the failure of students to be at the top in international tests.

These educational changes are occurring at the same time that huge budget cuts are taking place. For teachers, the government's motivation for the radical changes is not to enhance student learning, as suggested in the rhetoric, but simply to decrease costs regardless of the loss of jobs and the violation of the assumed rights of teachers. To add to teachers' frustration, the media generally attacks education as it is being practiced today and concludes that students are not being educated well enough to compete in a global economy. Members of the public quickly pick up on this anxiety and want schools to return to the practices that were in place when they went to school. The press rarely acknowledges that the good old days were never as good as the mythology that surrounds them (Bracey, 1997).

Educational Reform From a Larger Context

The perception of some teachers that we are regressing is understandable and affirmed by some immediate facts. I think that the bigger picture is getting lost in the seeming chaos of our everyday situations, however. The whole world is in the midst of fundamental change. Major professions are shifting their definitions and their roles in the workplace. Educators are finding themselves in no different positions than health care workers, lawyers, police officers, businesspeople, government employees, and church personnel. The old ways, or "old story," does not work any more. This is a result of a complex web of factors introduced into our society, such as a global community, instant communication technology, technological advances, exponential knowledge increases, redefinition of family, shifting demographics, and equity issues.

A first response to the call for educational reform has been new ways of assessment intended to increase accountability. Across North America, national, state, and district organizations are developing rigorous achievement standards for students. Demanding higher standards alone will not raise the quality of education, however. Much more is happening than simply an attempt to redefine standards—reform is penetrating all areas of education.

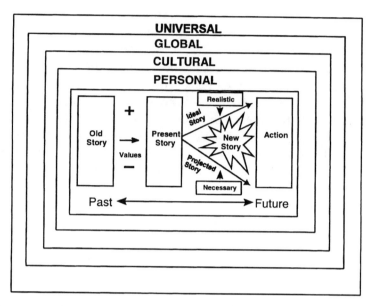

Figure 1.1. Story Model

Using the Story Framework

The story model (Drake et al., 1992) is a framework that is helpful in making sense of the changes. It is actually a curriculum model that is developed later in this book under transdisciplinary approaches, but it helps to understand the bigger picture (see Figure 1.1). The outside frames on Figure 1.1 indicate the filters that affect our learning and knowledge. The story model framework assumes that one way of knowing is through story. We make sense of the world that we live in by "storying" significant events in our lives. Storying is used as a verb to signify our ways of believing, valuing, and acting. Within these stories are our assumptions about the world, the assumptions that drive our actions.

In using the story model to explain the shifts happening in education today, we need to examine our ways of knowing. The first filter is the personal story. Our knowing is influenced primarily by the personal events of our lives. We construct knowledge and make meaning of it through the lens of our personal story, and that is why individuals interpret the same event so differently. Every educator has a different context and thus stories his or her perceptions differently. My own story includes all the experiences that I have had while developing new models of education. These include both research and hands-on experiences. As well, my story includes the mandates of the Ontario government, which are undergoing rapid change.

The second filter is the cultural story. The culture that we live in sends out powerful messages about what is "true." These assumptions and beliefs filter through our personal story, and we often accept these assumptions as fundamental truths. The media, government, schools, and churches perpetuate this cultural story. Ours is a North American story. In Japan, for example, there is a different cultural story. This cultural story influences how we conduct education—the beliefs and assumptions that we accept as unquestioned truths drive our behavior.

Because education is a concern across the planet, we need to consider the global filter, or story. It is by international standards that both American and Canadian students appear to be falling short, which is a catalyst for much of the current furor surrounding education. As well, it is important to know how other systems are adapting to changing times so that we can be aware of the educational picture in its widest sense. An international study looking at innovations in 13 countries notes that all countries participating were dissatisfied with their current system (Atkin & Black, 1997). Although there were different reasons for desiring reform, there were some strong similarities. All countries were putting greater emphasis on a real-life context and, as a result, many were attempting cross-curricular innovations.

Finally, there is a universal story; this is a story that connects us all as human beings regardless of time or culture. All humans demonstrate the same emotions, have similar needs and responses to great art, music, and story. Are there ways in which all people learn? Is this different from the traditional method of the teacher delivering material to passive students? How does this connect to the way in which we teach and assess?

Examining the Old Story

Today, education is in flux and transformation; in many ways, education is in crisis. The bottom line is that the old ways are not working for enough people. To understand what is happening, one needs to revisit the traditional or old story and deconstruct it to

TABLE 1.1 Old Story

Old Story Practices	Embedded Assumptions
The teacher lectures.	The teacher is the expert.
The student is a passive learner.	The student is a blank slate.
The classroom is set up in fixed rows.	The best way to learn is alone.
The bell curve is employed.	Only a very few will demonstrate exceptional success or failure; the majority of students will be average.
Pencil-and-paper measurements are used.	Knowledge worth knowing can be written. Knowledge is linear, sequential, with one right answer.
Standardized tests are emphasized.	Accountability gained through standardized testing allows us to compare students, teachers, districts, states, provinces, and nations.
The status quo is maintained.	A few people will do well, leaving the power structures in place.

discover the assumptions embedded in it. The old story consists of practices presented in Table 1.1.

Challenging the Assumptions

For many reasons, global competitiveness and equity issues among them, we are challenging the assumptions of the old story. At stake are the central questions that have been asked for centuries:

- What is the purpose of education?

- What is worth knowing?

- How do people learn best?

- How do we teach to insure that we are aligned with learning principles?

- Who is in control of education?

In-Between Stories

There will inevitably be tension between polarities as we move to a new story of education and its accompanying shifts in beliefs and practices. One side will be represented by those who want to hold on to the traditional ways of doing things; the other side will be calling for a radically different approach. At one end of the spectrum is the call for "back to the basics," more accountability, standardized testing, and the way things used to be. At the other end, we hear educators advocating a student-centered approach that is individualized and more holistic in nature.

For the past few years, many educators have experimented with innovative programs embedded in a student-centered, constructivist approach. In the view of many traditionalists, it is this student-centered focus that is failing our children. Advocates of the student-centered philosophy believe that this approach is aligned with the ways in which people learn most effectively, however. They contend that this approach has not had enough time to be implemented fully and that, at any rate, standardized student achievement tests are neither the best way in which to evaluate these programs nor the best way to measure what is worth knowing. For them, it is the old story that is failing our children and that will continue to fail them.

Toward a New Story

The new story is emerging and can also be deconstructed. Some practices being explored in the student-centered approach are presented in Table 1.2.

Understanding the Process

Many complex reasons explain why these changing times are so confusing. First, there is the tension between the two sides of this debate. The transformation involves a dialectical process between these two sides, and we will shift back and forth until we come to some acceptable position for all concerned. Second, the new story has not yet been created. We—all the stakeholders—are in the midst of creating the story. Only recently are there sufficient exemplary practices to give us an initial sense of where we are going. Third, the story involves all aspects of curriculum building: content selection,

TABLE 1.2 New Story

New Story Practices	Embedded Assumptions
The teacher is a facilitator of student learning experiences.	The student constructs meaning through relevant experiences.
The student is an active learner.	The student learns by being actively involved.
Teaching for understanding	The learning can be transferred to applicable contexts.
Collaborative learning	The student constructs meaning socially.
Ongoing assessment	Ongoing feedback is used as a learning tool.
Alternative assessments (aligned with instructional strategies)	Knowledge is ambiguous, indeterminate; there are multiple realities and no one right answer.
Emphasis on life and work-related skills	Assessment should demonstrate application of knowledge
Clear expectations	Explicit criteria facilitate student learning.
Cross-disciplinary approaches	The boundaries of discipline are artificial.

standards, assessment, instructional strategies, and reporting. Fourth, because this story is just emerging, it is difficult to understand and connect all pieces at once. There is so much to learn, and no one has all the answers. Most educators have been experimenting with only a part of the picture, be it assessment practices, reporting, curriculum integration, instructional strategies, or standards. In reality, all aspects must be aligned and grounded in a philosophy. This understanding of the interconnectedness of all the parts is only gradually being understood. When we change one aspect—if the change is grounded in a philosophical stance—all parts must change to reflect this.

How these different philosophies will be reconciled or synthesized is only just emerging. Why, for example, can't we teach the basics in a holistic, integrated way? Why can't we combine quantitative and qualitative reporting? Why can't we teach phonics within a whole language approach? Coming to a new story involves trying things in new ways, reflecting on these practices, and then modifying them to find the most effective way.

Parents, not fully understanding this, do not want their children to be experimented on. Teachers themselves often demand to be told the right way to deliver curriculum and resent the continual shifts in curriculum mandates. These shifts occur because curriculum developers and policymakers are learning by active exploration to find a process that accurately reflects their stated beliefs and assumptions. Teachers, not just policymakers, are an active part of creating the new story, and this is understood by most innovative teachers.

In spite of all the resistance, we are definitely moving forward. Some of the shifts that have happened in the personal stories of most teachers are

- An understanding of how outcomes or standards are used
- The importance of performance indicators or criteria
- The necessity of explicitly teaching the skills required to attain outcomes
- The need to explicitly teach life- and work-related skills
- What a rubric or scoring guide is and how to use it
- Alternative forms of assessment
- Variety in teaching strategies

In areas such as curriculum integration, however, the shifts into new ways are not as clear. There are various reasons for this. Integration can come in many forms, and there is no universal model; thus, it is impossible to develop a curriculum where everyone teaches the same content and skills in the same way in every classroom. Reform has usually started with assessment and standards because they address the accountability issues so crucial to a good educational system. Given the changing times and the abundance of new knowledge being generated, however, the adoption of some form of integration seems inevitable.

The current move to develop clear and measurable standards is definitely not a move backwards. Across North America, different stakeholders are developing such standards. Some misunderstandings initially arose from a lack of common definition of what the standards actually represent. The first round of state and provincial guidelines tended to be amorphous and ambiguous. Problems arose with outcomes that were neither measurable nor observable. Others argued that some outcomes fell within the realm of values; and although whether or not teachers should be teaching values is a moot point, it is clear that the attainment of values is very difficult to measure.

There is currently a remarkable similarity among guidelines being developed by all kinds of groups at all levels of education. Regardless of discipline or educational level, the standards tend to be generic, can be applied to a variety of contents, and address the doing aspect of learning. In other words, because it is doing, it can really be defined as a skill. Consider, for example, the following expectations:

- Use and verify estimation strategies (e.g., rounding) to determine the reasonableness of solutions to problems and justify the choice of strategy—grade 6 mathematics. (*The Ontario Curriculum*, Grades 1-8, Mathematics, p. 22)

- Explain their interpretation of a written work, supporting it with evidence from the work and from their own knowledge and experience—grade 8 language. (*The Ontario Curriculum*, Grades 1-8, Language, p. 31)

That the standards are being developed from a discipline-based perspective is seen as a problem by some. A quick glance at most documents, however, reveals that many of the standards are, in fact, cross-disciplinary and can indeed lead to interdisciplinary programming.

We are now in the midst of the dialectical process. Yes, we are going back to the basics, but we are doing so in a fundamentally different way. The basics are being deconstructed in a way that makes both the teacher's and the student's jobs easier; that is, we now acknowledge the criteria that make up the basic skills, along with the "new basics" that are work related or life related, such as organizational, communication, and interpersonal skills.

True, assessment methods have not yet been fully aligned with the new standards. Innovative curriculum seems to take a backseat as teachers move from covering the content to covering the standards. But this is part of the dialectical process as we weave back and forth from the old story to the emerging new story. It is important that we take the good things with us from the old story. Time is needed to reflect on what must be changed and what is worth keeping.

As educators, we have to be patient because real change takes a long time. We are all a part of creating the new story. This creation needs to be a collaborative process, and all the voices must be heard. The bottom line must be to act on our beliefs and continue to explore how all the parts interconnect in ways that facilitate students' optimal learning. It is only by our actions as individuals that the new story will become a reality.

Why Should Integrated Curriculum Be a Part of the New Story?

Curriculum integration belongs in the new story because it is usually aligned philosophically with other curriculum reforms. Another reason stands alone when considering some degree of integration at all levels of education, however: the knowledge explosion.

Education today is set in an ever-changing context. Reforms are occurring everywhere, including social security, health care, and welfare. Integrated studies can offer some solutions within this new context. With the present information explosion, it is impossible to teach everything. On the Internet, students can obtain information on any number of topics that cannot be divided neatly into discrete disciplines. Interdisciplinary curriculum helps teachers deal with the inherent complexity of the world, overcomes rigid perceptions of subject boundaries, and supports the claim that all knowledge is interrelated (Martin-Kniep, Fiege, & Soodak, 1995).

It Reduces Duplication

At a time when there is so much to know, there is a problem with duplication in the curriculum. For example, in one typical high school, the schedule allows for a student to study global warming in grade 10 geography, grade 10 science, grade 11 environmental studies, and grade 12 environmental science. An interdisciplinary program such as environmental science would eliminate these overlaps and allow students to explore the topic from a variety of lenses that are interconnected and connected to the real world.

Preparation for the Workplace

Public education is under severe stress. Public anxiety about perceived falling educational standards is coupled with increased demands for high school graduates with higher skill levels. The world of work is changing in fundamental ways. Dagget (1995) points out that 50% of the workforce was unskilled in 1950; in 1994, 33% were unskilled; and he predicts that by 2000 only 15% of jobs will be unskilled. What are the skills North American graduates must acquire? Certainly, we need students who are skilled with computers; however, given the speed of technological advances, it may be impossible to teach students the actual technological skills they will be using in the future. For example, auto mechanics teachers cannot teach the skills to fix the cars of the future because, by the time the students get into the workplace, the technology of the cars will have changed.

The U.S. Department of Labor (1991) published *What Work Requires of School: A SCANS Report for America 2000,* and in Canada, the Conference Board of Canada (1992) developed an *Employability Skills Profile.* Both documents outline the skills that employers deem necessary for the workplace. These work-related skills are cross-disciplinary and not connected to any particular subject area. They include

- Reading
- Writing
- Basic computation
- Listening
- Speaking
- Creative thinking
- Decision making
- Learning how to learn
- Responsibility for self
- Teamwork skills

The Purpose of School

Today's mandate is for students to "become productive citizens of the 21st century." This means more than just obtaining high grades in school; it means being able to apply the skills learned within real-life contexts. It means education that is concerned with what students know and can do, how they interact with others, and what they will face in the world (Delors, 1996: Drake, 1995). Further, there is a call for "success for all." This is not merely rhetoric; educators are trying to redefine success. Success means being the productive citizen of the 21st century and requires new skills—particularly life skills. Not everyone can be a doctor, but everyone has a talent or ability that can be developed so they will contribute to society.

What Is Worth Knowing?

Our rapidly changing world challenges us to reexamine the essential educational question, "What is worth knowing?" Schools have been charged not only with responsibility for their traditional subject areas, but also with such cross-disciplinary topics as multiculturalism, antiviolence, gender issues, racism, AIDS education, and conflict resolution. Living in a global world, students need to have a global perspective. Some people argue that we should teach only the classics such as Shakespeare; others insist that we include popular culture. In a world where students watch countless hours of television and are profoundly influenced by media, media literacy seems crucial (Duncan, 1996). Having an educated approach to these issues seems essential for the productive citizen of the 21st century.

As educators wrestle with vast amounts of content, there is a continuing shift to generic skills being the most important to learn. These skills do not preclude content; rather, the content is a vehicle for acquiring the skills. For example, it is imperative for students to be technologically literate in the 21st century. Technological studies no longer means just drafting and electricity classes designed for male students; these studies have shifted to a more broadly based technology—an activity-based, process-oriented, project-driven program for all students in which they learn technical knowledge, skills, and values through open-ended problem solving. Students might, for example, design, create, and market their own product using many skills and technologies. Computers can be used to enhance critical thinking and for a variety of educational purposes such as experimentation, inquiry, problem solving, interactive learning, drawing, composing, and role playing. Clearly, these uses are not subject or content specific. Similarly, language skills (reading, writing, and listening) are not specific to English classes, but apply to all classes. In interdisciplinary work, "technology across the curriculum" and "language across the curriculum" are not hollow phrases, but skills that all teachers can attend to.

How Do People Learn?

Relevant Curriculum

Traditional subject-based curriculum does not engage students in learning because it is often irrelevant and provides little challenge (Hargreaves, Earl, & Ryan, 1996). When teaching different subjects, teachers may present knowledge in a fragmented way. Often the only reason teachers give for learning something is that it will be on the test or it will be needed down the road. In contrast, interdisciplinary curriculum is often associated with real-life problems because life is not fragmented into subject areas. For example, the threat of nuclear war brought together scholars who study climate, population patterns, history of past disasters, and philosophy (Fosnot, 1996). A real-life context gives students a reason to learn. Courses that are more theoretical, such as the philosophy of science, offer a larger view of the world and tend to be more relevant, too.

Brain Research

Recently there have been many breakthroughs in understanding how the brain works. The latest theories suggest that there are more than 100 trillion connections in the brain circuitry (Begley, 1996). A baby's brain is 100 trillion neurons just waiting to be wired into a mind. Only 50% of these can be attributed to heredity; the rest are determined by life experiences. Certain types of experiences are necessary because without them, the circuits for music, math, language, and emotion will not form. Apparently there is a right time for different skills to be introduced to develop the proper circuitry that will serve us throughout our lifetime. Once this window of opportunity has passed, it is more difficult to learn. For example, math and logic skills are learned from birth to 4 years. The language brain is developed from birth to 10 years. Applying this research strongly suggests that we need to offer early education experiences.

For example, we need to teach languages before the age of 10 if we want to develop the brain circuitry for the child to speak the language properly.

It is crucial to offer the right experiences at the right time. And it is important that these experiences connect in meaningful ways because this is how the brain processes information to make sense of the world (Caine & Caine, 1997). The more connections we can make to previous knowledge and to our experiences, the more we learn and can apply our learning. This has tremendous implications for how we teach because it leads directly to connecting what we learn.

If we paid attention to brain research, we would not teach as we have been teaching (Hancock, 1996). For example, numerous studies show that students who exercise regularly do better in school. Knowledge also has an emotional component, and students retain more if they connect to the material not only aurally but also emotionally and physically. Music and physical education would occur daily and hands-on learning, drama, and projects would replace lectures and rote memorization. Complex subject areas such as new languages and difficult mathematical skills would be introduced before puberty. In other words, the curriculum would become more integrated.

Sylwester (1995) provides concepts from brain research that he applies to school. He makes a number of interesting connections. For example, teachers should do the following:

- Teach both controlling and releasing emotions in an appropriate way.
- Encourage students to talk about their emotions.
- Use activities that are social in nature.
- Develop activities with an emotional context.
- Avoid stress.
- Connect emotions and health.
- Use both passive and active teaching strategies.
- Teach what is important to know.
- Use discussion, debates, and storytelling activities.
- Attend to the contributions of others through cooperative learning.
- Use role-playing, simulations, songs, games, films, and novels.

- Use multiple intelligences to solve problems that involve temporal, spatial, and personal elements.
- Solve problems collaboratively.
- Use technology (e.g., hypercards, spreadsheets, statistical programs, calculator) to complement teaching the basic skills needed to solve problems.

Conceptions of Intelligence

Gardner's (1983) seminal work on multiple intelligences affects the way we teach. Gardner suggests that we all have at least eight intelligences and that only two, linguistic and mathematical-logical, have been taught and measured in schools. If we teach to incorporate the other six intelligences as well, students can learn more fully. These other six intelligences are musical, spatial, interpersonal, intrapersonal, naturalist, and bodily-kinesthetic.

Goleman's (1996) concept of emotional intelligence has had an effect on current thinking about teaching and learning. This concept corresponds with Gardner's (1983) interpersonal and intrapersonal ways of knowing. Goleman claims that IQ in the traditional sense accounts for only about 20% of the factors that determine life success—leaving 80% to everything else. Thus, it is imperative to teach emotional intelligence (O'Neill, 1996).

In a similar vein, Sternberg (1996) questions what it means to be smart. For him, "successful intelligence" is needed to succeed in the world, and this is not measured by IQ. Some characteristics of successful intelligence are goal setting, identifying strengths and weaknesses, and completing tasks. Most important, the skills for successful intelligence can be taught. (Sternberg, 1997). When teachers employ strategies that include all these intelligences, the curriculum becomes interdisciplinary and allows for students with different learning styles.

Sequential Skills?

Cognitive psychologists are challenging the assumption that the learning of skills is sequential in nature and must proceed from the basic to complex. Recent research (Means & Knapp, 1997) explores how disadvantaged students learn; these students come disproportionately from poor families and ethnic and linguistic minority backgrounds. Disadvantaged students are considered at-risk for school failure. Traditional models suggest that students need to master the basic skills before they can move on to more complex tasks. Newer models challenge these assumptions and suggest that, although disadvantaged students come to school with fewer experiences than other students, they can do more complex tasks before they have mastered the basics; they can be taught the basic skills within the framework of meaningful and relevant contexts; and they benefit with cognitive guided instruction where equal emphasis is put on both the answer and how the students got the answer.

This insight that complex skills may not need to be mastered sequentially is crucial for teachers who perceive their subject areas as sequential. It is these teachers who resist integration.

Means and Knapp (1997) offer principles of learning emerging from cognitive psychology:

- Focus on complex, meaningful problems.
- Teach the basic skills within the more meaningful tasks.
- Connect to the students' culture and out-of-school experiences.
- Model thinking strategies to students.
- Encourage more than one approach to answering a question.
- Modify tasks to provide scaffolding for students during complex tasks
- Dialogue rather than transmit to create the central medium of teaching.

Student Benefits

Interdisciplinary curriculum provides a vehicle for higher-level thinking. When students are challenged to move beyond memorizing facts, to pursue a topic in depth, and to see patterns and relationships, they are engaged in constructing knowledge rather than merely accumulating information. They are also acquiring analysis and synthesis skills (Erickson, 1995).

The emphasis is on *understanding* what we learn, which is demonstrated by what we can do with what we learn. True understanding is shown by the transferability of skills so that students can solve new problems in diverse settings. Understanding is increased by connecting to the real world. Ultimately, when students can transfer learning, they are more employable and they are more likely to become lifelong learners.

Teacher Benefits

When I talk with teachers who have begun to teach in integrated ways, there are two comments that almost always seem to go together. These teachers are exhausted, but this is more than balanced by the excitement they feel and the fact that they usually feel more energized than at any other time in their careers. Once they have planned their curriculum in this way for a while, it becomes second nature and the exhaustion fades.

Many of the rewards come from working collaboratively, often for the first time, with other teachers. Other rewards are derived from the reception of students. For the students, school becomes a more inviting place to be. There are fewer discipline and attendance problems because students tend to be more engaged in the learning.

When a teacher enters this territory, he or she also becomes a learner. New connections are made and new strategies are tried. The teacher is no longer necessarily the expert in the classroom; rather, he or she now models the lifelong learner that the students are encouraged to be. Thus, developing and implementing an integrated approach to curriculum can be professional development at its finest.

What Is Integrated Curriculum?

Integrated curriculum can be defined in many ways. Most experts believe that there is a continuum along which progressively more and more connections are made (Figure 1.2). Jacobs (1989), Burns (1995), and Fogarty (1991) all present a continuum that appears to be evolutionary in nature. Burns, for example, interprets the continuum as evolutionary, and she aligns each position with curriculum, instruction, assessment, and classroom culture. Erickson (1995) differentiates between a lower-level form of integration (multidisciplinary) and a higher form that calls for higher-order thinking (interdisciplinary). She agrees that teachers tend to start from the multidisciplinary and move to interdisciplinary.

Hargreaves et al. (1996) caution curriculum planners that one problem with continuums can be that they often embody implicit values that suggest that any movement along the continuum is growth, or growth toward a more progressive state. They warn that progress along the continuum may not be better; it may be worse. They point to Case's (1991) typology, which offers many dimensions with which to understand integration in all its possible complexities. Case offers four different modes or types of integration (fusion, insertion, correlation, harmonization), four forms of integration (content, skills-processes, school and self, underlying principles), four purposes (important issues, wider view of the subjects, seamless web of knowledge, reduced redundancy), and two dimensions (horizontal, vertical).

Case (1991) demonstrates that a common understanding of curriculum integration can be complex. Jacobs (1997) simplifies the task somewhat and offers a process for curriculum mapping that allows for both horizontal (across one grade) and vertical (K-12) integration. Jacobs claims that every teacher should go through the process of mapping his or her own curriculum, and *Mapping the Big Picture* reminds us that we have to consider the big picture.

Not everyone believes in a continuum or in many complex variations. Beane (1995) claims that there is only one form of integration, and that is an approach that uses students' questions to generate the curriculum. For him, any other form of integration is not authentic.

When I look back on my original work (Drake, 1993) I am aware that I, too, developed a continuum that moved from multidisciplinary to interdisciplinary to transdisciplinary. At the time, I saw distinct differences in the philosophy and techniques that educators use when they develop curricula; they seemed to move into more degrees of integration as they made more connections. Then, as now, it seemed clear that one position is not superior to another; rather, different approaches are more appropriate than others according to the context in which they are used.

Curriculum development has advanced since I developed these orientations. Whether one is planning for a discipline-based curriculum or an interdisciplinary one, many elements will exist in common, given the shift to a standards-based approach. Harris and Carr's (1996) book *How to Use Standards in the Classroom* offers a sound standards-based planning strategy that fits the entire range of curriculum planning.

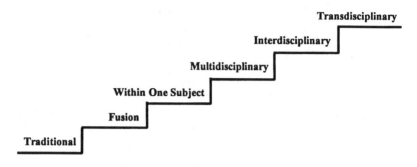

Figure 1.2. Continuum of Integration

Interdisciplinary studies have a wide range of definitions in different settings. In 1973, Pring differentiated between interdisciplinary (the use of more than one discipline to pursue an inquiry) and integration (assuming that knowledge is interconnected). Over time, these distinctions have become blurred. This book includes a range of definitions under the umbrella of integrated studies. It also uses the term *standards* as an umbrella to include terms that are currently in use, such as *outcomes, expectations,* and *competencies.*

The continuum, as it is being interpreted by many schools, is illustrated in Figure 1.2. A brief description of these positions follows.

- *Traditional.* The material is taught through the lens of only one discipline, such as science or English.

- *Fusion.* A topic is inserted into several subject areas. For example, one school fuses environmental issues, social responsibility, and social action into single courses such as geography or English.

- *Within one subject.* The subdisciplines are integrated within one subject area, such as physics, chemistry, and biology integrated as science.

- *Multidisciplinary.* The disciplines are connected through a theme or issue that is studied during the same time frame, but in separate classrooms (Figure 1.3). In elementary school, students may rotate through learning centers representing different subject areas. Generally, students are expected to

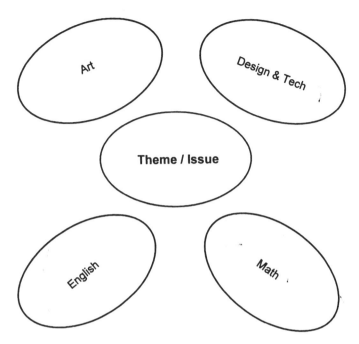

Figure 1.3. Multidiscplinary

make the connections among subject areas rather than having them taught explicitly.

- *Interdisciplinary.* Interdisciplinary curriculum has many different variations. The subjects are interconnected in some way beyond the common theme or issue. These connections are made explicit to the students. The curriculum may be tied together by guiding questions, a common conceptual focus, or cross-disciplinary standards (Figure 1.4).

- *Transdisciplinary.* This approach transcends the disciplines and is found in many different forms. It differs from the other approaches because it does not begin with the disciplines in the planning process; rather, the planning begins from a real-life context (Figure 1.5). The disciplines are embedded in the learning, but the focus does not start there. This approach can include cross-disciplinary outcomes, but often emphasizes personal growth and social responsibility.

Some examples of transdisciplinary approaches:

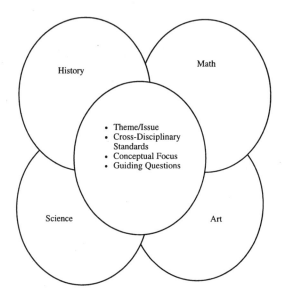

History

Math

• Theme/Issue
• Cross-Disciplinary
  Standards
• Conceptual Focus
• Guiding Questions

Science

Art

Figure 1.4. Interdisciplinary

■ The curriculum revolves around a social issue or problem in a real-life context.

■ Brady (1989) suggests we use the relationships among the environment, perceptions of reality, patterns of action, and humans as the organizing focus rather than the disciplines.

■ In the story model, students use a real-life context as the organizing focus (Drake et al., 1992). A topic such as "water" would be examined considering the influence of social, political, economic, media, global, environmental, and technological aspects.

■ In the project method, students actively solve a real-life problem such as building a house from scratch.

■ With the *negotiating the curriculum* approach, the teacher negotiates the knowledge, skills, activities, and assessment procedures with the students. The students begin with a predetermined content area such as demographics and determine their prior knowledge. They then negotiate with the teacher to establish what it is necessary to know, how to learn it, and

Figure 1.5. Transdisciplinary

how to assess what is learned. Allowing students control over their learning has been shown to increase academic achievement and well-being (Kohn, 1993).

■ Beane (1993) approaches integration through questions generated by students rather than predetermining the topic. He finds that students ask deep questions that revolve around social and personal issues and that sound curriculum can be built on these questions.

Summary

This chapter presented a range of different approaches to curriculum that can be considered integrated. These approaches represent a very different way of thinking about curriculum and all aspects of curriculum planning.

Education was explored from a larger context to understand the basic assumptions underlying the traditional factory model of education. This is referred to as the old story of education. The premises of the new story of education were also explored because curriculum integration is usually assumed (not necessarily correctly) to involve new ways of teaching and learning.

A rationale for integration was offered. Curriculum integration is only a small part of the large shifts occurring in educational thinking today. The world we are living in is changing, and education must change with it. If we live in an interconnected and interdependent world, it only makes sense that knowledge be presented as interconnected and interdependent.

2

✳✳✳✳✳✳

Does Integrated
Curriculum Work?

✳ ✳ ✳

International High in Queens, New York City, has 450 students who
come from 56 countries and speak 40 different languages. At ad-
mittance, all students have been in the United States for less than 4
years and have low English proficiency scores. The entire day is interdisciplinary and explores themes such as "the world of money."
Students participate in the development of the courses. The gradu-
ation rate is over 95%, and more than 90% of graduates go on to
college. Virtually all students pass the required New York State Re-
gents Competency tests in all subjects (Sadowski, 1995).

At Merritton High School in St. Catherines, Ontario, science
teachers integrated grade 9 science with other subjects. With the
advice of the English department, they taught a science fiction novel
while exploring scientific concepts and skills. They did traditional
science activities, but also incorporated drama, webbing, computer
graphing, and presentation skills. During the culminating activity,
students taught what they had learned to other students in a workshop setting. Teachers commented on how students demonstrated a
true understanding of their topics (Drake, Hemphill, & Chappell,
1996).

What Type of
Research Counts?

The first example illustrates the quantitative research evidence required before there is widespread public acceptance of an integrated approach. The second example is more common, but qualitative examples are often dismissed as anecdotal. There is not sufficient quantitative research to date that connects interdisciplinary programs with results on standardized tests. There are serious flaws in accepting only quantitative research in looking for new directions, however. Usually, teachers use an integrated approach to enhance relevance for students and to teach for understanding. An increase in test scores, however, does not necessarily reflect understanding. Research indicates that students may do well on standardized tests but actually have little comprehension of the material. In fact, evaluating the success of integrated programs solely on these measures may do more harm than good. It is well-known that teachers tend to teach to the test. This phenomenon is true of standardized testing as well. Because interdisciplinary programs do not, by definition, teach to standardized tests, they can be easy to dismiss.

Latham (1997) identifies the difficulty with quantifying gains on standardized testing in classrooms where teaching reflects the use of multiple intelligences (MI). For him, measuring these gains is antithetical to the MI theory that emphasizes teaching in ways that enhance the learning of all students. A truer measure would be to employ a variety of tools for evaluation such as those used at New City School (Hoerr, 1997). Here standardized testing is included in a comprehensive student profile that includes portfolios, MI profile forms, and progress reports.

Similarly, it seems that we are asking the wrong questions when we consider only standardized test gains as proof that integrated approaches work. The real issues should address whether the classroom has changed in ways that honor the principles of teaching and learning. Are we engaging all the students in the learning? How can we do this? Gretchen Dietz teaches in an integrated program at Port Townsend High School in Washington State. She comments that students who are in integrated programs are better thinkers and can think their way through standardized tests. Although her students did well on standardized measures in the initial 2 years that the program was taught, these tests did not measure the full potential of the students. She teaches how to think and problem solve, but the tests do not measure thought processes or communication skills. Most current research studies are qualitative. These studies often offer a definition of interdisciplinary studies, describe the development and implementation processes of the teachers, and describe results for students. Interdisciplinary programs tend to use alternative assessment procedures such as performance assessment, portfolios, self-assessment, peer assessment, interviews, and rubrics (scoring guides that offer the criteria for skills). These are difficult to standardize. Educators are currently developing measures that capture a full and accurate picture of what a student can do, rather than rely solely on standardized tests. Standardized tests do not accurately measure achievement levels for interdisciplinary studies.

What Is the Background of Integrated Studies?

Interdisciplinary studies are not new. They date as far back as Plato and were particularly championed for educators in the 1920s and 1930s. John Dewey (1938/1969) criticizes the narrowness of disciplines and proposes a dynamic educative process that prepares the student to participate in the democratic process. His philosophy can be seen in many integrated ventures today. Dewey recognizes that there is a unique relationship between education and society. Education that uses the scientific method could promote positive social change. Intelligence is developed by interactions with the social environment, especially those that require problem solving. Both core curriculum and the 8-Year Study evolved from Dewey's (1938/1969) concept of experiential problem-based inquiry learning that promoted democracy. In the late 1930s, the 8-Year Study, a venture of progressive educators, demonstrated the promise of interdisciplinary education for preparing students for postgraduate destinations. The National Association for Core Curriculum has been recommending interdisciplinary studies for over 40 years.

There is a growing global interest in interdisciplinary studies. In Australia, the development of such programs has accompanied the school reform movement (Vaille, 1997; Williams et al., 1994). Israel is moving toward an integrated approach (Levin, Nevo, & Luttzatti, 1996). Across Canada and the United States, schools are experimenting with interdisciplinary programs. Interdisciplinary studies have been recommended by such national American organizations as School Science and Mathematics and the National Council of Teachers in Mathematics. Interdisciplinary studies are most popular at the elementary level. High schools have been less receptive because of a variety of obstacles, such as the admission requirements of universities. In 1994, only one fifth of U.S. high schools had interdisciplinary curriculum in practice (Sadowski, 1995). This is rapidly changing as universities move toward more interdisciplinary programming and shifts in their acceptance criteria.

In 1996, U.S. Secretary of Education Richard W. Riley called on states and communities to explore ways of creating "new American high schools" ("Top Ten," 1996). This occurred at the New American High School Conference, where 10 schools were showcased as new American high schools. These schools were selected from among 300 nominated schools by researchers from the University of California at Berkeley. These schools based their innovations on the national school-to-work program. The programs were interdisciplinary and students achieved high standards in both academic and technical skills; prepared for college and careers; learned in the context of careers or special interests; learned by doing; enhanced learning through technology; were organized in a school within a school; and were supported by adult mentors.

Two contrasting positions have emerged that support integrating curriculum. Many argue that interdisciplinary studies enhance the traditional system and are particularly good for at-risk students. In contrast, others see integrated studies as replacing the current system altogether (see Beane, 1995; Dagget, 1995).

The 8-Year Study

The 8-Year Study convincingly demonstrated the effectiveness of interdisciplinary curriculum in high schools. Thirty secondary schools participated in this study in the 1930s. Carnegie, Rockefeller, and other foundations contributed over $1 million to the Progressive Education Association for this research. Schools were given the freedom to decide how to present curriculum. They followed two major principles:

1. School life would conform to what was known about teaching and learning: "A human being learns through doing things that are meaningful to him (sic); that the doing involves the whole person . . . ; and that the growth takes place as each experience leads to greater understanding" (Aikin, 1942, p. 17).

2. School life would provide students with the skills and social orientation for a democratic way of life. It was most important that students gain a vision of democracy followed by the 3 Rs and other subject areas.

The adoption of these principles required small schools, increased teacher decision making, and a core curriculum in almost all schools. The teacher and students planned the curriculum collaboratively. Many schools committed to experiential learning. Progressive educators encouraged experience-based pedagogy because it not only motivated students but also reflected student choice and integrated subject matter.

Universities and colleges dropped admission requirements, subject and credit prescription, and, in most cases, entrance examinations. This was very important to the success of the study because then, as now, high schools claimed that they could not provide innovative programs because they did not prepare students for university. Success was ascertained by comparison of 1,475 matched pairs (in study and not in study) on 18 variables. The results indicated that the graduates of the 30 schools had done "a somewhat better job than the comparison group" (Aikin, 1942, p. 112). These measures included grade average, academic honors, objective thinking, and resourcefulness in new situations. The graduates of the schools who were most experimental (interdisciplinary studies being an important characteristic), were "strikingly more successful" (p. 113) than their matches and all the other schools in the study. The graduates from the least innovative schools, on the other hand, showed no consistent differences from those in the comparison group.

Why this study had little influence is not clear. It was a longitudinal study with ample quantitative evidence to support progressive theory. Renowned names in education were associated with the process such as Ralph Tyler and Hilda Taba. One suggestion is that the timing of the study doomed it to obscurity until the 1990s. The study ended just as the Second World War was beginning, and educators were preoccupied with other events. Another suggestion is that those who set policy after the war were not progressive educators at heart and therefore did not want the results to be widely known. (Kahne, 1995).

How Do Interdisciplinary Studies Relate to Postsecondary Destinations?

Although most universities are anchored in the traditional disciplines and specializations, they are on the brink of change. The information explosion has had a tremendous effect. Data found on the Internet blur the boundaries of the disciplines and subdisciplines. New knowledge has been developed by disciplinary linkages such as southwest studies, Asian-Pacific studies, Canadian studies, women's studies, neuroscience, and environmental studies. Discipline research procedures are also becoming blurred; scholars have found that methodologies from different fields can be very useful (Fosnot, 1989). For example, developments in higher mathematics research have united many of the sciences.

Some universities already offer interdisciplinary programs. Colorado College offers 17 interdisciplinary programs, most of which have a strong independent aspect and include community-based projects and study abroad. The University of Texas at Arlington offers a BA in interdisciplinary studies; students choose a theme and an advisor and then design an individual course of study. The University of Guelph offers a curriculum in human-computer interaction. In the second edition of *Interdisciplinary Undergraduate Programs: A Directory*, 410 programs are described, up 74.5% from the 1986 first edition. The definition of program is interpreted broadly (including study groups and learning communities), but all are institutionally recognized (as cited in Vars, 1997). Some other conclusions that Vars (1997) notes:

- In the last decade, many programs have been created and occupy meaningful positions in spite of downsizing and retrenchment.

- New topics and study areas are growing faster than traditional ones.

- New forms of interdisciplinary programs are emerging; for example, interinstitutional programs.

In some universities, there is a movement toward interdisciplinary medical education that is grounded in problem-based learning (PBL). Knowledge is acquired in the format or real-life context that it will be used. These programs use case studies and emphasize self-learning rather than instruction. They are student centered rather than faculty centered, topic oriented rather than discipline oriented. The role of the student is to ask the right question. The learning tools used to answer the question include academic faculty, clinical and basic science textbooks, computer-assisted learning, videotapes, Internet sources, and the knowledge of other students (Tobin, 1997).

Research on problem-based programs demonstrates that these programs are more than viable. Students in PBL programs score higher in factual knowledge, differential diagnosis, performing a physical task, and organizing and expressing information than students in lecture programs (Richards et al., 1996). Students from PBL programs are better at diagnosis skills than their counterparts, and this becomes increasingly so as training progresses (Schmidt et al., 1996). Finally, students in PBL have significantly higher scores on enthusiasm, student interaction. and curiosity about sciences (Kaufman & Mann, 1996).

Funding cuts are forcing universities to rethink their ways of operation. Colleges and universities are collaborating to allow for easy transfers. Universities are moving into skill development more typical of colleges, whereas colleges apply high standards in the knowledge components. Instead of looking the same, institutions of higher education are stressing their uniqueness (in a real-life and interdisciplinary context) to attract funding. For example, Brock University, where I teach, is situated in the heart of wine-making country. It recently created the Cool Climate Oenology and Viticulture Institute in partnership with local industry, provincial and federal governments, and other educational institutions in the region.

Other higher education institutions are following suit and capitalizing on the expertise available in their regions.

When Doesn't Integration Work?

Many current problems revolve around educators not having enough experiences or exemplars to guarantee sound interdisciplinary curriculum. Superficial curriculum can be developed with superficial topics, and subject areas can get short shrift. Certainly, this could be a charge leveled at some current attempts (Case, 1994).

There have been unsuccessful examples of integration. Roth (1994) valiantly joined an effort to include science in an interdisciplinary unit on 1492. She found that science got superficial treatment in this theme and recommended that science be taught by itself. In British Columbia, when social studies was integrated with English, foreign languages, health, and guidance, there was nothing for students to develop disciplinary understandings so that they could apply what they learned to new problems (Seixas, 1994). As a result, interdisciplinary studies were not ruled out, but teacher colleges were urged to teach how to teach such an approach in a substantive way.

The attitudes of teachers make a difference. At a middle school in Texas, at-risk students were put into either a grade 7 or a grade 8 interdisciplinary class (Scroth, Dunbar, Vaughan, & Seaborg, 1994). The teachers of the grade 7 students were willing to try new alternatives and were open to the opinions of all team members. The grade 8 teachers did not appreciate the benefits of an interdisciplinary program. They thought they should be preparing students for high school and dropped this approach midstream. The grade 7 students demonstrated significant gains in academic improvement over a control group and had half the absences of the control group, and discipline referrals dropped dramatically. In contrast, there was no significant academic improvement over the control group for the grade 8 students. As well, there was more absenteeism than the control group, and discipline referrals increased.

Many programs do not have enough rigor to ensure that students learn worthwhile knowledge and skills. Martin-Kniep et al. (1995) developed three criteria for interdisciplinary programs: substance, relevance, and coherence. In analyzing 20 New York City schools, the authors found only three that produced thematic units that fulfilled these requirements. The researchers noted that the success of such units depended on the craftsmanship of the teacher. They found that curriculum that promoted a connection to the self led to powerful learning. They did not recommend abandoning teaching interdisciplinary units, but advised block scheduling, allowing more time to understand the perspectives of others on the teaching team, and using substance, relevance, and coherence as criteria for evaluation of the unit.

Student Benefits

Academic Gains

A preliminary body of evidence is beginning to accumulate on the results of integrated programs for students. Vars (1995, 1996) reviews more than 100 studies that took place from 1956 until 1995. He cautiously concludes that students in integrated programs do as well as, and often better than, students in conventional programs. Other patterns emerged in Vars's study. Almost without exception, students in any type of connected curriculum program do as well or better on basic skills than students in traditional programs. The results of standardized tests follow the same pattern. Thus far, there have not been enough studies to identify whether integrated or multidisciplinary approaches produce superior results. Weaker students do better with one teacher who teaches all subjects, however. Academic students do better with a teacher who is discipline based. Vars's findings are very important because they represent the most extensive review to date. Recent efforts have not been well documented. In part, this is because the research has focused on how to integrate and has been concerned with organizational factors and teacher beliefs. As well, because educators are just beginning to move into this territory, there are few examples of programs that fully qualify as interdisciplinary or integrated.

Early research on interdisciplinary work in middle schools indicates that, although the evidence is limited and inconclusive, there are indications of academic gains. Arhar, Johnston, and Markle (1992) review the research on the effect of interdisciplinary teaming on middle school students. They cite the following findings:

■ The results of 13 studies and three large-scale reviews show that interdisciplinary team teaching, as compared to the traditional arrangements, is equally effective at enhancing student achievement (Cotton, 1982).

■ The vast majority of early studies show no difference in student achievement (Cooper & Sterns, 1973; Gamsky, 1970; Georgiades & Bjelke, 1964; Oakland Public Schools, 1964; Zimmerman, 1962).

■ Other studies show academic gains: higher achievement was reported on the California Achievement Test (CAT) among eighth graders (Georgiades & Bjelke, 1964). Ninth graders increased CAT scores in language arts but not social studies (Noto, 1972). Higher achievement in math and reading was achieved for fourth and fifth graders on the Iowa Test of Basic Skills (Sterns, 1969).

■ In a study of 100 effective middle schools, 62% reported consistent academic improvement (George & Oldaker, 1985). Twenty-eight percent supported these claims with the results of the Iowa Test of Basic Skills and CAT scores.

■ Ten years of research examining the grades 10, 11, and 12 interdisciplinary Humanitas Program in the Los Angeles Unified School District shows a statistically significant improvement in student writing and increased content knowledge over a year (Aschbacher, 1991). The more time students spent in the program, the more their writing skills and knowledge improved, attendance improved, and drop-out rates decreased. The humanitas students liked school better than the comparison group even though the program was considered more demanding.

■ At the independent New City School (Hoerr, 1997), teachers base their program on the MI. They expect students to demonstrate understanding and use innovative evaluation methods such as a portfolio of student achievements on videotape and an annual autobiography. They also administer standardized tests that indicate their students perform far above grade average. This school emphasizes that standardized tests are only one facet of evaluation techniques.

■ An elementary school in Maryland adopted MI in response to a statewide test, the Maryland School Performance Assessment Program (Greenhawk, 1997). Unlike standardized tests of the past, these tests measure the ability to apply basic skills to solve difficult real-life problems. Programs such as grade 5 creating its own business were implemented. This was followed by rigorous performance assessment in math, reading, social studies, and writing. In one year, the test results rose by 20%.

■ Using a brain-based approach, observations were noted in two case studies (Caine & Caine, 1997). Reading scores at Dry Creek jumped 10 percentiles in a year and 6 percentiles in the second grade for grade 1 students. Math scores also increased, although not as much. Students were more engaged in the learning, and projects were completed more frequently. At Park View, the grade point average rose by one full point for grade 7 students in the brain-based program. When these students advanced to eighth and ninth grade, they continued to achieve higher grades than would be predicted statistically. This class included a large proportion of special needs students. Scores on standardized tests showed an upward trend for both groups. Caine and Caine (1997) noted that a different type of test is probably needed to measure learning in the kinds of schools they are advocating.

■ One recent study of an Ontario grade 9 integrated program documents the following achievements for math skills: the number of As and Bs increased each year (drawing comments that the standards must have been lowered), grades of females increased dramatically, and results on the Canadian Achievement Tests rose each year (Warren, 1996).

■ Integrating technology into the curriculum for students with physical and cognitive disabilities has proved fruitful using DECtalk (Latham, 1997). The teacher can program this high-quality speech synthesizer to read aloud, sound out words, or give feedback on spelling. Groups using DECtalk gained an average of .6 in grade level in word recognition skills compared to .3 in the control group, which was reading using conventional methods.

■ A 3-year integrated science (IS) program was designed at the University of Alabama's Center for Communication and Educational Technology. There are over 1,400 teachers and 170,000 middle school students from grades 6 to 8 enrolled in 15 states and Canada. The program is delivered via weekly 20-minute telecasts in which the perspectives of biology, chemistry, physics, and earth-space science are interconnected. The Southeastern Regional Vision for Education (SERVE) studied a Florida group and an Alabama group enrolled in the program for 3 years ("Summary Report," 1997). This study employed a matched pair design to compare race, age, gender, and academic ability of 121 students from the IS programs with their non-IS student counterparts. The study indicated that

- students significantly outperformed their counterparts in science process skills.
- students performed better on the grade Stanford Achievement Test, at 4 percentiles higher (marginally significant).
- students reported a significantly more positive attitude toward science classroom experiences and their teachers.

Studying the arts can stimulate both learning and the ability to learn. Oddeleifson (1989) refers to a number of studies that strongly support this assertion:

- A study by the College Board concludes that students who pursued more than 4 years of music and arts scored 34 points higher on SAT verbal and 18 points higher on SAT math than students who took these subjects for less than a year (cited in Royal Conservatory of Music, 1994).

- Research by the Center for Arts in the Basic Curriculum (cited in Royal Conservatory of Music, 1994) indicates that students who study the arts perform 30% better in basic academic skills than those who are not involved.

- The Center for Arts in the Basic Curriculum offers several examples of schools with students considered below average but who achieved substantial academic improvement when a comprehensive approach to the arts was added to the curriculum. For example, in 1979, Elm Elementary in Milwaukee was in the bottom 10% in academic performance until it added a comprehensive approach to the curriculum. It then ranked first out of 103 schools for the next 10 years.

Additional Evidence

The arts do not have to be studied in isolation to be effective; for example, music can be an effective medium to teach students with reading and writing difficulties at the primary level (Anderson, 1992). Other examples:

- The introduction of song has been used effectively for the language arts curriculum at the early childhood level (Pirie & Opuni, 1992).

- The arts taught in a diverse inner-city school in San Francisco led to significant enhancement of self-concept, positive observable behavior, and respect and tolerance for others (Trjillo, 1981).

- Drama in New York schools reduced prejudice and increased students' knowledge and acceptance of another culture (Grimmestad, 1982).

- Angela Elster of the Royal Conservatory of Music in Toronto coordinates the Learning through the Arts program. She presents many stories of how preliminary research that uses student journals indicates increased self-esteem, better coping skills, and enhanced emotional development.

An increasing amount of research (Hancock, 1996) indicates that the study of music enhances the capacity for higher-order thinking. Hancock (1996) discusses research that indicates that students who take music lessons dramatically increase their spatial reasoning—the cornerstone of mathematical thinking. According to Hancock, young children aren't ready to be taught higher mathematics or chess, but they can learn music and be exposed to classical music. This, in turn, excites inherent brain patterns and enhances use in complex reasoning. Other research indicates that there are many benefits to integrating the program:

- Benefits for grade 9 students in the integrated math, science, and technology program, compared to a control group, included the ability to apply shared concepts, student motivation, the ability to work together, and a better understanding of selected science concepts for female students (Ross & Hogaboam-Gray, in press).

- In an outdoor program, students learned that transcendent qualities are independent of the disciplinary content. They learned a complete process of making a product, valued the real-life context, gained interpersonal skills, and became more responsible human beings (Horwood, 1992).

- In Wright's (1997) economics classroom, students acted as citizens and became members of a fictional town called Livengood.

How would they develop a gift of 600 acres of land? Students took on the roles of city governance to solve the challenge. They learned research skills and found that learning was fun. Initial results on SAT and ACT tests were impressive: These students scored significantly higher than other students in the area.

■ In Mexico, high school students wrote in English to explain Mexican culture and then used the Internet to send their writing to English-speaking people around the world. Because they were writing to real people, these students made significantly more progress than the control group working with a textbook. They cared about what they said, so they made sure they had the correct grammar and necessary vocabulary. The teacher reports they also increased knowledge about their own culture (Meagher, 1995).

■ At Radnor Middle School in Pennsylvania, about one fifth of the seventh graders study at the watershed all year. Except for foreign languages, the entire curriculum is integrated. Students study a water treatment plant, a power plant, and a local landfill. They visit battle sites, study the art of area native Andrew Wyeth, and canoe on the local river. Watershed students consistently (over 9 years) show the greatest writing improvement of all seventh graders. Their standardized test scores are equal to or better than those of students who are in the traditional program (Sadowski, 1995).

■ Special educators promote integrated programs for students with learning disabilities. This type of learning builds on student strengths rather than being limited to remedial techniques (Vaille, 1997).

■ Interdisciplinary programs enhance learning for the gifted (Clark, 1986), and MI is an effective way to plan programs for gifted children because it allows for challenging real-life problem solving (Reid & Romanoff, 1997).

■ The Writing to Read (WTR) program developed by John Henry Martin is a literature-based language arts program. It uses computers in a process writing environment to foster literacy in young children. Casey (1994) compares classes using WTR in networked classroom settings with students using the program in a lab setting and with primary students who are not using computers at all. Students who experienced classroom WTR wrote at higher levels than either other group. Both WTR groups outperformed those without computers, however. Students in the WTR program had a significantly more positive attitude toward reading than students in the control group. Parents of students in WTR reported significantly higher levels of reading at home than parents in the control group. Students with special learning needs achieved the same benefits from the WTR program as other students. Using a similar program, Martin (1994) found that her grade 3 students became prolific writers in science and social studies. As well, they learned the skill of editing.

Nonacademic Benefits

Ontario teachers who were interviewed believed that, although an integrated approach may not lead to substantial gains in standardized test scores, there is a substantive difference in the quality of school life (Miller, Drake, Molinaro, & Harris, 1997). Students are enthusiastic and more motivated to learn. Other researchers note similar benefits:

■ In one school, there was improvement in nonacademic outcomes such as interracial relationships and enthusiasm for school and teachers (Arhar, Johnston, & Markle, 1989).

■ When science was integrated with dramatic arts in a grade 11 class in Portland High School, Connecticut, the students researched the life of a chemist and used this information to generate and produce a play that was performed for an audience (Budzinsky, 1995). Students reported more self-confidence, increased student cooperation, mutual respect, and having more fun. All students preferred this mode of delivery over lecture style. They believed that they had greater recall and understanding of the material and could transfer skills to other subject areas.

■ Teachers at the middle school level used James Beane's (1993) model to construct the curriculum with the students. They provided adolescent literature to answer student-generated questions. They found that this was the "hook" that allowed students to be motivated active learners (Smith & Johnson, 1993).

■ In an interdisciplinary program delivered in Newfoundland, there was more effective use of innovative teaching strategies, students discovered that the learning was fun, and there was less disruptive behavior. Teachers noted the necessity for longer time blocks for successful programming (Cole, 1994).

■ In a review of the effectiveness of computers in schools (Bialo & Sivin, 1991), the following results were documented: both mainstream and learning-disabled students liked working on computers, the perception of learners being in control was increased, students were motivated to remain on task, positive attitudes toward school increased, math anxiety was reduced, and self-esteem was increased.

■ Four groups of elementary students participated in a curriculum designed around the arts. A tribal theme integrated drama, history, science, social studies, language, and physical and social development. Students learned to respect others and value their opinions. They understood the new knowledge that they learned and developed as individuals (Geoghegan, 1994).

■ The Blue Wolves Core received the Secretary's Commission on Achievement of Necessary Skills (SCANS) Award. This was an interdisciplinary project at Desert Sky Middle School in Arizona where teachers instructed in a microsociety. Students were paid to come to school and used a banking system to negotiate school life. Small businesses, court systems, and student government were the core of math, science, language arts, and social studies. During the 9-week program, students learned basic skills, higher-level thinking skills, creative thinking skills, research skills, and social skills (Alteritz, 1994).

■ Student feedback from over 700 sixth-, seventh-, and eighth-grade students was collected over 5 years of interdisciplinary units. Students enjoyed the learning, found topics interesting, learned from working in groups, and expressed high quality in their work (Davies, 1992). Successful interdisciplinary units included relevant topics, clear goals and objectives, variety in activities and groupings, choice, adequate time, development of products, skill development woven into the topics, field trips, organized group work, sharing results with others, and community involvement.

Effect on Teachers

Improving student learning requires deep change (Sparks, 1998). Teachers have to learn to think and teach in new ways. This will not be an easy or quick task. According to Sparks (1998), the key ingredient is ongoing support of the teachers who have to implement the changes. The following are dramatic changes that occurred with teachers in our study (Miller et al., 1997).

Collaboration

Schools that successfully effect change do establish a collaborative culture. In fact, the most striking change in our study of four school boards (Miller et al., 1997) is that teachers learned to be collaborative during the 3 years we observed them. This finding was duplicated by Rebecca Burns (R. Burns, personal communication, October 18, 1997) at the Appalachian Educational Laboratories in Charleston, West Virginia. In quantitative measures based on a survey, teachers were asked about their experiences on integrated curriculum teams. The survey measured reflective dialogue, deprivatization of practice, collective focus on student learning, shared norms and values, and collaboration. Although all variables showed a positive difference, there was a significant difference in the amount of collaboration experienced.

Teachers not only experienced collaboration, they valued it. A typical comment from our research:

> You know it's funny; I find the more I work with teachers the more I want to work with them. It's becoming natural in this school. I also find that collaboration helps me to think in a more integrated way. So, as I work with other teachers I can see how we can work together to better integrate our courses.

Teacher as Leader-Learner

Our research (Miller et al., 1997) indicates that the role of teacher is fundamentally changing. The first finding is that the teacher is emerging as a leader in many school situations. This is in part because there is an emphasis on shared leadership and site-based management. Teachers are taking responsibility for new roles.

The second important factor is that the teacher is learning throughout changes. One teacher said, "You are learning all the time. Probably half the job is learning." The fact that teachers are learners is emphasized in Elmore, Petersen, and McCarthey's (1996) study on the effects of restructuring on teachers in their classroom. Fifty-eight teachers in Israel demonstrated a significant change in thinking after 3 months of training to teach integrated programs. Their thinking shifted from thinking of the curriculum as an object to thinking of curriculum as activity, and from the teacher as expert to the teacher as a person who is a guide and fellow explorer (Levin et al., 1996).

Professional Development

Another dramatic change is in professional development. Previously, professional development activities were one-shot efforts where teachers worked with an outside expert. Often the effect of the speaker was quickly lost. Now, partly because there is less money to bring in experts, professional development shifts in-house. A teacher who has been sent to a train-the-trainer conference teaches the staff. We (Miller et al., 1997) found that most staffs were receptive to this approach because the teacher was usually enthusiastic about what he or she was presenting. Or a consultant from central office would work with the staff and establish an ongoing relationship. This led to an increase in teacher leadership and was appreciated by most teachers as being more effective for real change.

Summary

This chapter explored some of the existing literature in an attempt to discover if integrated approaches work. Although there are different opinions on what kind of research counts, a survey of the literature (Vars, 1995, 1996) indicates that students slightly improve their academic scores with integrated approaches. What is apparent from the existing literature is that there are definite rewards for students. Although these rewards may not always be academic in nature, they include a better learning environment and better relationships among students and teachers. Academic scores do not dip, and there is a positive change in the school culture. Given this evidence, it is hard to understand why the mainstream, including some educators, resists an integrated approach and a definite shift in teaching methodology and assessment. It does indicate the complexity of implementing major change into the institution.

3

XXXXXXX

Creating Multidisciplinary Programs

✳ ✳ ✳

This chapter explores different ways in which educators have created multidisciplinary programs. The main criteria that define a multidisciplinary program include the following:

- The procedures of the disciplines are separate entities.

- The disciplinary procedures influence how a subject is taught and assessed.

- The content is labeled as belonging to one subject area.

- The reporting is precise. English is English and history is history.

There also is a blurring of the boundaries, however. Much of this blurring occurs when teachers begin to make connections as they plan together. If there is no collaborative planning, the connections among the disciplines remain obscure.

Fusion

Fusion occurs when specific issues or skills are infused into different subject areas. No subject area is dependent on any other area in this process. For example, one school infuses global awareness into every grade and every course. Another school commits itself to presenting environmental stewardship in every course.

Other schools adopt a fusion strategy in one grade or in several subjects. An example is AIDS awareness taught in several subject areas such as health, science, and social studies as mandated by a district policy. These teachers may never need to consult each other on the results or how they have taught this, however. Some schools infuse skills into the curriculum. For example, all teachers in grade 9 emphasize work habits, although each teacher may do this differently.

Applying the Model

At North York Board of Education, the "artist educator" is integrated into the curriculum in a unique way. The program is called Learning Through the Arts: Fusing Artists Into the Curriculum. This is a community partnership with the Royal Conservatory of Music and seven schools. It also involves arts organizations, foundations, and corporate sponsors. This is a 5-year commitment where every student in each of the seven schools participates in the program.

This program is not just about bringing an artist into the classroom to do his or her stuff. A great deal of planning and thoughtfulness is needed to connect what artists do with the general school curriculum. In many ways, the venture is about changing the culture in schools. The philosophy behind the venture includes promoting other learning through involvement in the arts; integrating the curriculum; building on skills sequentially; building on the previous year's experiences; and developing artist, teacher, and student learning.

During the school year, each class hosts a minimum of three different artists who each come for 3 days. Their skills as artists are integrated into the classroom through professional development workshops. The teachers have a lot to work with between sessions. The process is as follows:

1. The teacher reflects on his or her own curriculum and on where and how an artist might enhance the skills being taught. In the

final analysis, teachers have their choice of both the theme and the artists who will be joining the class.

2. Teachers and artists meet and discuss the needs for the classroom. The program is planned collaboratively.

3. The artists meet for a professional development program to help facilitate the needs of the students they will be teaching.

4. Each artist gives a half-day workshop for the teachers with whom they will be working. Here the teachers learn the skills that the artist educators will be teaching the students. The teachers are then able to help the students during the artist's visit.

Sample programs give a flavor of the students' experiences. In grade 1, the theme is community-family. The artists introduce drama, African drumming and storytelling, visual arts, and ensemble (e.g., violin, viola, cello). Additional activities include a field trip to the Milk International Children's Festival and a trip to an RCM Orchestra Rehearsal.

In grade 6, the theme is values, influences, and peers. The visiting artists offer global percussion, storytelling, and composition. Additional activities include a visit by a reporter for an entertainment magazine and a field trip to a local television and radio station.

An example of how this program works comes from a grade 9 class at Westview Centennial High School. This school is multicultural and in a lower-income area. Although only two artists participated in the first year, the school will be adding an aboriginal filmmaker this year. The arts skills tapped in the first year were voice and global percussion. First, the students listened to a well-known local blues singer who focuses on black history. She disclosed interesting facts about the obscure history of slavery in Canada. The next artist, a percussionist, taught students drumming techniques from different countries. Students then completed a research project on different drums from around the world. How was a particular drum used? Math calculations were performed to understand how the drum creates sound. The image of the drum sound then was transferred as a picture on a computer, and this fit with a previously existing program called "Cyberarts." Finally, an African Canadian teacher on staff joined in by demonstrating tribal dancing. During this time, the regular teacher made conscious connections in the curriculum with the learning from the artists.

Qualitative analysis indicates that everyone benefits from this program. Teachers are learning from other teachers. They are also learning from the artists. Now it is not uncommon for artists and teachers to go out for lunch together. Student journals indicate that students are acquiring coping skills and emotional development. Initially, teachers trained as music and arts specialists felt threatened by this program. Since the implementation of this program, however, parents, students, and teachers have recommended including arts in the curriculum.

Integrating the Subdisciplines

Some subject areas strive toward a more interdisciplinary program by integrating their subdisciplines. Science and math programs often take this approach to make their courses more relevant to the student. They usually connect the subject area to a real-life context rather than to a textbook. An interesting story I heard crushes the myth of the sequentiality of the sciences (Dagget, 1995). When an august educational body was pondering the question of what order biology, chemistry, and physics should be taught in, no one could think of any good reason why one should precede the other. The members decided to go by alphabetical order. Today, it is a deeply ingrained truth that the order of teaching these subdisciplines is crucial because of the nature of each area and that one must precede the other.

Applying the Model

An integrated science program has been developed by the University of Alabama Center for Communication and Educational Technology (www.ccet.ua.edu). This innovative middle school curriculum integrates perspectives of physics, chemistry, biology, and earth sciences. This multiyear program for grades 6 to 8 is based on recommendations from the American Association for the Advancement of Science and the National Science Teachers Association. The program has a positive effect on both student achievement and attitudes toward science.

The goal of the program is to rekindle student interest in science and to produce adults who are scientifically literate. This non-profit program comes to teachers via weekly telecasts, teacher manuals, and student books. The teachers take summer workshops and have support on electronic mail. There are 1,400 enrolled teachers in 16 states and Quebec; more than 170,000 students are taking the program.

The instructional strategies adopted are appropriate for all learners, represent constructivist learning (students construct their own meaning), provide hands-on activities with familiar phenomena, and encourage family involvement in science activities.

Teachers are given training in strategies such as cross-curricular opportunities, cooperative learning, alternative assessment, hands-on activities, higher-order thinking skills, tournaments, interactive video, class projects, and student incentives. It is important to note that this program works with radically different techniques of teaching and learning from the traditional model. At the same time, it supports multiple opportunities for cross-curricular work. Many of the ideas embedded in this approach will be seen again in later chapters. Teachers who are comfortable with this program are open to further integration because they have already acquired many of the skills necessary to teach interdisciplinary programs successfully.

An outline of the 3-year program is presented in Table 3.1.

Parallel or Multidisciplinary?

In parallel disciplines, related content is taught in two or more subjects during the same time period. In multidisciplinary disciplines, connections are made among subjects. These connections are made by both teachers and students. Often the subject areas are connected by the culminating activity. Figure 3.1 illustrates this difference.

In elementary school, parallel organization is often displayed in learning centers. For example, the teacher is discussing a topic such as water. The students go to different centers where they take part in activities that explore the topic of water through the lens of science, language arts, social studies, and art. In high school, the students move from class to class to study the same topic from the lens of different subjects. For example, they may explore a theme in visual

TABLE 3.1 3-Year Overview of Integrated Science

Block 1	Sixth Grade Clues	Seventh Grade Patterns	Eighth Grade Waves
Integrating Concept: The universe has regular and predictable patterns.	**Theme:** Observations provide clues. **Topics:** Senses/ perception Neurons/ archeolgy Paleontology Digestive system Symmetry Scientific inquiry	**Theme:** Form and function are related. **Topics:** Scientific investigation Classification Circles/spheres Cylinders/spirals Triangles/fractals Circulatory and respiratory systems	**Theme:** Waves have measurable properties in a repeating pattern. **Topics:** Wave similarities/ differences/ behavior Water waves/ seismic waves Sound waves Electromagnetic waves Sensory organs— ears and eyes
Block 2	*Machines*	*Forces*	*Energy*
Integrating Concept: Matter and energy can change forms.	**Theme:** Work requires energy. **Topics:** Properties of matter Work/energy Forces Simple machines Skeletal system Muscular system	**Theme:** Forces act on matter. **Topics:** Gravity/friction Types of matter Periodic table Electricity Magnetism Nervous system	**Theme:** Energy holds matter together. **Topics:** Forms of energy Energy present in matter Chemical reactions Energy in living systems' alternative energy sources

arts, music, and drama, but teachers do not deliberately make connections for the students. They are left to do this themselves.

Sturch (1996) presents a good example of a successful multidisciplinary arts unit. The first 3 days brought together the students (from grades 9 to 11) who were taking art, music, and drama classes. They experienced icebreaker activities as a large group and were introduced to the theme of "the journey" for the unit. They were

TABLE 3.1 *Continued*

Block 3	Sixth Grade Cycles	Seventh Grade Change	Eighth Grade Stages
Integrating Concept: Change is the universal constant.	**Theme:** Change can operate in cycles. **Topics:** Universe—Seasons, tides Earth—weather, geographic cycles Organisms—cells, life cycle	**Theme:** Change is ongoing. **Topics:** Universe—solar system/planets asteroids/comets Earth—Earth's structure/crustal movement weathering/erosion organisms—cell division/heredity human life cycle	**Theme:** Some change has no timelines. **Topics:** Universe—models of the universe Galaxies/stars/uncommon objects earth—geologic time, radiometric development, rock cycle organisms—embryonic development evolution and extinction

Block 4	*Environment*	*Environment*	*Environment*
Integrating Concept: Environments balance the living and nonliving.	**Theme:** The biosphere supports life. **Topics:** Biosphere Biomes/climate Adaptations Relationships	**Theme:** Ecosystems are both fragile and complex. **Topics:** Soil/water Food chains/webs Niche/habitat Succession	**Theme:** Human activities affect the environment. **Topics:** Population growth Environmental degradation Global concerns Environmental economics

rearranged into three new groupings; the groups rotated through 5-day blocks in visual arts, music, and drama. In each block, students learned content and skills that prepared them for the culminating activity. This was a live performance that integrated the sets, music compositions, and dramatic storytelling that they had created in the blocks.

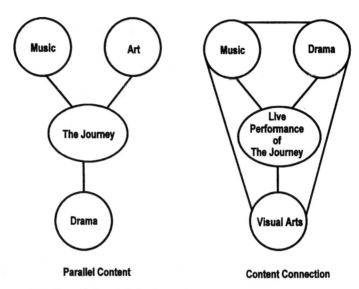

Parallel Content   **Content Connection**

Figure 3.1. Parallel or Multidisciplinary?

Standards-Based Multidisciplinary Curriculum

This particular version of multidisciplinary curriculum uses a reliable standards-based approach offered in Harris and Carr (1996). This is an excellent book on how to plan any curriculum and is described further in Resource A.

Harris and Carr's (1996) approach is not specifically intended for a multidisciplinary curriculum. It is curriculum planning for an individual subject that emphasizes beginning with standards.

The steps for one subject area are:

- Identify theme or question.
- Select standards.
- Brainstorm for activities and resources.
- Decide on the necessary knowledge and skills needed to achieve each standard.
- Select activities that enable students to achieve the standard.
- Choose appropriate assessment tools.

Several teachers used this standards-based process to plan a multidisciplinary curriculum. Representing science and technology, language, and history, these teachers began by planning with the theme Olympics. They made many different connections. These teachers felt that it was difficult to separate subject areas when they worked together to decide on the theme and brainstormed for activities and resources. This example did not include assessment, although it is an essential part of the process.

Key Ideas

Central to this model is the selection of the standards at the beginning of the process. It is the standards that are most important. This is a very different way to think about curriculum development, and is initially difficult for teachers to do. There is great merit in this approach, however. The knowledge and skills required are selected and aligned with the standard. Likewise, all the activities lead to gaining the necessary knowledge and skills. This eliminates activities that are done for the sake of the activities themselves. In the past, teachers tended to plan curriculum by selecting content and activities first. Once teachers apply a standards-based model, it becomes very easy to do again. An important feature of this design is to teach the skills that students will need to achieve the standard explicitly. Students like this approach because they are made aware of what standards they have to achieve and how they are to achieve them.

Applying the Model

The following example was created by Michael Gagliardi, Helen Rust, Mary Durnford, Josiane Beckles, and Simone Gravesande.

1. Select a topic or essential question (Figure 3.2).
2. Select appropriate standards for science and technology, language, and history (Table 3.2).
3. Brainstorm for activities and resources (Table 3.3).
4. Decide on necessary knowledge skills and enabling activities to achieve standards in each subject area (Tables 3.4, 3.5, and 3.6).
5. Decide on assessment for these activities (not included).

(text continued on p. 56)

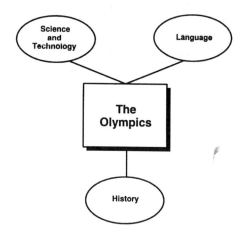

Identify a Unit Topic or Essential Question

Figure 3.2. Olympic Web

TABLE 3.2 A Unit on Olympic Games: Selected Standards

Science/Technology	History	Language (Reading and Writing)
1. Students know and understand inter-relationships among science, technology, and human activity and how they can affect the world.	1. Students understand that societies are diverse and have changed over time.	1. Students write and speak for a variety of purposes and audiences.
	2. Students understand how science, technology, and economic activity have developed, changed, and affected societies throughout history.	2. Students write and speak using conventional grammar, usage, sentence structure, punctuation, capitalization, and spelling.
	3. Students understand political institutions and theories that have developed and changed over time.	3. Students apply thinking skills to their reading, writing, speaking, listening, and viewing.
	4. Students know that religious and philosophical ideas have been powerful forces throughout history.	4. Students read to locate, select, and make sense of relevant information from a variety of media, reference, and technological sources.

TABLE 3.3 A Unit on the Olympic Games: Brainstorming Activities/Resources

Improving International Relations	*The Nature of Competition*	*Body, Mind, Soul of Athletes*	*Politics in Sport*
Promoting multiculturalism	Making an Olympic bid (who gets the games)	Use/abuse of drugs (steroids, etc.)	Research the history of the Olympics since 1970
Designing Olympic Village	Sponsorship	Research past Olympic stars: Where are they now?	Examine the economics of the
Designing their own flag	What it means to win; the positive and the negative aspects	Taking competition to the limits—what does it mean?	Olympics
Composing national anthem; Olympic song	Interview school student athletes and team coaches	How important is nationalism?	Who participates and who is excluded and why? Should politics and sports mix?
Researching a competing country	Tracking the road to the Olympics	Measuring fitness level: heart rate, lung capacity, etc.	Examine the ethics of Olympic funding for competitors
Determining what role nationalism really plays	Group cohesion (teamwork)	Debate nature vs. nurture conflict	
	Defining sports: What is an Olympic sport (i.e., beach volleyball)?	Research abuse of body in training for Olympics (i.e., eating disorders resulting from desire for perfect competitive weight)	
		Are gender barriers an issue? Examine women's roles in sport (stereotyping, limitations, etc.)	

NOTE: Resources: "Chariots of Fire" or "Cool Runnings"; International/American/Canadian Olympic Association; Olympic athletes: Donovan Bailey, Carl Lewis, Michael Johnson, Silken Laumann, Florence Griffith-Joyner, Otto and Maria Jelinek; television/radio news/videos/newspapers/magazines' sports museums; library, Internet.

TABLE 3.4 A Unit on the Olympic Games: Sample Enabling
Activity: Language Arts

Standard	Necessary Knowledge and Skills	Enabling Activities
Standard 1: Students write and speak for a variety of purposes and audiences (rationale: use of essential tools for learning).	Writing stories, letters, and reports with greater detail and supporting material Choosing vocabulary and figures of speech that communicate clearly	Write and present a "bid" for hosting the Olympic Games in your city. Outline the process; for example, approaching the city's mayor, submitting the bid to the IOC, researching number of other countries vying for this honor.
Standard 1: Students write and speak using conventional grammar, usage, sentence structure, punctuation, capitalization, and spelling (rationale: students needs to know and be able to use standard English).	Drafting, revising, editing, and proofreading for a legible copy Applying skills in analysis, synthesis, evaluation, and explanation to writing and speaking Incorporating source materials into speaking and writing (e.g., interviews, news articles, Internet) Writing and speaking in the content areas (e.g., science, history, literature) using the technical vocabulary of the subject accurately Recognizing stylistic elements such as voice, tone, and style Identifying the parts of speech Punctuating and capitalizing titles and direct quotations, using possessives and correct paragraphing in writing	Discuss the intricacies of hosting the Olympics, such as creating local public awareness. (impact) Create an advertising campaign and sponsorship aimed at recruiting volunteers, lobbying at home, and staging events sponsored by national sporting companies aimed at demonstrating your city's facilities and organizing capabilities. Discuss and write an essay on the economic and cultural impact on your city. Should the Olympic Games be hosted there?—Tourism, improved infrastructure (airport, roads, freeway, landscaping, etc.). How would you make your city the world's multicultural showcase? A boost to the cultural and educational exhibition through dance, music, visual art, featuring international and North American artists.

TABLE 3.4 *Continued*

Standard	Necessary Knowledge and Skills	Enabling Activities
Standard 2: continued	Using prefixes, root words, and suffixes correctly in writing and speaking Expanding spelling skills to include more complex words	
Standard 3: Students apply thinking skills to their reading, writing, speaking, listening, and viewing.	Making predictions, analyzing, drawing conclusions, and discriminating between fact and opinion in writing, reading, speaking, listening, and viewing Using reading, writing, speaking, listening, and viewing to define and solve problems Recognizing, expressing, and defending points of view orally and in writing Identifying the purpose, perspective, and historical and cultural influences of a speaker, author, or director Evaluating the reliability, accuracy, and relevancy of information	View and discuss a video (e.g., "Chariots of Fire," "Cool Runnings") related to the topic and critique. Complete a scavenger hunt on the details of the movie. Examine issues: moral of the story; what makes someone a winner? Assign reflection and journal writing about the movie. Write your own ending to this movie. Discuss the issue of competition in sport and reflect on the tradition of the Olympic Games as embodied in the words of the founder of the modern games, Baron Pierre de Coubertin: "The important thing in the Olympic Games is not winning but taking part. The essential thing in life is not conquering but fighting well." How does this relate to the movie's theme?

(continued)

TABLE 3.4 *Continued*

Standard	Necessary Knowledge and Skills	Enabling Activities
Standard 3: continued		Have a class debate: "On the joy of victory and the agony of defeat." Does a medal make you a winner and make your competitor a loser? What does it take to be a winner?
		Interview student athletes and submit a written report.
Standard 4: Students read to locate, select, and make use of relevant information from a variety of media, references, and technological sources.	Selecting relevant material for reading, writing, and speaking purposes	Assign a project on information collection of media portrayal and coverage of the Olympics.
	Understanding the structure, organization, and use of various media, reference, and technological sources as they select information for their reading and writing	Prepare a technology log of research, recording dates, and events and problems you encountered during your search, at the library, on the Internet, etc.
	Paraphrasing, summarizing, organizing, and synthesizing information	Present by way of audiovisual materials (graphics, PowerPoint, etc.) the different views presented by the media on the Olympics.
	Giving credit for others' ideas, images, or information	
	Using information to produce a quality product	Submit a bibliography of all reference information used.

Summary

This chapter has explored variations of the multidisciplinary approach. This approach ranges from bringing a community artist into the classroom to a fully developed integrated science program to a standards-based multidisciplinary program. This chapter

TABLE 3.5 A Unit on the Olympic Games: Sample Enabling
Activity: History

Standard	Necessary Knowledge And Skills	Enabling Activities
Standard 1: Students understand that societies are diverse and have changed over time.	Demonstrate an understanding of the ways in which one's own cultural traditions have shaped one, and an appreciation of one's own uniqueness and that of others. Analyze the ways in which immigration has influenced and continues to influence American society.	Present opening ceremonies based on cultures represented in the class. Bring flags, family pictures, Olympic stories from home.
Standard 2: Students understand how science, technology, and economic activity have developed, changed, and affected societies throughout history.	Analyze the ways in which diverse groups have contributed to the historical, cultural, and economic development of the United States. Engage in and describe responses to recreational activities in natural environments.	List positive and negative aspects of multiculturalism. Investigate cultural makeup of the United States. Define "sport." Categorize sports. Physically play some of these sports and evaluate whether categories are appropriate.
Standard 3: Students understand political institutions and theories that have developed and changed over time.	Present a case for a particular position on a local, national, or global issue, basing the case on research. Analyze power relationships in the past and in the present between individuals, groups, or countries.	Examine sponsorships, ethics, and funding research, and debate "Should Sports and Politics Mix?"

(continued)

compared parallel disciplines and multidisciplinary programs. All examples are important to consider. All approaches lead to more

TABLE 3.5 *Continued*

Standard	Necessary Knowledge and Skills	Enabling Activities
Standard 3: continued		Lobby for sport activity (divide the class into groups of three, each group representing a country or Olympic organization). Each group finds a popular sport of its country that is not represented at the Olympics and then lobbies to have it included at the Olympic Games.
Standard 4: Students know that religious and philosophical ideas have been powerful forces throughout history.	Assess the role of the United States in international affairs.	Roundtable discussion and vote on "Should Politics Play a Big Role in the Olympics?" (End-of-unit project because students need many facts to have a useful discussion.)

integrated possibilities if the teachers are ready. A multidisciplinary approach is not only an excellent starting point, but it can often stand on its own as an effective way to educate. In these examples, students are being taught in ways that enhance learning.

TABLE 3.6 A Unit on the Olympic Games: Sample Enabling
Activity: Science and Technology

Standard	Necessary Knowledge and Skills	Enabling Activities
Standard 1: Students know and understand interrelationships among science, technology, and human activity and how they can affect the world.	Explain the connections among the systems within the human body and describe the effects on the body system of different lifestyle choices. Assess some of the effects of technology on environment and society, and indicate whether these effects are positive or negative, including ethical issues and predictions of the consequences of the continued use of these technologies. Gather information from various sources, make decisions based on the information, and communicate the decisions, using appropriate methods.	Measure the heart rate and the changes in the body when the heart rate increases/decreases. Measure and create a zone and try to get into it. Design an ideal piece of sports equipment and make an ad to promote it (poster, commercial, etc.). Research the effect of technology on the Olympics (e.g., score keeping, speed/accuracy measurement, instant replay, level playing field, ability to know opponents in advance of competition, etc.).

4

×××××

USING INTERDISCIPLINARY
APPROACHES

✳ ✳ ✳

Most existing approaches to integration tend to be interdisciplinary. Interdisciplinary curriculum includes the following characteristics:

- The disciplines are readily identifiable although content is interconnected.

- One or more commonalities connect the disciplines; for example, a theme, guided questions, concepts, essential learnings, standards, or skills.

- Connections are made explicit to students.

- All aspects of curriculum are interconnected. The assessment and reporting reflect selected standards and instructional strategies.

- There are different emphases and varying degrees of sophistication in existing approaches.

This chapter presents four different approaches to interdisciplinary planning. All begin with a theme or issue that connects the subject areas, and all are concerned with developing a full curriculum. In each approach, however, a different organizer is emphasized to connect disciplines. In Fogarty's (1991) work, a theme is the key factor in the integration process. For Taylor (1996), human activities are interconnected with the theme as areas for study. Jacobs (1989) stresses the guiding, or essential, questions that limit and shape a topic while bringing the different subject areas together. Finally, Erickson (1995, in press) uses concepts and essential understandings as an umbrella to connect subject areas. A standards-based interdisciplinary model is explored in Chapter 6, "Connecting Standards to Curriculum."

A Theme Approach

Robin Fogarty (1991) offers a continuum of 10 models of curriculum. She presents these different models in a simple and easy-to-understand format that is very helpful to educators struggling to discover the meaning of integration in their situations. What these models lack in sophistication is compensated for by their simplicity. Her continuum moves from subject specific to interdisciplinary to intrinsic models for individuals. Subject-specific models are shown in Figure 4.1. Interdisciplinary models are portrayed in Figure 4.2. Intrinsic models for individuals are illustrated in Figure 4.3.

This chapter examines the webbed model. Although it is possible to consider the shared, threaded, or integrated model as interdisciplinary, these models are not as typical as the webbed model. The shared model, for example, does not share concepts generated from a selected extrinsic theme. The threaded model is skills based and does not connect content. The integrated model begins with screening ideas in each subject area's content and finding overlapping skills, concepts, and attitudes. A prerequisite for this model is participants who have worked together previously and are comfortable making these connections.

Key Ideas

In the webbed model, teachers consciously select the theme and construct the curriculum from a starting point. Fogarty and Stoehr

1 PERISCOPE

Fragmented
Periscope — one direction; one sighting; narrow focus on single discipline

Description
The traditional model of separate and distinct disciplines, which fragments the subject areas.

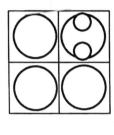

Example
Teacher applies this view in Math, Science, Social Studies, Language Arts, OR Sciences, Humanities, Fine and Practical Arts

2 OPERA GLASS

Connected
Opera glass — details of one discipline; focus on subtleties and interconnections

Description
Within each subject area, course content is connected topic to topic, concept to concept, one year's work to the next, and relates idea(s) explicitly.

Example
Teacher relates the concept of fractions to decimals, which in turn relates to money, grades, etc.

3 3-D GLASSES

Nested
3-D glasses — multiple dimensions to one scene, topic, or unit

Description
Within each subject area, the teacher targets multiple skills, a social skill, a thinking skill, and a content-specific skill.

Example
Teacher designs the unit on photosynthesis to simultaneously target consensus seeking (social skill), sequencing (thinking skill), and plant life cycle (science content).

4 EYEGLASSES

Sequenced
Eyeglasses — varied internal content framed by broad, related concepts

Description
Topics or units of study are rearranged and sequenced to coincide with one another. Similar ideas are taught in concert while remaining separate subjects.

Example
English teacher presents an historical novel depicting a particular period while the History teacher teaches that same historical period.

Figure 4.1. Fogarty's Four Multidisciplinary Models

Adapted with permission of the publisher from Fogarty and Stoehr (1995), from the chart on page 24 in Fogarty (1991), extrapolated from Jacobs (1989).

62

5 | BINOCULARS

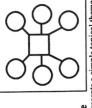

Shared
Binoculars — two disciplines that share overlapping concepts and skills

Description
Shared planning and teaching take place in two disciplines in which overlapping concepts or ideas emerge as organizing elements.

Example
Science and Math teachers use data collection, charting, and graphing as shared concepts that can be team-taught

6 | TELESCOPE

Webbed
Telescope — broad view of entire constellation as one theme, webbed to the various elements.

Description
A fertile theme is webbed to curriculum contents and disciplines; subjects use the theme to shift out appropriate concepts, topics, and ideas.

Example
Teacher presents a simple topical theme, such as the circus, and webs it to the subject areas. A conceptual theme, such as conflict, can be webbed for more depth in the theme approach.

7 | MAGNIFYING GLASS

Threaded
Magnifying glass — big ideas that magnify all content through a metacurricular approach.

Description
The metacurricular approach threads thinking skills, social skills, multiple intelligences, technology, and study skills through the various disciplines.

Example
Teaching staff targets prediction in Reading, Math, and Social Studies teacher targets forecasting current events, and thus threads the skill (prediction) across disciplines.

8 | KALEIDOSCOPE

Integrated
Kaleidoscope — new patterns and designs that use the basic elements of each discipline

Description
This interdisciplinary approach matches subjects for overlaps in topics and concepts with some team teaching in an authentic integrated model.

Example
In Math, Science, Social Studies, Fine Arts, Language Arts, and Practical Arts teachers look for patterning models and approach content through these patterns.

Figure 4.2. Fogarty's Four Interdisciplinary Models

Adapted with permission of the publisher from Fogarty and Stoehr (1995), from the chart on page 24 in Fogarty (1991), extrapolated from Jacobs (1989).

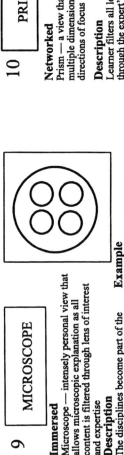

9 | **MICROSCOPE**

Immersed
Microscope — intensely personal view that allows microscopic explanation as all content is filtered through lens of interest and expertise

Description
The disciplines become part of the learner's lens of expertise; the learner filters all content through this lens and becomes immersed in his or her own experience.

Example
Student or doctoral candidate has an area of expert interest and sees all learning through that lens.

10 | **PRISM**

Networked
Prism — a view that creates multiple dimensions and directions of focus

Description
Learner filters all learning through the expert's eye and makes internal connections that lead to external networks of experts in related fields.

Example
Architect, while adopting the CAD/CAM technology for design, networks with technical programmers and expands her knowledge base, just as she had traditionally done with interior designers.

Figure 4.3. Fogarty's Two Intrinsic Models

Adapted with permission of the publisher from Fogarty and Stoehr (1995), from the chart on page 24 in Fogarty (1991), extrapolated from Jacobs (1989).

(1995) mention that this is the most popular approach; certainly it is the easiest. Within her models, Fogarty puts a lot of emphasis on such skills as thinking, social, study, organizing, and the multiple intelligences (MI) skills.

The theme can be a topic, concept, event, novel, project, film, or song. Fogarty and Stoehr (1995) encourage planners to pick fertile themes. For example, "argument and evidence" is a fertile theme, whereas transportation is not (Perkins, 1989). Argument and evidence can be found within and throughout all subject areas, but transportation is not broad enough to teach in all subject areas. Perkins (1989) describes fertile themes.

- They apply broadly to many subject areas.
- They relate to all aspects of a topic.
- They reveal patterns fundamental to subject areas.
- They disclose fundamental similarities and contrasts within and across disciplines.
- They intrigue both teachers and students.

In her 10 models, Fogarty (1991) does not suggest a step-by-step procedure that includes all the elements necessary for today's curriculum. She adds a procedure in *Integrating Curricula With Multiple Intelligences* (Fogarty & Stoehr, 1995) and includes MI as a way to plan for activities.

Applying the Model

The following web model was developed by Joanne Graham, Mira Coghlan, Leigh Ann Sullivan, and Jennifer Staats.

1. Brainstorm for themes.
   - Environment
   - Endangered species
   - Transportation
   - Decision making
   - Fire
   - Hockey

- Inventions
- Community
- Argument and evidence
- Baseball
- Valentine's Day
- Gender issues

2. Streamline the list into topics, concepts, and issues.

- Topics: fire, Valentine's Day
- Concepts: change, patterns, interdependence
- Problems or issues: gender issues, environmental issues

3. Choose a fertile theme.

- Environmental issues
- Valentine's day

4. Manipulate the theme into a question. The question should begin with "how" or "why" to ensure that it is a higher-order question.

- Environment: How can the planet survive?
- Valentine's Day: Why does love make the world go 'round?

5. Expand into activities using a web (Figure 4.4).

6. Select goals and assessment.

- In the science area, endangered species will be studied.
- The goal will be to learn and apply research skills.
- The assessment will be a written research report with a presentation of the report.

This model can be combined with the threaded model and have a skill threaded through it. For example, research may be taught in every subject area, not just in science. As well, it can be webbed according to the eight intelligences. An example of webbing the intelligences is found in Chapter 7, "Aligning Teaching, Learning, and Assessment."

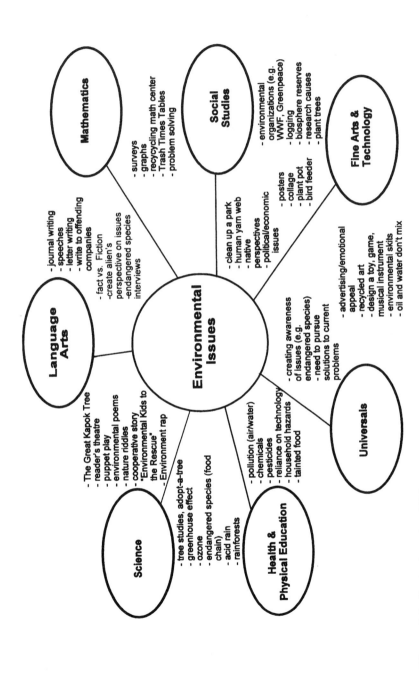

Figure 4.4. Brainstorming Web

67

The Human
Connections Model

The human connections model analyzing human activities (AHA) was created by Roger Taylor (1996). It uses themes in more than one context. It also employs moral and ethical reasoning and critical-creative thinking as the organizing centers to integrate the disciplines. The model focuses on creating strategies that fit into prescribed categories rather than webbing or brainstorming. Taylor's suggestions guarantee a rich curriculum where teaching and learning are transformed from the old model.

Key Ideas

Taylor (1996) recommends beginning with a universal theme to integrate the curriculum. He suggests that universal themes are cause and effect, celebration of pluralism, citizenship, government and authority, human rights, scarcity and choice, survival issues and future alternatives, and equal opportunity.

The universal theme is then matched with the 10 human activities (analyzing human activities, AHA!). Activities are generated for each of the 10 areas. The same process of matching the universal theme can be followed with the disciplines. These activities are producing, exchanging, and distributing; transportation; communications; protecting and conserving; providing education; making tools; providing recreation; organizing and governing; moral and ethical religious behavior; and aesthetic needs.

For each of these areas, activities are created in four categories: knowledge, comprehension, application, and higher-order thinking skills (HOTS).

AHA is only one way of exploring the universal theme. A second exploration is moral-ethical-philosophical reasoning (morality). This is done by providing ethical dilemmas involving the universal theme. A third investigation is productive-creative reasoning (creativity) to explore interdisciplinary connections. This uses creative problem-solving strategies.

Taylor's (1996) work includes many of the latest theories of teaching and learning. Some key elements:

- Books and the arts: Taylor places heavy emphasis on using good literature and music to involve students in the project and to ensure cultural literacy.
- I-search research: The "I-search paper" is a type of research that narrates the process of discovering information while simultaneously explaining how it was uncovered (Macrorie, 1988). This is an independent research project.
- Mastery learning: The student contracts to do certain tasks and repeats the tasks until they are acceptable.
- Bloom's (1956) taxonomy
- Synectics: the process of connecting something to another thing where there is no obvious connection. It is similar to using metaphor. For example, an evergreen tree can be compared to a clothing factory.
- HOTS (higher order thinking skills)
- MI
- Portfolio-authentic assessment
- Inclusion
- Cooperative learning

Applying the Model

Activities are planned for human activities categories and selected disciplines that include knowledge, comprehension, application, and HOTS. For example, the universal theme of "peace" would be explored under organizing and protecting with activities such as the following:

- Knowledge: Using an atlas and your readings, label a map to show the countries that have been at peace in the last 2 years.
- Comprehension: Using a map and your readings, summarize the difference between pre-World War II Europe and today.
- Application: Construct a collage that depicts the type of behavior that leads to peace.
- HOTS: Compare and contrast the pre-World War II United States and the United States of today. Through a group discussion, decide how peace can be maintained.

TABLE 4.1 AHA Planning Chart

	Critical and Analytical Reasoning	Moral-Ethical-Philosophical Reasoning	Productive Creative Reasoning
Producing, exchanging, and distributing			
Transportation			
Communications			
Protecting and conserving			
Making and using tools for technology			
Providing recreation			
Organizing and governing			
Moral, ethical, and spiritual behavior			
Aesthetic needs			
History/politics			
Literature/theater			
Religion/philosophy/ learning			
Visual arts			
Music			
Science/technology/ growth			
Daily life			

SOURCE: Curriculum Design for Excellence, Inc., P. O. Box 4505, Oak Brook, IL 60522, 630-852-8863.

Table 4.1 could be used as a guide for the options that Taylor (1996) suggests.

The Interdisciplinary Concept Model
With Essential Questions

Heidi Hayes Jacobs (1989) presents a comprehensive interdisciplinary concept model that is similar to Fogarty's (1991) model in that it uses a theme and curriculum wheel to develop the content. A version of her model is also found in the video *Integrating the Curriculum* (Video Journal of Education, 1993).

Key Ideas

Jacobs (1989) goes a step further than Fogarty (1991). She emphasizes the guiding or essential questions as an additional umbrella that enables students to connect the content. These guiding questions are intended to be broad, usually two to five, rich enough for several lessons, in logical sequence, understood by all students, often selected through student input, a step toward the learning outcomes, and posted for all students to see.

Jacobs' (1989) approach offers three other aspects that are helpful.

1. It is beneficial to begin brainstorming by having everyone do it alone to allow for personal reflection. This is followed by the teacher sharing his or her thoughts and further brainstorming. Finally, student brainstorming can be added to the procedure. This process facilitates the richest database from which to choose curriculum possibilities.

2. Teachers might create a data box and leave it in the room while the curriculum is being taught. Students could bring in contributions from the real world and their own experiences that connect to the topic and ensure their interest. The data box would be used periodically. This is a wonderful teaching strategy for all ages.

3. Jacobs employs Bloom's (1956) taxonomy methodically to ensure that there is a wide range of activities moving into HOTS. She distinguishes between knowledge that is consumed and knowledge that is produced. The lower levels of Bloom's taxonomy lead to consumer knowledge; the higher levels lead to the production of new

knowledge. A richer description of Bloom's taxonomy is in Chapter 7, "Aligning Teaching, Learning, and Assessment."

Applying the Model

Alan Foster, Katie Flockhart, Dianne Stevens, and Josephine Virgilio decided to design an integrated curricular unit based on Jacobs' (1989) model of curriculum integration. Their process required thoughtful and creative planning while following four important steps. They prepared the unit for middle school students, and the unit was successfully implemented. Their description follows.

Organizing Center

The first step in planning our integrated unit was to identify a problem, issue, or theme for curricular webbing. This theme was to be a focal point for learning, our workbench on which to plan, and a recipe book from which we would create all the learning activities. During an early discussion, one of our group members suggested the theme of Valentine's day. Although somewhat apprehensive at first, we all were delighted with the challenge of developing creative and integrated activities centered around a theme that, for us, had previously elicited somewhat dull and repetitious activities.

Together we reviewed our organizing center criteria and agreed that this theme effectively established a link between a variety of subject disciplines. Given our collective decision to focus on students in the intermediate grades, we also felt that the activities we designed would reflect achievement outcomes identified for students by the end of grade 9 (Table 4.2). In addition, we knew that many of the materials that we would need were available to us within our homes, schools, or local libraries. As well, we all felt that planning an integrated unit on Valentine's day would definitely meet the needs of intermediate students in our classrooms and that we could design activities to last a reasonable length of time (i.e., 4 to 6 weeks).

TABLE 4.2 Long-Range Planning

The 10 outcomes are considered essential for all students. By the end of grade 9, students will . . .	*History*	*English*	*Science*	*Music*
Communicate effectively				
Solve problems and make responsible decisions using critical and creative thinking				
Use technology effectively				
Demonstrate an understanding of the world as a set of related systems (system: ecological, social, or economic unit)				
Apply the skills needed to work and get along with other people				
Participate as responsible citizens in the life of local, national, and global communities				
Explore educational and career opportunities				
Apply aesthetic judgement in everyday life				
Make wise and safe choices for healthy living				
Use the skills of learning to learn more effectively				

SOURCE: Ontario Ministry of Education and Training, *The Common Curriculum*, 1995.

Brainstorming

Our next step involved brainstorming, first on an individual level and then with our group members. (Note: If we were planning this unit with our own classrooms, a further step would involve brainstorming with the students.) Our brainstorming was enhanced by using the "Brainstorming Wheel" (Figure 4.5), with our chosen theme at the center. On a large sheet of paper, we drew arrows that connected this theme to a variety of subject disciplines, such as language arts, history, science, mathematics, art, music, and physical and health education. Then, under each subject heading, we created a point-form list of a number of activities that would enhance student learning.

Guiding Questions

The third step in designing our integrated unit required the creation of essential questions. Our goal was to develop two to five questions that were general in nature, connected to a range of disciplines, and flowed in a logical sequence. We also aimed to design questions that were understandable to students and would provide answers that they needed to know. Finally, it was important that we avoid repetition and devise our questions in such a way that they were sensitive to time constraints.

After carefully considering these criteria, we decided on the following guiding questions:

1. What is the theme of Valentine's Day and how is it celebrated in different cultures?
2. What images are associated with Valentine's Day?
3. What is the story of Valentine's Day from the past, to the present, and the future, and what is my story?
4. How does Valentine's Day affect consumerism?

Planning Activities

The final part of the process of designing our integrated unit was planning the activities. For each guiding question, we generated a list of related learning activities. In devising these activities, we always kept the equation complete. Specifically, learning activi-

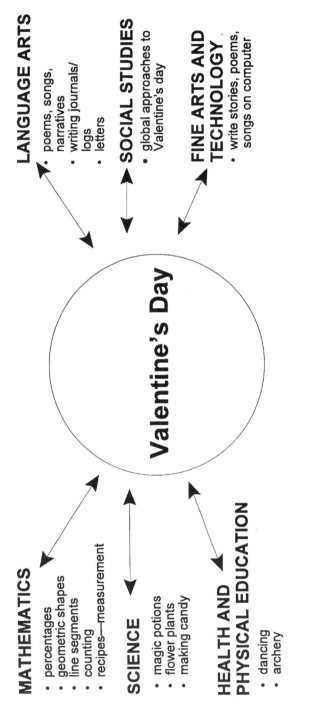

INTERDISCIPLINARY WHEEL

LANGUAGE ARTS

· poems, songs,
  narratives
· writing journals/
  logs
· letters

SOCIAL STUDIES

· global approaches to
  Valentine's day

**FINE ARTS AND
TECHNOLOGY**

· write stories, poems,
  songs on computer

Valentine's Day

MATHEMATICS

· percentages
· geometric shapes
· line segments
· counting
· recipes—measurement

SCIENCE

· magic potions
· flower plants
· making candy

**HEALTH AND
PHYSICAL EDUCATION**

· dancing
· archery

Figure 4.5. Valentine's Wheel

ties needed to include thinking processes and content that lead to a desired product, performance, or behavior outcome. The equation is written in more concrete terms by Jacobs (1989), as follows:

$$T + C = O$$

Thinking processes + Content learning = Outcomes

For each activity that we listed, we also identified the encompassing subject areas as well as all required resources and materials.

An overview of our guiding questions and activity strands brought us to a point where we could synthesize our collaborative efforts. This stage focused on one aspect of the Jacobs (1989) model that is unique in comparison with other models. Specifically, we considered each guiding question within the context of Bloom's (1956) taxonomy, thus developing an interdisciplinary concept model matrix (Table 4.3). The knowledge and experience of one of our group members in this regard became helpful at this time. Although we filled in every category in the matrix, we noted that Jacobs does not insist on filling the boxes. Rather, there should be a balance across the matrix.

All activities were created by following the interdisciplinary activity plan (individual) as shown in Jacobs' (1989) integrated curriculum design plan. For us, it was a priority to design each of these activities with careful attention and sensitivity given to the needs of special populations. Our last step involved the creation of a rubric that would assist us in evaluating our completed Valentine's day unit for intermediate students. For all of us, the process of designing our own integrated curriculum unit was a challenging, exciting, and enjoyable learning experience.

Concept-Based Integrated Units With Essential Questions

This approach is the most complex one explored in this chapter. Although it is referred to as *integrated*, it actually falls into the category of interdisciplinary as defined in this book. It is developed by Lynn Erickson in *Stirring the Head, Heart, and Soul* (1995) and *Concept-Based Curriculum and Instruction* (in press). A version of it is also presented

TABLE 4.3 Matrix: Guiding Questions and Activity Strands

Guiding Questions	Knowledge	Comprehension	Application	Analysis	Synthesis	Evaluation
What images are associated with Valentine's day?	X	X	X	X	X	X
What is the theme of Valentine's day and how is it celebrated across different cultures?	X	X	X	X	X	X
What is the story of Valentine's day from past to present, the future, and my story?	X	X	X	X	X	X
How does Valentine's day affect consumerism?	X	X	X	X	X	X

TABLE 4.4 Activity Plan (Master)

Unit Title: Love Makes the World Go 'Round			
Subject(s): All Grade 7 Level			
Guiding Question 1: What is the theme of Valentine's Day and how is it celebrated across different cultures?			Dates:
Activities (number, description, subject area) *Sequence activities in order of delivery*			
Activities	Description	**Subject(s)**	**Materials/Resources**
1.1	Valentine's cards	Language arts	Library resources, novels, CD-ROMs, Internet, videos, newspapers, magazines
1.2	Stone of knowledge	Language arts	
1.3	Time capsule	Language arts	
1.4	Personal time lines	Language arts	
1.5	Valentine puzzles	Language arts	
1.6	Valentine word power	Language arts	
1.7	Graphing and map reading	Mathematics	
1.8	Valentine banners	Language arts	
1.9	Secret Valentine math	Mathematics	
1.10	Tableau	Visual arts/ drama	
1.11	Bird activity	Language arts	
1.12	Paired novel study	Language arts	

TABLE 4.4 *Continued*

Unit Title: Love Makes the World Go 'Round Subject(s): All Grade 7 Level			
Guiding Question 1: What is the theme of Valentine's Day and how is it celebrated across different cultures?			Dates:
Activities (number, description, subject area) Sequence activities in order of delivery			
Activities	Description	**Subject(s)**	**Materials/Resources**
1.13	"Love" literature	Language arts	Library resources, novels, CD-ROMs, Internet, videos, newspapers, magazines
1.14	Collection heart expression	Language arts	
1.15	Magic mood music	Music/ language arts	
1.16	Keep a journal	Language arts	
1.17	Design a romantic menu	Language arts	
1.18	Valentine's cards	Language arts	
1.19	Cupid	Language arts	
1.20	Paper making	Language arts/science	

in the video *Planning Integrated Units: A Concept-Based Approach* (Video Journal Curriculum, 1997).

Key Ideas

Erickson (1995, in press) incorporates most of the ideas that I have already investigated, but adds a new component by revisiting the question of what is worth knowing. The guiding questions direct

TABLE 4.5 Hugs and Handshakes: Teaching Grammar Using Valentine Imagery

Guiding Question 2: What images are associated with Valentine's Day?	
Activity Plan:	Grade: Intermediate
Subject: Language arts	Bloom's Taxonomy: Know, Comprehend, Apply

Some students come to grade 7 with excellent skills in grammar usage; frequently, these are the same students who read widely and continuously. Other students, less enamoured with the written word, also have less facility writing in the traditional mode; proper use of punctuation may elude them. The approach in this lesson is designed to link the use of quotation marks and semicolons to symbolic gestures with which students are familiar, such as the handshake, in an attempt to make connections that will assist understanding.

Semicolons are like handshakes!

Most often, when people shake hands, they have something in common. It may be that two businesspeople are greeting each other; perhaps two acquaintances are saying hello. A third person may be introducing two people to each other. Pick one of these examples; see the picture in your mind.

Think of the handshake that joins two similar people together as being like a semicolon that joins two sentences that have something in common. Whenever a semicolon is used, it must connect two sentences that are closely related.

Example: Valentine's Day is celebrated in North America. It is always on February 14th.

Both these sentences talk about Valentine's day. It is correct to leave them as two separate sentences, but because they are closely related by their similar topic, Valentine's day, it is also correct to remove the period and the second capital letter and replace the period with a semicolon.

Example: Valentine's Day is celebrated in North America; it is always on February 14th.

the unit as they did in Jacobs' (1989) approach, but they are linked with essential understandings, or generalizations. For Erickson, facts and skills are important; but we need deeper understanding if we

TABLE 4.5 *Continued*

Assignment

1. Use semicolons to join the following sentences, if it is appropriate. Explain your decision.

   a. Many images are associated with Valentine's Day. Often chocolates are in the shape of these images.

   b. Many people don't exercise. It is usually cold on February 14th.

2. Work with partners. Make up pairs of sentences; have some of the pairs relate to each other and some not. Switch sentences with your partner; rewrite the sentences, using semicolons if it is appropriate.

3. Work with partners. Each person is to write the first sentence only of what will be a pair of sentences. Use something that you have learned about Valentine's Day in this unit as your subject. Exchange sentences with your partner; he or she is to write a second sentence that is related to your first sentence and join it with a semicolon.

4. Work individually. Write a paragraph (journal entry, letter, etc.) about some aspect of Valentine's Day, using semicolons when you can.

want to transfer knowledge. She places greater emphasis on the structure of knowledge and how to get at a deeper understanding of the content.

Skills do not rely on any outside structure such as Bloom's (1956) taxonomy or MI. Instead, Erickson (1995, in press) emphasizes complex performances that are needed in the real world. If, for example, the student needs to act as a historian to complete the task, he or she must learn the skills necessary to be a historian. These skills must be taught explicitly. Several complex performances may be needed in a curriculum unit.

Erickson (1995, in press) differentiates between process and content and provides an effective method to distinguish between the two. This is especially important because a curriculum document does not always separate them.

Content

Content is understood through the structure of knowledge. This structure is hierarchical, moving from the lowest level to the most complex. The lowest level of knowledge is represented by facts; a topic includes a number of facts. Concepts represent a higher level of knowledge and serve as organizing ideas. They answer the question of "so what?" Concepts are broad, abstract categories under which many examples with similar attributes can be categorized. They are universal and timeless.

- Concepts: change, interdependence, cause and effect, models, probability, patterns
- Topics: China, green plants, World War II, Valentine's Day, Who am I?, our community

The essential learnings of the unit represent a higher level of knowledge called *generalizations,* or *essential understandings.* Essential understandings are the "big ideas" that synthesize the learning. They state the relationship between two or more concepts. Creating essential understandings is not easy because some generalizations can still represent a lower level of knowledge.

Compare "Interactions between seals and commercial fisheries have political and socioeconomic implications" and "Interactions between humans and nature have political and socioeconomic implications."

The second example represents a higher level of knowledge. Generalizations that are universal in application are timeless, broad, and abstract. They are usually true, can be supported by varied examples, and do not have proper nouns in them.

When teachers use concepts, students shift from memorizing isolated facts to incorporating higher-order thinking skills to understand the universal generalizations. Teachers generally encourage students to discover these essential learnings inductively rather than explicitly telling them what they are. Assessment of content involves critical facts and conceptual understanding.

Process

Process skills are internal abilities that students acquire over time. Examples of process skills are computing, reading, writing, listing, drawing, dramatizing, thinking, creating, analyzing, synthesizing, and hypothesizing. By using process skills, students construct

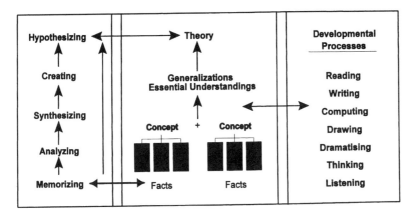

Figure 4.6. Content/Process Interactions

meaning around the content. They are developmental in nature and need to be recognized as such in the assessment process. Erickson (1995, in press) cautions us that, if we are to increase conceptual understanding and the developmental process skills, we need to allow sufficient time to teach these skills. This will necessarily reduce the amount of content that can be taught.

My understanding of Erickson's (1995, in press) proposed relationship between content and theory is illustrated in Figure 4.6.

Applying the Model

This application was developed by Shawna Hopkins and Cheryl Riddell for a grade 11 class. Note that Shawna and Cheryl have integrated the sciences and also have included other subject areas.

1. Select a significant topic. The topic identifies the content. For example, "fishing in the Atlantic." Limit the content by adding more words: "Perceptions of fishing in the Atlantic."
2. Identify a universal concept: "Perceptions."
3. Create a web to determine the content. The web may revolve around subjects of areas connected to content (Figure 4.7).
4. Brainstorm for key generalizations to guide the study. Key generalizations or essential understandings:

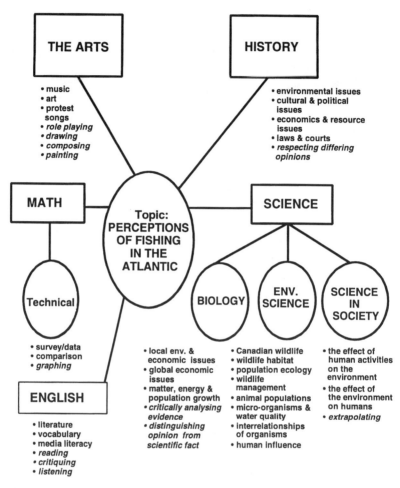

Figure 4.7. Brainstorming Concept-Based Model

- Life experiences bias perceptions.

- Interactions between humans and nature have political and socioeconomic implications.

- Societal values and interest groups influence scientific research.

5. Write guiding questions linked with the essential under-standings. These questions guide the unit and ensure that essential understandings are being taught. Note that "what"

and "when" questions usually lead to fact-based answers relating to the topic. "How" and "why" questions, on the other hand, lead to the big ideas. The following examples connect generalizations and guiding questions:

Essential understanding: Life experiences bias perceptions:

- What is bias?
- What is perception?
- What are various seal-fishery interactions that are perceived to exist?

Essential understanding: Interactions between humans and nature have political and socioeconomic implications:

- How have changes in the natural environment (e.g., depletion of fish stocks and increases in seal population) affected politics and socioeconomics?
- What are the perceived causes of these changes in the natural environment?

Essential understanding: Societal values and interest groups influence scientific research.

- Why do some "facts" in the seal-fishery controversy appear questionable?
- How do personal and professional opinions bias what and how information is transferred and interpreted?
- What role do interest groups play in Atlantic controversies?

6. List complex performances and key skills. The complex performance to be demonstrated is the student acting as a scientist. The necessary key skills are analysis, compare and contrast, evaluation, research, and presentation.
7. Develop the unit outcome and the culminating performance that will demonstrate the outcome.

Unit outcome: In a small group or alone, the students research the interactions among seals, commercial fisheries, and interest groups in the Atlantic. They analyze by comparing and contrasting positions to evaluate the underlying controversies. They choose the position of one group and develop a presentation to deliver to the class that will convince them of the validity of their position. As experts, students will address questions from the audience. Their product will include a written report as well as one of the following: presentation of a role-play; preparation of a public awareness pamphlet; creation of a radio or television commercial; or critique of a video program, newspaper, or magazine article on seal-fishery interactions.

A rubric to assess the presentation is included (Table 4.6). This rubric does not address the skills necessary for the research component of the topic. Teachers need to give the necessary direct instruction for the process skills.

   8. Create the daily activities that link outcomes to the content and generalizations of the unit.

Core courses involved in this activity will require approximately 12 hours to complete this unit, with other courses needing between 3 and 5 hours.

The Activities

1. The survey: The survey consists of a number of questions on attitudes and knowledge of marine mammals and marine mammal issues. It should act as a benchmark and is given to students before any information on the study unit is provided. At the end of the unit, students will repeat the survey and compare the results graphically.

2. Introduction: The video *Seals, Fish and You—The Nature of the Story* is shown to all classes at the most appropriate time. The video presents the perspective of the Marine Mammal Association on the relationship between killing seals and fish stocks. Students are made aware that there are other perspectives on this topic. A discussion about bias follows. Students are encouraged to question what they read and hear.

3. A brief story outlining sealing and fishery industries is read. This introduction provides historical perspectives of the various fishing and sealing industries and introduces students to the con-

cepts of seal-fishery interactions. Objectives, evaluation schemes, study planners, and strategies are included to help students organize their time. A glossary of terms is distributed.

4. Activity 1: By providing students with literature from numerous sources around the world, the teacher introduces students to marine mammal-fishery interactions. Examples include articles from various journals, professional organizations, newspapers, and government transcripts. A variety of reading materials must be provided to introduce students to different ways an issue can be addressed. The teacher must stress that the source (author, affiliation) is vital to the interpretation of information because personal and professional opinions tend to bias what information is included in a report and how it is presented. Students must be encouraged to question continuously what is read and attempt to familiarize themselves with all sides of an issue. From these readings, students should be able to understand why interactions exist or are perceived to exist and what interest groups are involved.

5. Activity 2, information sharing: Literature is again provided to students from a variety of sources. This material introduces students to specific interactions that exist (e.g., seals and commercial fisheries, human effect on prey availability, codworm effect on fish, seals, public health, economics and employment, and operational interactions). In addition, students will become familiar with the roles that interest groups (fisheries, scientists, the government, and animal welfare and environmental groups) play both in the controversies and with political, biological, social, and economic forces. Analysis and compare-and-contrast skills are taught explicitly. Classes or subject areas may be divided into expert groups, with each group researching one type of interaction. For example, a history class may examine political forces, whereas a science class may study biological forces. The format for sharing the data is negotiated with the classes.

6. Activity 3, independent research: Students do their own independent research to prepare for the culminating activity. The skills necessary for the final presentation are taught explicitly here.

7. Activity 4, culminating activity: This activity allows students to integrate what they have learned in a creative form and then share

(text continued on p. 91)

Table 4.6 Evaluation Rubric

Ministry Level	Below Expectations	Meets	Expectations		Beyond Expectations
	One	Two	Three	Four	Five
Marking Scheme	0/1 Inadequate/Poor	2.5 Adequate/Marginal	3.5 Good	4.5 Very Good	5 Excellent/Outstanding
Information Content 1. Demonstrates student awareness of seal-fisheries interactions. 2. Organization of evidence-based information in a logical, persuasive format.	■ Did not submit product. ■ Blank, off-topic, or unreadable response. ■ Understands issue only slightly. ■ Some information inaccurate. ■ Content mostly complete.	■ Incorporation of a position a group has taken. ■ Supporting arguments based on emotion.	■ Information was complete and accurate. ■ Inclusion of a group's position and the rationale behind it. ■ One objective reason for rationale included.	■ Information complete, accurate, and well summarized. ■ Objective reasoning backed up with evidence that supports it.	■ Information beyond level 4 in completeness and accuracy. ■ Multiple objective reasonings with evidence cited. ■ Validity of evidence from other groups questioned.

Presentation of Information 1. Topic clarity evident. 2. Well organized. 3. Superior command of the language.					
■ Layout lacked organization and was difficult to understand. ■ Poor and ineffective use of materials. ■ Terminology and vocabulary lacking or confused. ■ Organization needs to be improved. ■ Materials could have been better chosen. ■ Little use of appropriate vocabulary.	■ Acceptable layout of presentation. ■ Materials used appropriately. ■ Adequate use of the language and appropriate vocabulary utilized.	■ Layout logical, concise, and could be followed easily. ■ Materials used appropriately and effectively. ■ Good use of vocabulary and terminology.	■ Layout self-explanatory. ■ Very effective use of materials. ■ Proper and effective use of language, vocabulary, and terminology.	■ Data beyond level 4 in clarity and confidence. ■ Command of language, vocabulary, and terminology superior. ■ Able to extrapolate.

Table 4.6 *Continued*

Creativity 1. Presentaion included some original ideas. 2. Novel methods used to convey information.	■ Lack of creativity in both topic and resources. ■ Incomplete and unimaginative use of resources.	■ Standard approach. ■ Adequate treatment of current topic.	■ Standard approach. ■ Good treatment of current topic.	■ Imaginative, extension of standard approach, use of equipment or materials.	■ Original, resourceful, novel approach. ■ Creative design and use of equipment and materials.

Comments/Observations/Conference_____

_____

_____

Student Signature _____   Teacher Signature _____

it with the rest of the class. There are four projects to choose from: a role play, information pamphlets, a commercial, or a critique of literature. The message (content) will vary, but it must include at least one interaction discussed in class and it must provide a group's position with its rationale. Positions must be supported with appropriate references. The presentation may be evaluated with a scoring guide by peers, the teacher, or both.

Summary

This chapter introduced the reader to four interdisciplinary models. Each one emphasizes a different way to approach the integration. In each of the models, the disciplines are central. It is important to note that rich connections rather than forced fits can be made in all these models. What is important in making each approach work is that the teaching strategies are aligned with how people learn.

5

✳✳✳✳✳✳

EXPLORING TRANSDISCIPLINARY APPROACHES

✳ ✳ ✳

Many use the word *integrated* to describe the level of integration beyond multi- and interdisciplinary approaches. I prefer to use the term *transdisciplinary*, meaning "beyond the disciplines," rather than integration of the disciplines into a whole. Beyond the disciplines implies that, although the disciplines will be embedded in the topic, they are not the main focus. All "categories" that I describe in this book blur easily, including the transdisiciplinary one. Transdisciplinary approaches can be found in a classroom with a disciplinary focus or one that is free of subject area definition. Characteristics of the transdisciplinary approach include the following:

- The disciplines are not the organizing center.
- The disciplines are embedded within the unit and can be separated if desired.
- The real-world context is of utmost importance.
- The student as researcher is a core concept.
- Student input and choice are crucial.
- Standards can be built into the curriculum as needed.
- Most examples can be applied at the multi- or interdisciplinary level.

■ Many transdisciplinary approaches challenge the central tenets of the traditional model.

This chapter considers several transdisciplinary approaches. It is organized by moving from the models that can be adapted to more traditional frameworks to those that espouse a very different approach to education, where there is no middle ground.

Problem-Based Learning

Problem-based learning (PBL) has its roots in the project method, which was advocated as early as the 1920s. PBL began in the 1970s at the medical school at McMaster University in Ontario, and has since been a model for other universities. Students tackle course content through real-life problems rather than lectures. The entrance procedures for this program at McMaster are interesting. Students from a wide variety of backgrounds are admitted; for example, philosophy degrees are valued. This means the students who enter the program are generalists who are not locked into the medical model with an objective scientific perspective. As a result, they are often better able to tackle the ill-structured problems that they encounter in the real world. As well, this method tends to produce doctors and nurses who are interested in a more holistic approach to health care and acquire good bedside skills.

Educators are taking this lesson from the medical field and offering students real-life problems as curriculum. Although schools have always been interested in problem-solving skills, it is interesting how these skills have moved from formula problem solving using a procedure such as the scientific method, to complex problem solving, to ill-structured problem solving. This speaks to the nature of problems in real life. The scientific method is not abandoned—it remains at the core—but students have many more variables to consider and more ambiguity to navigate. One advantage of this approach is that students learn to think like an expert. Given the problem, students may need to think like a historian, mathematician, archaeologist, or architect. Students learn skills such as reasoning, collaboration, and persistence. Teachers are the facilitators in the process.

Key Ideas

Vars (1993) outlines the following process for a problem-centered unit.

1. The teacher designs the unit with student input.
2. The teacher introduces the unit in a motivating way.
3. The teacher engages students with active participation.
4. The teacher develops problems through active discussion.
5. The teacher forms groups based on preference for a topic.
6. The groups then plan their procedures for problem solving.
7. The groups engage in research and study.
8. The groups plan and prepare reports of problem solving.
9. The groups present their findings to the class in an interesting way, such as a skit, panel, or video.
10. Class discussion on unit topics follows.
11. The class then plans and implements a culminating activity to share results.
12. The class and teacher evaluate the unit.

A recent version of PBL is called the *problem based learning as co-development (PBL-CD) model* (Jones, Rasmussen, & Moffitt, 1997). This version views problem solving as a progressive skill. It is a series of cycles consisting of four fundamental thinking processes:

1. Understanding and planning
2. Acting and sharing
3. Reflecting
4. Rethinking and revisioning

These cycles are applied to both teachers developing curriculum and students engaged in problem solving. They involve developing expertise in the area, doing progressive action research, using a critical friend to provide feedback, and using a rubric or template to build on one's work.

Building on previous models, PBL-CD includes the following elements:

- Open-ended questions
- Authentic tasks
- Progressive problem solving
- Performance-based assessment
- Codevelopment (teams of teachers, teachers with students)
- student centered
- Graphic representation of text (advanced organizers, summarizing, and debriefing)
- Community service

Applying the Model

There are some concerns with this approach. It is a very messy, time-consuming process. PBL must occur with enough regularity that students gain the necessary skills and can make connections among subject areas. By its nature, PBL delves into issues and values, and some parents are anxious if their child is exposed only to learning of this sort. Therefore, parents need to be informed that the student will be undergoing this process. They are usually delighted, however, when children display obvious enthusiasm for their work.

PBL can be done within one discipline or at any of the levels of integration offered in this book. Examples of classroom situations follow.

■ How can we improve the image of Urbana? This grew from a 4- to 6-week unit in a year-long program. Teachers Kathy Norviel and Joanne Petty used this problem with grades 4, 5, and 6. Students defined community and wrote poems to identify perceptions of their hometown. They interviewed people who lived in the community, graphed the data, then presented it to the business community for evaluation. They created a community Internet Web site at the request of the businesses (Rasmussen, 1997).

■ What should happen to the driver involved in a prom night drunk driving car accident? At Indian Trail Junior High School, grade 8 students were put in charge of this fictional accident. They were all investigators who had 5 days to review existing evidence and investigate further. All grade 8 students were involved with 15 teachers from different content areas. Students worked individually and in groups to come up with their recommendations, which were presented at a mock press conference (Rasmussen, 1997).

■ What is the probability that a volcano in Yellowstone National Park will erupt and wipe out one third of the United States? What would be the effect of this on the jobs and politics of the region? In Rick McKelvey's grade 12 geoscience class, students were encouraged to address this question by finding information on the Internet and presenting their research to the class (Rasmussen, 1997).

■ How could we send a group of 190 students to Mars to develop and establish a permanent colony? Students at the Center for Technology and Communication in California researched and prepared a specialty master plan to accompany the colonizers during the first flight (Glasgow, 1997). All subject areas were included, although science, engineering, and government were emphasized.

■ How can we produce a *Sixty Minutes* pilot on a relevant issue? Students researched an issue of choice, and composed and communicated through an oral and visual interpretation that emulated the television show's approach (Glasgow, 1997).

■ How can we develop a "living document" that will act as a resource to preserve the cultural landscape in the local village of Blair? Grade 12 students at Galt Collegiate Institute in Ontario are attacking this problem in a unique and interesting way. Students are engaging their families in a study of genealogy and community memorabilia. As well, they are connecting to businesses to reconstruct the community's history. They are also developing a database on the Internet for monitoring cultural and environmental heritage information. The environmental aspect revolves around monitoring water quality and the identification of the local ecosystem's flora and fauna. This project involves partnerships with many local businesses and industry.

■ What do we need to know to plan for a trip from Northern Ontario to Old Crow, Yukon? This example of PBL involved many teachers and two schools. Students hypothetically traveled different legs of the journey for 3 weeks in grades 7, 8, and 9. Students planned their trips—largely on back roads—in vehicles that they had researched before "buying." They kept daily logs and reported a detailed breakdown of the route, including temperature, precipitation, winds, local features, local urban centers, and history of the area, and wrote postcards in both English and French. Costs of food, fuel, and maintenance of the vehicle were calculated. Five special features of each area also had to be noted. In each grade, different skills were learned over the 15-day trip (Numbers, 1996).

■ How can grade 6 improve its Illinois Goal Assessment Program scores and preserve the school's accreditation? To do the seemingly impossible task of connecting PBL with improving rigid statewide assessment exams, Paula Bulli used this question as the problem for her students (Ewy, 1996-1997). Students decided on the following 2-month regime: They practiced the subjects, looked for resources on reading and math testing, interviewed educators who could tell them the criteria of the test makers, and set up a tutoring program. In the end, the students felt confident in taking the exams and even commented that the process was fun. They met or exceeded state math, reading, and writing goals. As well, their average scores surpassed their grade 3 scores.

This last example is an ingenious way to connect standardized testing with an open teaching approach. It also indicates the amount of time needed to prepare for standardized tests. Paradoxically, this innovative approach is still teaching to the test.

Story as an Organizing Center

Two different approaches to curriculum are offered using story as the integrating framework. The narrative curriculum method works with a story that already exists and may be historical, problem centered, or literary. In the story model approach, the curriculum is created around personal, cultural, and global stories. Both approaches have some common assumptions:

■ Story is the way we make meaning of our lives.
■ Stories are good tools for remembering things.
■ Stories allow for learning in a meaningful context.
■ Everyone can connect to story.

- Stories provide a sense of community because of the universal human elements within them.

- Stories promote a constructivist approach.

- Authentic student inquiry emerges from stories.

- Broad curricular goals such as thinking critically, creatively, and reflectively can be embedded in a story curriculum.

- Curriculum can be negotiated.

- The disciplines will be embedded in the stories and in the questions emerging from the stories, but they are not the organizing center.

- Narrative curriculum is marked by its recursiveness. Learners return again and again to the story to link their explorations, that is, the story of their lives in the classroom, to the story in the book.

The Narrative Curriculum

Lauritzen and Jaeger (1997) developed the narrative curriculum approach. This opens with a story that has been selected by the teacher; interactive reading of the text occurs, where shared student listening, questioning, and hypothesizing are encouraged. The teacher (or students) can organize the questions so that they are under the umbrella of larger questions similar to Jacobs' (1989) guiding questions. Students then brainstorm how they can answer these questions, aided by teacher input. They create scoring guides by which their work will be assessed. The teacher gathers resources and materials to help answer the questions the students have addressed. Students then commit themselves to answering a specific question.

Key Ideas

The narrative curriculum begins with a story or storylike context. Stories are selected to interest learners as well as to spark wonder. The natural wonder of learners provides the basis for generating specific or general questions that can be investigated from a variety of disciplinary perspectives. Learners pursue their questions in much the same way a scientist probes a hypothesis or an author crafts writing. The culminations of these explorations are the communications students make with others in the learning community. The shared findings of all contribute to the context, and thereby inform and transform the story. The narrative curriculum model honors learner interests and variable routes to knowing while considering the broad purposes and goals of schooling.

What are the key features of the narrative curriculum? The curriculum begins and ends in story. Reading the story aloud in a collaborative manner invites the children to bring their own life experiences, their personal stories, to interact with the original story. The children's responses—their puzzles, their wonderments, their desire to know—lead to explorations of new aspects that add to the children's life stories. The rereading of the story, with all the new experiences intertwined, creates a new version of the text. In the narrative curriculum design, the story is more than an anticipatory set to introduce areas of study. It is more than a springboard to launch children into inquiry. It is instead a context that both invites and surrounds learning and gives meaning to all the children's investigations and explorations. Not only are stories long remembered, but the learning that is generated from the story and intertwined with the story is long remembered.

A second feature of narrative curriculum is that the learner's natural wonder and desire to know are central to the curriculum. Students are encouraged to make connections between their own lives and the story. Their responses are sought and their questions are honored. Their authentic desire to know becomes the focus of study. What they learn is blended with what they already know to construct new meaning.

Explorations are another key feature of narrative curriculum. They are open-ended routes developed with the students to help them meet the challenge of an inquiry. The teacher does not have to know all the answers. Rather, the teacher gathers resources and materials and facilitates the students' learning. Disciplines are used as a heuristic in this approach. The purpose of the narrative is to encourage asking questions. The students use the tools of the discipline that are needed; they act as scientists, historians, artists, or authors as dictated by the question asked. Lauritzen and Jaeger (1997) offer examples of studies that began with a story of the Canadian North that inspired scientific questions. Students then developed inquiries where they acted like scientists.

Applying the Model

A template that was developed to plan curriculum helps teachers see how goals, narratives, and disciplinary heuristics interconnect is shown in Figure 5.1.

The Story Model

The story model (Drake et al., 1992) can be taught at any level and can originate in any subject area or areas. Its main focus is past, present, and future. It explores any topic through personal, cultural, global, and universal lenses. This framework is generic and can be adapted in many ways. It has been modified for use at the kindergarten level to the graduate-student level. The teacher is in control of the amount of the curriculum that is self-directed and how much the teacher wishes to teach necessary knowledge and skills.

The story model has two major objectives—personal growth and social change. These act as an umbrella for the daily curriculum plan. The framework assumes the following:

- The world as we know it is undergoing flux and change.

- We make meaning though story.

- Knowledge is interconnected.

- Knowledge is laden with cultural values, beliefs, and assumptions.

- Most of these values, beliefs and assumptions are held at an unconscious level.

- Our actions are driven by these beliefs.

- To change actions, we have to become conscious of our cultural values, beliefs, and assumptions.

- We can consciously create a "new story" to live by.

The fact that most people wear seat belts and most students recycle automatically at school are good examples that new stories are possible. We story these new behaviors in new ways. A key element in new stories is education.

Goals: Interpret human experiences through literature and the arts. Think creatively and imaginatively when framing problems and seeking solutions. Social Science--Describe an event or issue from multiple points of view. Science--use interrelated processes to pose questions and investigate the world.

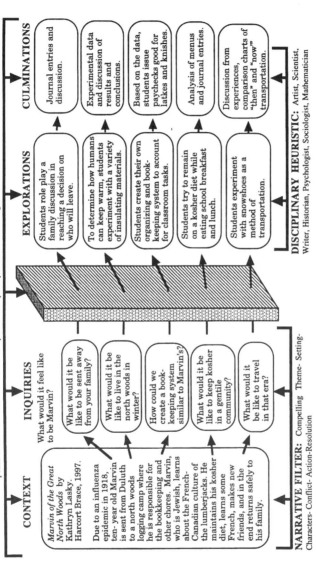

CONTEXT

Marvin of the Great North Woods by Kathryn Lasky. Harcort Brace, 1997.

Due to an influenza epidemic in 1918, ten-year old Marvin is sent from Duluth to a north woods logging camp where he is responsible for the bookkeeping and other chores. Marvin, who is Jewish, learns about the French-Canadian culture of the lumberjacks. He maintains his kosher diet, learns some French, makes new friends, and in the end returns safely to his family.

INQUIRIES

What would it feel like to be Marvin?

What would it be like to be sent away from your family?

What would it be like to live in the north woods in winter?

How could we create a book-keeping system similar to Marvin's?

What would it be like to keep kosher in a gentile community?

What would it be like to travel in that era?

EXPLORATIONS

Students role play a family discussion in reaching a decision on who will leave.

To determine how humans can keep warm, students experiment with a variety of insulating materials.

Students create their own organizing and book-keeping system to account for classroom tasks.

Students try to remain on a kosher diet while eating school breakfast and lunch.

Students experiment with snowshoes as a method of transportation.

CULMINATIONS

Journal entries and discussion.

Experimental data and discussion of results and conclusions.

Based on the data, students issue paychecks good for latkes and knishes.

Analysis of menus and journal entries.

Discussion from experiences, comparison charts of "then" and "now" transportation.

NARRATIVE FILTER: Compelling Theme- Setting-Characters- Conflict- Action-Resolution

DISCIPLINARY HEURISTIC: Artist, Scientist, Writer, Historian, Psychologist, Sociologist, Mathematician

Figure 5.1. Narrative Curriculum Planning Template

Used by permission of Carol Lauritzen and Michael Jaeger, copyright 1997.

101

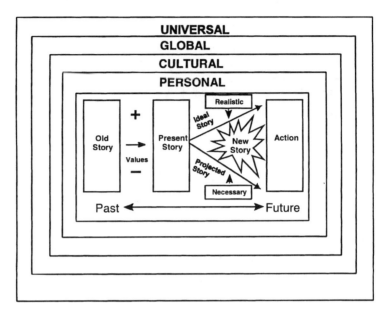

Figure 5.2. The Story Model

Key Ideas

The story model (Figure 5.2) assumes that we all make sense of our lives through the process of storying. We all have a personal story, and this is our primary way of knowing. This story is filtered by a cultural story that we are often unaware of but that colors our perceptions in powerful ways. The assumptions and beliefs of our society are embedded in these perceptions. Much of this curriculum framework involves uncovering these assumptions and beliefs. The next lens of the framework is the global story. Living in a global world, we must consider topics globally. The final lens is the universal one; this refers to narratives that have appealed to humans throughout time, such as mythologies.

We "story" to understand what happens in the real-world context. The "hook" for this model is the story aspect. Students are encouraged to tell personal stories about each topic. As the topic is explored further, stories are told as often as possible. These may come from many sources, such as personal experiences, newspapers, movies, or books.

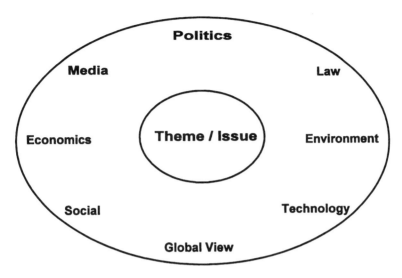

Figure 5.3. Real-World Web—Theme/Issue

Planned activities include stories found in such places as novels, interviews, role playing, drama, photographs and videos, songs, and journals. The creation of stories is often used as an assessment tool.

It is best to start the story model curriculum with a concrete topic rather than a concept. For example, "tree" is better than "environment." This is atypical of most approaches, but once the real-life context is revealed, the topic becomes global very quickly. An issue or problem also works very well as a topic.

The cultural story or real-life context is identified in the real-world web (Figure 5.3). It is important to use this web as it is. The focus words on the outside of the web ensure that any topic will be situated in its real-world context, or cultural story. The focus words can be adapted, but the emphasis needs to be the real-life context. For younger children, the focus words can be simpler. For example, "economics" could become "money."

Students brainstorm around the focus words on the outside of the real-world web. This answers the question of what they already know. To ensure that a topic is wide open, students must push whatever they are studying to its global edge. For example, the story of bicycles can be very limited, and the use of bikes instead of cars that pollute can seem like a new story. When the topic of bicycles is pushed beyond its local context into the third world, however, students can begin to see the inequities and power issues that revolve around who has motorized transportation and why.

Next, students draw lines to make connections among facts on the web. These connections need to be made explicit. Each real-world web will reveal endless connections. This illustrates, in a very visual way, that knowledge is interconnected and interdependent.

A sophisticated addition to this model is to ask what values, beliefs, and assumptions are embedded in the web. This step is very difficult. Younger children can do it best. In essence, this task is done by identifying the "old story," or the actions that have brought us to where we are today but are not working very well. It is necessary to look at what is happening, not at what we believe should be happening. Although many new stories are emerging now that have positive and sustaining values, most old stories are dominated by autonomy, individualism, personal pleasure, inequities, status, consumption, power, greed, and violence.

Following this theme, students select values, beliefs, and assumptions that they believe (through consensus) should ground stories and thus drive behavior. Note that the intention is not to throw out the old story totally, but to keep what has been valuable from the old story and add what is realistic from the ideal story. Values that are usually selected for the new story are autonomy, love, caring, compassion, freedom, equality, justice, and respect for self, others, and the environment.

Overview of Steps of the Story Model

The story model has personal growth and social change built into the model as "being" goals. This aspect of the curriculum acts as an umbrella for everything that is taught. (See Chapter 6, "Connecting Standards to Curriculum," for a further explanation of being goals.)

1. Choose the content area to be covered; this may be teacher directed or left to student interest, depending on how the model is implemented.
2. Select a major goal or standard for the unit. This should be a complex cross-disciplinary skill such as information management, reading and listening, or using technology.

3. Decide how the "being" characteristics and complex skills can be evaluated. How can students demonstrate these criteria? Create rubrics or suitable instruments that allow students to know what is expected of them. Or give students the opportunity to develop the criteria themselves.

4. Brainstorm for content. Decide on a culminating activity that demonstrates desired goals or standards. Decide on appropriate activities that lead to these standards. As you are doing this, determine ongoing assessment practices that are aligned with the rest of your planning.

5. The following steps are key to the story model and should be done by both students and teachers.

   a. Tell your personal stories about the topic under exploration. Call on personal stories throughout the unit whenever appropriate.

   b. Begin to develop the cultural story. The cultural story colors and filters the knowledge we can obtain on our topic. To do this, use the real-world web. Brainstorm what you know about the topic and the focus words. Make connections within the web; draw lines to all the connecting ideas, facts, or concepts. What do these connections tell us about the world? What values, beliefs, and assumptions are embedded within the web? How do people act? Is there a difference between what we say and what we do? Do we want to change the cultural story?

   c. Follow the story model map and develop the present (crisis), the past, the preferred future, and the projected future. Identify the values, beliefs, and assumptions that drive each of these. Develop the new story by considering what is really possible and what we consider to be necessary.

   d. Develop an action plan for "my story." What can you, as an individual, do to make the new story happen?

6. Develop activities that can be done while teaching the unit. One key activity is the student as researcher. The student develops a question of interest from the real-world web and uses research skills to answer the question. It is particularly powerful if students use the story model visual as a framework for their research. Presentations often have both a written part and a "creative" presentation component.

Applying the Model

The following application was developed by Anne Armstrong and Brian Speed. They have adapted it for use with both junior and intermediate students.

Theme: Food

Cross-disciplinary expectations (standard): Students will know how to build healthy lifestyles and demonstrate this knowledge while applying a global perspective in both attitude and behavior.

Assessment:

- Students make judgments related to packaging, production, and the effect on personal health when selecting food to purchase or eat through use of a matrix.
- Students prepare and present individual presentations.
- Students plan and prepare a community meal that demonstrates an understanding of the effect of food selection on health and the environment.

Activities: Introduction, familiarization, exploration. These introductory activities are designed to help students become familiar with the subject matter so that they will later be able to make connections. Typically, with intermediate and senior students, the story model is taught after a brief unit introduction. With younger students and with weaker students, however, it is important to teach more introductory (familiarization) activities so that the overall learning experience is richer and the pupils are equipped to make connections and competently complete a research project. There is, accordingly, no set rule as to the number or order of activities that should be taught.

The introduction includes storying. Teachers tell meaningful stories about an experience with food, such as the personal importance of meals or how one cooks for oneself, or personal experiences concerning the diet of the poor. After teachers tell their stories, students can share their stories using think, pair, share, or small group sharing of food stories.

1. Importance of food: Students work in groups toward an understanding of the role of food in their lives. They pull together for a total group share. They work with concepts such as favorite

foods, healthy foods, and hated foods (ideal for concept formation lessons).

2. Continuity

   ■ Barbecue day—possibly initiating activity

   ■ Rice and beans day—possibly middle of unit for contrast

   ■ Planned food day (thought about meal, encourage pasta)—concluding activity with staff and parent community involvement

3. Reading aloud: *Anansi the Spider* (Sherlock, 1954)
4. Familiarization: sharing recipes
5. Perk days: Popcorn Day, Treat Day, Baking Day, Pizza Day
6. Etiquette: Work with students on eating etiquette.
7. Packaging, processing, producing, transportation

   a. Trace the present story. (This is an awareness-level activity only. More extensive connections will be made later; but to see the global implications, students need to be familiar with today's factory environments.)

   b. Visit a food processing factory.

8. Food chains: Look at food chains. In particular, look at food we consume, such as beef, pork, bread, and fish.

Present Story

The present story is our view of the country, society, world, and universe today. The perceived past is part of the present story, as is the anticipated future. The present story acts as our link to understanding ourselves and our universe. It can be viewed through a global, cultural, or personal lens, that is, our perspective can shift.

1. Food distribution: Divide students into continents and into proportions that reflect population distribution. Divide a loaf of bread in the same ratio and distribute it to the students. Incorporate mapping. For intermediate students, incorporate division and proportion.

2. Real-world web

   a. Develop the present story by examining the inquiry topic through the real-world web illustrated in Figure 5.4. Use a visual model if possible. For junior-level students, develop the connections separately. Intermediate students

Figure 5.4. Real-World Web—Food

can handle the entire web. Go over the model so that pupils not only understand the scope of the model but are able to share a common vocabulary during the rest of the unit.

b. In a group, introduce the real-world web. Use the theme "food" in the center. Begin by brainstorming food and family with the class so that they understand the process. In small groups, have pupils continue the brainstorming process with the remaining focus words. Younger students will work with each real-world context (media, community, etc.) separately. Come together for total class sharing (use chart paper so results may be displayed). Remember to introduce the real-world web at a modified (structured) pace for junior division classes. Focus words are media, jobs, family, community, and the environment.

c. When all focus words have been completed, compile the results in the large group. Ask pupils to make some connections between the various focus word areas. When the teacher feels confident that the process and concepts are understood, pupils can continue to connect ideas with a magic marker. Post the results.

3. Research

   a. Discuss research questions using key words. Suggested key words are kinds, characteristics, purposes, conditions, consequences, purpose, functions, adaptations, past, influences, significance, causes, styles, present, types, changes, roles, value, future, relationships, and consequences.

   b. Students select an area that they would like to explore in greater depth by referring to the posted real-world web. Using a small-groups approach, have groups come up with questions and return to large group. Alternatively, pupils could choose their topics individually.

   c. Begin the research topic. This becomes an ongoing activity while minilesson input continues, culminating in the preparation of a creative presentation of students' findings that is shared with the whole group toward the end of the unit. Multiple intelligences are encouraged in the choice of presentation.

4. Examine the present story

   a. Look at the behaviors in the web and elicit values inherent in the described behavior. The present story is no longer working. Organize a whole group or small group discussion as to what is wrong with the way we eat in regard to our health and the health of the planet.

   b. Have students identify both the positive and the negative aspects of the present story. Create a chart to organize the information suggested by the pupils. The headings of the chart are negatives, positives, valuable, and cost.

   c. Have students refer to the diagram of the story model. Discuss the values that are evident in the present story. Some examples are money (capitalism), convenience, image, status, and thinness. Do this by looking at behavior (implicit values revealed) as compared to what we espouse to value (explicit values).

Old Story

Values and beliefs of the past influence us today. In some cases, the values remain. To see conflicts in the present story, it is important to trace the path of the issue (food) under study.

1. Comparison: Work in small groups describing how life is better and worse since fast foods have come into our lives.
2. Pantomime—life before processing: Make up a food story involving up to four people and present it in a pantomime. Consider a time perspective where students portray eating before the advent of processed and packaged food. The mime might include food preparation to help the audience interpret or guess the setting.
3. Diary—A day in the life of . . . : Write a diary entry while assuming the role of someone living at the turn of the century. Use the process described by Donald Graves (1983) (model, work in pairs sharing, role play, total class sharing, then write taking on the role rehearsed). During sharing, note behaviors (what people say and do). From the behaviors, one can deduce implicit values; by examining what the characters say, one can locate explicit values. These can be listed.
4. Timeline: Examine the present story and old story values. Develop a simple timeline illustrating these values.
5. Story breakdown: Locate problems with the present story and explain how these problems evolved.

New Story

The new story can be seen as a compromise between the projected story (where we are heading if things don't change) and the ideal story (which is presumably the impractical realm of the dreamer). To create the new story, students must decide on what is necessary (the good things in the projected story) and what is realistic (what we can practically hope to attain from the ideal story).

1. Probable story: Using the real-world web, project the state of the world in 2010 assuming directions don't change.
2. Ideal story: Using data from the real-world web in the preceding activity, students suggest how they would like to see the world in the future.
3. New story: By focusing on what is realistic and necessary, have students create a new story. Use a chart with the following columns: worst, new story, and ideal.

Action (Personalizing the Story)

The action stage is intended to make the final connections. Here, abstractions become personal because the students invest themselves in what they have learned.

Working in groups, the students suggest actions that a society, class, or individual can take to help bring about the new story.

Rubric for Assessment

1. Personal engagement: Does the student initiate activities? Show excitement during learning? Make personal comparisons? Go beyond classroom contexts to extend personal inquiry? Encourage involvement with others? Show evidence of reflection?
2. Ability to make connections: Does the student connect cause-effect relationships? Identify how focus can be extended to the theme? Make connections among personal, cultural, and global stories? Involve himself or herself in visualization and relaxation activities?
3. Change management: Does the student show a tolerance for ambiguity during the change process? Adapt to change in a positive way? Take positive risks?
4. Self-direction: Does the student generate "big" questions for inquiry? Form intentions to act? Make plans? Seek assistance and resources when necessary? Use reflection to redirect and improve the learning process?
5. Willingness to collaborate: Does the student develop a collective story? Share individual learning with others? "Piggy-back" ideas in a group? Demonstrate individual accountability?
6. Awareness of values in story: Does the student recognize his or her personal story? Recognize the cultural global story? Recognize how the cultural global story shapes his or her personal story? Extract values from stories? Act on personal stories?

Evaluation Strategies

1. Observation

- Ongoing observation by teacher using "class at a glance" sheets
- Recorded observations of pupils' interactions when working in cooperative groups
- Observation of attentive listening strategies when teacher or other students are presenting

2. Teacher-student conferences: Teacher conferences with pupils at either predetermined or spontaneous times. Examples of predetermined times are when the pupil has developed a big (worthwhile) question or the individual or group is ready to present its findings to the group.
3. Peer and self-evaluation: Students develop criteria to assess their group work. In the past, pupils have used criteria such as:

- Did everyone share the work?
- Did everyone practice attentive listening skills?
- Did everyone respect the opinions of others?
- Did the group complete its task in the allotted time?

As an initial attempt to evaluate other groups' presentations, students could comment on the areas of the presentations that they particularly enjoyed or that especially helped them learn something new.

4. Response journals: Students are expected to write in their "food journals" every 2 days, or more often when they have the need or the desire. The teacher could consider the following criteria when evaluating the personal entries:

- Does the entry show evidence of thought and effort from a junior-age student?
- Does the student "wonder" or pose questions in his or her journal?
- Is the student willing to share his or her reflections during sharing time?
- Do entries show connections to the student's reality?
- Is he or she attempting to create personal meaning from the study of the integrated food unit?

5. Independent study project: During the inquiry phase of the unit, students research and present findings of personal in-

quiries. Teacher assessment and feedback and group assessment provide guidance for other inquiries.

6. Graphic representation: Are students able to understand the use of graphic representations as a tool to gain or present new learnings, for example, in the distribution of bread to the world's have and have-not continents?

7. In-basket simulation: Pupils have the opportunity to role-play connected scenarios as they explore the present and predict the future story.

Negotiating the Curriculum

At the far end of a curriculum integration continuum is negotiation of the curriculum. It is an idea popularized by Garth Boomer (1992). Negotiating the curriculum calls for a different model of education. Its intent is shared power and the demystification of the hidden curriculum of traditional teaching. Students become aware of the power dimensions in teaching and learning and share planning in a democratic process. Outcomes cannot be specifically prescribed; rather, the aim is a deep understanding of key principles and concepts.

Lester's (1992) comparison of cooperative and collaborative learning illustrates the fundamental philosophical gulf between negotiation and "American schooling." In her view, cooperative learning reinforces the status quo by

- Continuing to "track" students in small groups
- Using transmission, memorization, and regurgitation as teaching strategies
- Emphasizing the right answer
- Predetermining outcomes
- Using outcomes for classroom management
- Not challenging why schools accept the status quo

Key Ideas

In negotiating the curriculum, students answer four key questions. The curriculum is developed from the answers to these questions.

- What do we know?

- What do we need to know?

- How will we learn it?

- How can we assess it?

It is important to note that the teacher can determine the amount of control that he or she wishes to exert over the process. The teacher may establish control over the topic of study, the skills to be taught, the subject areas to be involved, or any aspect of curriculum—this is a negotiation process and not a process developed solely by the students.

Applying the Model

Katy Smith (1993) describes what happened when she and coteacher Ralph Fleece negotiated the curriculum in their grade 11 American studies class. Students were asked to design the perfect class. The teachers suggested the first topic, but by midyear they had moved to student topics. Students produced a solid unit outline based on a KWL strategy. KWL stands for "what I already know, what I want to know, and what I learned." The teachers became the "guide on the side," although they did teach some skills, brought in resources, arranged for speakers, and arranged for time in the library. Alternative assessment was used; however, students had to take a criteria-referenced departmental test, and they had not covered all the content. The average scores of both Smith's and Fleece's classes were identical to those of the traditional classes. Smith reports that it was a worthwhile exercise. Students took responsibility for their own learning; they learned to ask good questions and answer them. There was noticeably less moaning and groaning than in the past.

Subjects such as mathematics can also be negotiated. When Hyde (1992) negotiated math with a grade 8 class of mixed ability, almost everyone covered the year's set course and many did considerably more than required. Hyde notes that the class covered the work in a different way than traditional classes. She allowed for time to develop class and group discussion skills. She also found that there had to be an emphasis on meaning in math—students needed understanding of what they were doing. This was achieved by students writing rules, definitions, and explanations of the processes they were learning.

Negotiating the curriculum is an interesting concept. I have found that teachers who use this process are surprised and delighted with the results. Although students may be distrustful of the teacher's motives, once they "buy into" what is happening, they are more productive and happier than before. The following is Simone Gravesande's description of her classroom when she tried the first step of the process.

September 16, 1997: After working through the exercises on "negotiating curriculum" last Saturday in my graduate education class, I was wary as to whether or not kids could actually do this, seeing as how we had struggled with the concept as adults.

Due to reorganization at our school, I was in a position where I was teaching a newly formed class and, in a sense, our "first day of school" was yesterday. It was the perfect time to try out this new idea.

Starting the day with language arts, my grade 7s engaged in a conversation on "what is language arts." I purposely added as little to the conversation as possible. At times it was painful watching them argue and debate what "LA" (as they call it) is and has been to them in their academic careers. Finally, they agreed that, "Language arts is learning how to communicate properly. Communication can be writing different types of things. It can be speaking and expressing yourself clearly, and it has to do with reading and understanding what you've read." Not bad . . . they had pretty much the same idea about language as I did.

Next, I broke them down into groups, and I asked each group what they needed to learn to communicate properly. Their lists were extensive, but what astounded me was that they all had very similar and important ideas:

- ■ Correct our own writing mistakes before they get marked.

- ■ Increase our vocabulary.

- ■ Learn to use the dictionary properly.

- ■ Learn to speak with confidence.

- ■ Learn to understand what we read.

- Learn to choose books/novels that are challenging and interesting.
- Improve our spelling.
- Learn to like reading and writing.
- Improve grammar and punctuation when we use them in writing.

It was amazing . . . I couldn't believe it . . . they came up with the same goals that most teachers, parents, administrators have for students in language arts. I repeated the exercise with a second class, one that the school has deemed "highly exceptional." This was a risk. Even more surprisingly, these students came up with the same list, although I sensed that they would prioritize the goals differently than my first class. I posted their lists with the title "Goals for the Language Arts Program." Next, the kids will have to decide how they are going to learn these things.

Judging from yesterday, I'm sure they'll have great usable ideas.

The question is, what did I learn from all this? Teachers (myself included) don't often give students credit for what they are able to do. I've always thought of myself as a teacher who scored high on the caliber of challenges I gave my students, particularly in the area of language arts. Now I have to question if I have challenged my students in a meaningful way. We all say that kids need to be involved in their education; but how many of us have involved them in the most basic way . . . negotiating their own curriculum? I've just begun this process with my students, but I can already sense the feeling of ownership of their learning. Even if the students are not successful at defining how they will attain their outlined goals, the goals will remind me of what is important to them. It is also a reminder to them of what they think is important. In the final analysis, we are both account-able for the success of the program. Negotiation definitely leads to a different type of classroom, and no doubt a better, more focused program.

Collaborative Planning Process

The collaborative planning process is similar to the negotiation of the curriculum because both challenge the traditional tenets of teaching and learning. This method of curriculum development was popularized by James Beane (1993, in press), who works closely with teachers in the classroom. He offers a thoughtful scholarly basis for his work. The collaborative planning process has it roots in core curriculum and in progressive education. Core programs emerged from the 8-Year Study; they were a way of organizing education requirements for high schools. The leading advocates of core programs called for problem-based experiential learning that was planned collaboratively with teachers and students. A major goal of progressive education and core curriculum was the promotion of a deep understanding of democracy.

Most of Beane's (1993, in press) work is at the middle school level. Collaborative curriculum planning can be applied at any level, however, because it leads to substantive and rigorous curriculum. Beane's approach is more radical than negotiating the curriculum, where planning usually starts with a teacher's choice of subject or topic and the course is negotiated from that point. Beane always starts with the same two questions:

- What questions or concerns do you have about yourself?
- What questions or concerns do you have about the world?

Although Beane (1993, in press) begins with student questions, he does not ignore the disciplines. He believes that, in true curriculum integration, the disciplines are used as resources from which to examine the theme and then create activities. The disciplines are used to service the theme being studied, rather than the disciplines being central. In this context, Beane suggests that ideas that are drawn from the disciplines are the most relevant ones because they are being used in a real-life context.

Key Ideas

- What questions or concerns do you have about yourself?
- What questions or concerns do you have about the world?

Students write their questions individually first and then participate in small groups, where they brainstorm for common questions. The group then tries to find organizing centers or themes that incorporate both the self and world questions. A list of themes is explored by the whole class and a vote is taken to see which theme will be addressed first. Questions relevant to the chosen theme are selected for exploration. Students brainstorm for activities that will lead to answering the questions. A final plan is formulated, the unit is taught, and the students then move to the next theme.

Beane (1993, 1997) suggests several themes that work well with students. Each theme emerges from the intersection of personal and social concerns:

- Transitions
- Identities
- Interdependence
- Wellness
- Social Structures
- Independence
- Conflict Resolution
- Commercialism
- Justice
- Caring
- Institutions

To explore these themes, Beane (1993, 1997) suggests that students will need to know and apply several skills, such as thinking reflectively, identifying the ethics in problem situations, problem finding and analysis, identifying personal beliefs that influence decision making, taking action toward solving the problem, and searching for completeness and meaning.

Beane (1993, 1997) makes several observations about the process:

- The curriculum is maximally contextualized to the student's experiences and therefore is relevant.
- A community of trust with the students must be developed before this type of planning can be completed.
- The curriculum must be issue centered, not interest centered. The focus is not on the interests of the students, but on their concerns.

- The teachers are in a negotiation position. They can add elements to the curriculum that the students may have over-looked or that are unknown to the students.

- A large project or culminating activity integrates a wide array of knowledge that also allows for diverse learning styles.

Applying the Model

Anne Reid (1996) followed this process in a grade 7-8 class for 3 hours a week for 4 months. She was astounded by the range of issues and concerns that emerged. Typical concerns were community and global violence, bad hair days, relationships with the opposite sex, death and dying, and the search for personal identity.

The "mess" was organized into one big question suggested by a student: What does it mean to be a male or female adolescent in today's world? Students organized their questions into six catego-ries: physical, social, emotional, intellectual, economic, and spiritual. Research groups were formed by Reid after she asked each student to submit names of three males and three females with whom he or she would like to work. Groups classified class questions to fit into two or three of the six categories the class had selected. They then created a learning plan for answering the questions and included demonstrations of the learning.

One group tackled spiritual questions that it categorized into four topics: religion, cults, death and the afterlife, and the supernatu-ral. It decided that library research was the best way to answer most of the following questions:

- Do our friends believe in God?

- What customs and rituals are in different religions?

- What architecture is in different religions?

- What cults had human sacrifice, begged for money, etc.?

- Do humans have souls?

- Is there life after death?

- What really happens after we die?

- Are there ghosts or other forms of supernatural beings?

Clearly Beane (1993, 1997) is right—students do have valuable questions. Reid (1996) reports that her students found this process empowering, intriguing, and authentic. Teacher and students were exhilarated, even though the work was very demanding. Like Beane, Reid is convinced that this is the way education should go.

A Study of Reality:
A Supradisciplinary Approach

A view of curriculum development that totally rejects the disciplines as organizers is presented by Marion Brady (1989, 1993). He advocates a holistic curriculum that integrates all disciplines, all knowledge, into a single, systemically integrated, conceptual framework. He maintains that this framework already exists in our minds, and the instructional task is to make this view of reality explicit. His master conceptual framework has five components that include everything that is in our reality:

- Where?—location, environment
- Who?—actors or objects
- What?—action, state, or condition of actors or objects
- Why?—ideas and assumptions of actors or observers
- When?—time frame

These five categories should be thought of as distinct disciplines, but disciplines so interdependent that they must be studied simultaneously. Each category has a vast expanding conceptual substructure. Ultimately, students are provided with clear pictures of their reality, skills to refine those realities, and the ability to expand the relationships among various parts of the framework. Figure 5.5 is a modification of Brady's (1989, 1993) framework. The full framework is available on his Web page at http://ddi.digital.net/mbrady/index.htm. In Figure 5.5, concepts basic to education are in the far left columns. The other columns elaborate on these concepts. If space permitted, the conceptual framework could be extended to include all knowledge. Figure 5.6 shows how one concept can be extrapolated to create curriculum.

Levels of Generality				
1	2	3	4	5
	Time Frame	Duration		
		Interval		
		Frequency		
		Point		
		Geographics		
		Climate	Residential	
		Resources	Commercial	
		Constructions	Production	
	Environment	Wealth	Infrastructure	
		Tools	Recreational	
		Art	Honorific	
		Symbols	Sacred	
		Clothing	Educational	
		Other societies	Military	
		Waste	Shipping	
		Sounds and smells		
		Number	Distribution	Mean
	Actors	Age	Average	Median
		Sex	Range	Mode
		Physiological		
		Characteristics		
		(Inherent)		
		Working		
		Worshipping		
		Educating	At level 4 and beyond, space permits only illustrative categories	
	Action	Making		
		Decisions		
	(Patterns for)	Owning		
		Playing		
		Residing		
		Distributing/ Exchanging wealth	Time	
		Communicating	Frequency	
		Waste disposal		
		Physical reality		
		The supernatural		
		Time	Nature	
	Ideas, beliefs,	Space	Developmental	
	and assumptions	The individual	stages	
	about	Others	Structure	Integrated
		The good life	Value	Unintegrated
		Acceptable	Role	
		Action	Efficacy	
		Purpose of existence	Rhythms of action	
			Boundaries of existence	

Figure 5.5. Brady's Conceptual Framework

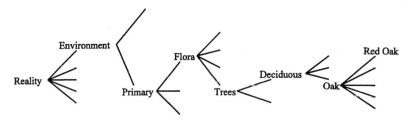

Figure 5.6. Extrapolation Example

Applying the Model

Over the years, students in Brady's classes or in the classes of teachers with whom he has worked (from the eighth grade through college) have been helped to make explicit their comprehensive conceptual models of reality. Some of the concepts he recommends are in Table 5.1. These teachers have then used their models to guide their descriptions and analyses of whatever was at hand. Some applications Brady recalls: their own classes, nearby neighborhoods, a military installation, a Coast Guard cutter, mythical societies in literature (e.g., *Lord of the Flies*), historical eras or societies (a comparison of ancient Athens and Sparta), ethnic enclaves, a village in western Samoa, and places where students have worked (M. Brady, personal communication, December 18, 1997).

TABLE 5.1 Brady's Concepts

Cause/effect	Duration	Lag	Rate
Change	Dynamic	Model	Rhythm
Chaos	Equilibrium	Rhythm	Duration
Complexity	Feedback	Multiple	Stasis
Component/element	Frequency	causation	Static
Critical mass	Function	Organization	Structure
Cumulative	Inertia	Pattern	Subsystem
causation	Institutionalization	Polarization	System
Cycle	Interaction	Process	Trend

Summary

This chapter has focused on the transdisciplinary approach, offering several examples. Some can be used within disciplines, such as problem-based learning, story approaches, and negotiation of the curriculum. The work of James Beane (1993, 1995, 1997) and Marion Brady (1989, 1993) cannot begin with a discipline, although Beane uses the disciplines as different lenses to view the theme. These models challenge the traditional model of education and go about teaching and learning in a very different way.

6

✳✳✳✳✳✳

CONNECTING STANDARDS
TO CURRICULUM

✳ ✳ ✳

This chapter explores ways that standards can connect with integrated approaches to curriculum. The standards are not an independent part of the design process. They must align with content, teaching strategies, assessment, and reporting. Chapter 7, "Aligning Teaching, Learning, and Assessment," examines the process of alignment in more detail. Standards and assessment are intimately linked. The learning principles should underlie how we approach creating both standards and assessment processes, however. Standards need to be a part of a dialogue toward a major rethinking of school and teaching practices.

Standards have been given many different labels. In some jurisdictions, they are referred to as *outcomes.* In others, they are *competencies.* In Ontario, they are now called *expectations,* not outcomes as they were referred to previously. This chapter will use the term *standards.*

Regardless of the term applied, standards have the same general purpose. They are in place to ensure some degree of accountability. Ideally, standards should not only measure student learning, but actually improve it (Darling-Hammond & Falk, 1997). In the traditional model, accountability is clearly defined. The quantity of knowledge a student can regurgitate is measured by pen and pencil measures. It can easily be quantified and standardized. When we consider that people also learn by doing, however, it makes sense to assess this doing. Doing often involves complex performances that demand a different way of assessing performances. Wiggins (1993) calls this "authentic assessment" to capture the essence of doing in an authentic or real-life context.

Two key questions must be addressed when we think of assessment. Are we measuring what we want to measure? If not, how do we measure what we want to measure?

Are we measuring what we want to measure? The conventional guidelines no longer apply. A checkmark for a right or wrong response is not an accurate measure for complex performances. When the team I led in developing the story model approached assessment, we as a group scoured existing reports and searched unsuccessfully for exemplary models on how to assess. We were not concerned with content, because content always changes according to the theme taught. We wanted students to demonstrate personal growth and be able to adapt to change. The books on evaluation were primarily focused on content, so we had to disregard them as an ideal source. Beginning from scratch, we asked what we wanted to measure and how we could be sure we were measuring it. How would we identify personal growth? Ability to handle change? We had to analyze what personal growth and change management looked like when someone had achieved it. This was the crude beginning of a standards-based curriculum. The scoring guide that we devised is found in Chapter 5, "Exploring Transdisciplinary Approaches."

During the last few years, many other educators have gone through the same process and asked the same questions we did when designing the story model. At every level, from national to the classroom, educators have developed criteria for skills. They have analyzed complex skills in an effort to assess in an accountable way. As a result, these complex skills have been broken down into a subset of skills. These subsets have been related to students as criteria on rubrics or scoring guides. What is amazing about these attempts is the amount of congruency evident when comparing most lists. There still is no widespread consensus, however.

There is a continuing and necessary dialogue about how standards can act as a catalyst for reform. The process of developing standards has been a time of trial and error. Not understanding the necessity for this process has been frustrating for both teachers and the public accustomed to the traditional model and clear mandates from the top.

What Is Worth Knowing?

When we create standards, we confront a fundamental question in education. What is worth knowing? The answer to this question is changing at the same time as the world is changing. The knowledge base is exponentially increasing. There is simply too much knowledge for any one person to know today. This factor alone is a great challenge to traditional approaches to curriculum. Also, our curricula tends to be Eurocentric and about the experiences of white men. Why would this type of learning be relevant in our multicultural classrooms?

What is worth knowing? To answer this question, I like to refer to personal stories to see what people really learned in school.

"What did you learn in school that you really know today?" I assign this question to small groups about to create integrated units for the first time. School can refer to any level of schooling. The important part of the question is what people really know today. This activity stimulates dialogue around school memories. I have asked this question to hundreds of educators working in groups and had them collate their responses. The answers are almost invariably identical. They learned literacy and numeracy, organization skills, social skills, leadership skills, how to play the game, whether they were smart or dumb, how girls or boys behaved, how to memorize, how to cram for the test.

It is important to note that this list is basically content free. The things that people consistently know today are skill based, attached to their self-concept, or relevant today. Occasionally someone will say that he or she learned something specific such as physics, history, or Spanish. Often this person is teaching this subject or using this knowledge in his or her real-life context.

When everyone is clear about what they really learned in school, the next step is easy. Given what you learned in school, what is it that we should teach our students to be productive citizens of the 21st century? Again the results produced by the groups are almost identical; they consist of knowledge skills such as reading and writing, computation skills, communication skills, problem solving, decision making, social skills, a sense of history and place, ability to deal with change, collaboration skills, negotiation skills, learning how to learn, information management, and presentation skills.

It is no accident that this list corresponds to the cross-disciplinary lists currently emerging in different arenas. In the United States there are the Secretary's Commission on Achievement of Necessary Skills (SCANS) skills (U.S. Department of Labor, 1991), and in Canada the Employability Skills Profile (Conference Board of Canada, 1992). Both lists evolved from concerns that schools were not teaching the skills necessary for the workplace. They are described in detail in Chapter 1, "What Is Integrated Curriculum and Why Is It Important?" These skills also correspond to the list above describing what people really learned in school. In the traditional model, knowledge was formally the only thing worth knowing. The skills that we acquired were incidental to the curriculum. Today, we acknowledge that these skills are worth learning and therefore worth teaching explicitly.

What Is a Standards-Based Approach?

A standards-based approach is different from the traditional approach in some of the following ways:

- Curriculum planning begins with the standards.
- Standards, teaching strategies, and assessment are aligned.
- The focus is on what students will do, not what the teacher will do.
- The standards are observable and measurable knowledge and skills.
- There is not a strict time limit to acquire standards.
- The content is the vehicle to achieving the standards.
- The teacher is free to teach in any style as long as it leads to the standard.
- Diversified teaching techniques facilitate inclusive education.

The Problems With Standards

The universal establishment of accepted standards has been problematic. As more and more educators turn their attention to standards, however, these problems are being alleviated. Current concerns are

- There are competing definitions on what standards actually are.
- There are too many standards created at too many levels of education.
- Subject areas are territorial about the importance of "their" discipline's standards.
- Not all standards are worth achieving.
- The standards are often ambiguous and not clear enough for teachers to follow.
- Not all students can achieve the standards in the same way at the same time.
- Teachers report covering the standards in the same spirit that they cover the content.
- When teachers are constrained by heavy content and many prescribed standards, it is very difficult to integrate the curriculum.
- Standards must be related to assessment.
- Standards should also promote standards for excellent teaching and equal resources.
- "Success for all" demands a redefinition of success.

Defining Standards

Once we determine what is worth knowing, standards can be developed for critical knowledge and skills. Creating standards is a task defined differently by different theorists, however. Wiggins (1989) perceives a standard to be a robust task that requires the use of important knowledge and skills to demonstrate the standard through a meaningful performance. Ravitch (1995) defines *content standards* as what the teacher should teach and the children should learn. *Performance standards* are the degrees of proficiency that students attain for the content standards. *Opportunity-to-learn standards* define the resources that should be available for students to achieve the content and performance standards.

Marzano, Pickering, and McTighe (1993) explore the differences between current definitions. They differentiate between curriculum standards, content standards, and lifelong learning standards. *Curriculum standards* define the processes that could be used to develop a skill. *Content standards* describe the information and skills essential to the content domain. There are two types of content standards: declarative and procedural. *Lifelong learning standards* refer to knowledge and skills that not only cross the disciplines but are used in the real world.

Lifelong standards are the complex skills worth knowing. They are also echoed in the school-to-work movement as workplace competencies. These are the cross-disciplinary standards not specific to academics and used in all aspects of life.

There are content standards for declarative and procedural knowledge (Marzano et al., 1993). Declarative knowledge is content and can be thought of as information. Content can be categorized hierarchically: Specific facts fall under concepts and generalizations. Procedural knowledge involves complex skills rather than just one skill, because a subset of skills is incorporated into the complex skills. This definition of content standards is discipline based.

A good way to understand a content standard is to analyze what a student must know and do to achieve the standard. Knowledge is the "know" and the procedural is the "do." This type of analysis may seem unnecessary because often we assume that students already possess the skills required in a standard.

Consider the following typical content standards:

Standard: Students understand mathematical structure concepts and the properties of various mathematical systems.

Know: Mathematical structure concepts and the properties of various mathematical systems

Do: Nothing

Standard: Students evaluate music and music performances.

Know: Evaluation criteria for different categories of music and musical performances

Do: Evaluation

Standard: Students understand the processes of scientific investigation and design, conduct, discuss, and evaluate such investigations.

Know: Scientific investigation processes, how to evaluate, how to communicate these processes

Do: Conduct, communicate, and evaluate scientific investigations.

Standard: Students understand the effects of interactions between human and physical systems and comprehend the resulting changes in use, distribution, and the significance of resources.

Know: Human interactions between human and physical systems, and the resulting changes in use, distribution, and significance of resources

Do: Nothing

Standard: Students read and recognize literature as a record of human experience.

Know: Criteria of good literature, the concept of a record of human experience

Do: Read good literature and categorize good literature.

Standard: Students know that religious and philosophical ideas have influenced history.

Know: Religious and philosophical ideas, the influence of these ideas throughout history

Do: Nothing

Interdisciplinary or lifelong learning skills cross all the disciplines and determine success in life. They have the same two characteristics that the content standards have. To be able to do or execute a skill, one must know certain information. The procedures are generic and they transcend the disciplines. Many skills at this level

TABLE 6.1 Information Processing

What the Student Must Do	*What the Student Must Know*
Do: Use information gathering strategies and information resources.	Know: Different information gathering strategies Information resources How to access those resources
Do: Interpret and synthesize information.	Know: How to interpret information How to synthesize information
Do: Assess the value of the information.	Know: How to evaluate information
Do: Add information when needed over time.	Know: Where and how a project would benefit from additional information

are complex and involve a large subset of skills. The student must be taught both the knowing and the doing aspects of the standard. For example, information processing could be analyzed into a subset of skills with four major parts (Marzano et al., 1993). A further analysis could look like Table 6.1.

Character Standards

I have found it helpful to conceptualize standards in a pyramid structure (Figure 6.1). The bottom of the hierarchy has numerous

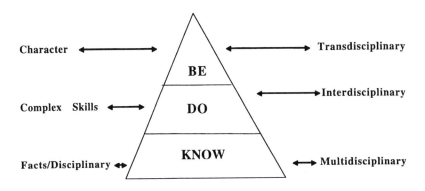

Figure 6.1. Standards Pyramid

content standards that are discipline based. Although there is procedural knowledge involved, they are primarily about knowing. The next level involves the interdisciplinary complex skills. These are far less in number and are composed of a subset of skills. They are primarily about doing. The top of the hierarchy has the standards that involve how we want students to be as they go about their school tasks. These are primarily about being.

The being level is admittedly problematic because it falls into the territory of values. The controversy revolves around whose values should be taught. Some parents believe that teaching values does not belong in the schools. Many states have removed any mention of values from their documents because of public sentiment. Some are dealing with values with a revival of character education. Others incorporate values by teaching citizenship.

The reality is that values are taught in the school every day, whether we acknowledge it or not. If, for example, the teacher negotiates the curriculum, students experience democratic values. Looking back at what people really learned in school, self-concept issues are always mentioned. Students learn if they are good or bad, smart or dumb. Teachers also have expectations of students that are value-laden, such as good work habits and respect for others.

Some schools and districts address this aspect of the curriculum by explicitly naming values that they wish to instill in the students. When the Waterloo Board of Education in Ontario began to develop student outcomes, it identified ethical values at a meeting that included the community. The consensus for desired values to act as an umbrella for all curriculum were honesty, integrity, trustworthiness, loyalty, fairness, caring, respect, citizenship, pursuit of excellence, and accountability.

It is impossible to teach a value-free curriculum unless learning remains at the lowest level of regurgitation of facts. As soon as higher levels of thinking are demanded, students have to apply values. How does one evaluate without some value base? Process information? Problem solve? Apply life skills?

When we are clear about how we want students to be, we can allow these values to guide our curriculum planning. This being level can act as the core of all curricula. Therefore, we can focus upward to the being aspect of curriculum at any level of curriculum implementation. For example, a high school that highly values the environment has adopted the value of respecting the environment. This value permeates all courses regardless of content. The explicit expectation is that students will act as environmental stewards.

Connecting Standards, Assessment, and Integration

As curriculum planners review and revise observable and measurable standards, these standards are more concrete and easier to measure and teach. Content standards that are focused on a discipline can often be assessed traditionally. The emphasis on performance requires alternative assessments, however. Many scoring guides and rubrics are available now to guide us. Most list the criteria or performance indicators that indicate the achievement of the standard. For every standard, there are usually benchmarks or levels to mark the degree of success the student has achieved.

Because this level is concerned primarily with the procedures of the disciplines, it connects most readily with the multidisciplinary approach. Teachers can continue to remain in the familiar territory of their discipline and begin to connect and collaborate with other teachers from other subject areas.

At the interdisciplinary level, assessment strategies still tend to be ambiguous. The lifelong learning or complex skills have not been identified clearly because they are often difficult to define. For example, a complex performance from a student could be to wrestle with an ill-structured complex problem. This skill goes far beyond the traditional definition of problem solving. Many find it hard to understand what an ill-structured problem is, and therefore difficult to define the criteria for solving such a problem. (The problem is very complex with multiple layers and difficult to limit or define. This is the type of problem we find in a real-life context.) When the criteria for a skill are not readily accessible, creating a valid assessment tool is problematic. It is much easier to measure the amount of knowledge that has been memorized than it is to assess how well a student has done demonstrating ill-structured complex problem solving in an authentic context.

Using a standards-based approach, complex skills connect the curriculum together along with the common theme. This is a large leap from designing an interdisciplinary project such as those described in Chapter 4, "Using Interdisciplinary Approaches," that begin with content as the focus.

At the character level, assessment becomes even muddier. How do we assess whether someone is caring? Can we observe it? What are the measurable criteria? What happens outside of school? Does behavior outside of school count? Given these ambiguities, and the controversy around teaching values, being is easy to ignore.

Some are treading into this territory because they believe that it is important to address values even if they are not explicitly assessed. Usually this occurs at the transdisciplinary level. Both James Beane's (1993, 1995, 1997) process and the concept of negotiating the curriculum expect students will experience the democratic process so that they understand how these values are acted out in the real world. The story model is concerned with personal growth and social change. All these curricula are built with components of the first two levels. The being level guides the process, however.

Figure 6.2 offers a template for planning that considers the being outcome as an umbrella for teaching what a student should know and be able to do.

How Do I Cover Required Content, Achieve Standards, and Integrate?

This is a difficult problem and I have no easy answer. Many teachers believe that they are required both to cover huge amounts of content and to maintain or develop new standards. Unfortunately, this expectation belongs to the traditional model. Teachers feel this pressure because their students must write standardized tests, and they believe that teaching to these tests guarantees the best results.

"Less is more" is a phrase often quoted by those who teach for a deep understanding. Some teachers go ahead with innovative teaching plans in spite of mandates. These teachers run the risk that their students will not do as well on the standardized tests as they might have. The risk is escalated by parents and administration who demand high scores and traditional models.

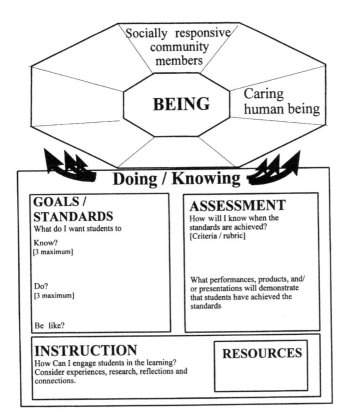

Figure 6.2. Planning Template

There are some ways that teachers may alleviate these concerns. Communication with parents is essential because they need to be a part of the curriculum development process. Parents should know the following:

- Current research shows that students in integrated programs do as well or slightly better in standardized testing.
- Teaching to the test does not increase student understanding.
- An explicit list of the skills the students are actually accomplishing is helpful.
- Parent-teacher-student conferences are an ideal way for parents to know what students are learning.

- Ongoing action research can increase parents' confidence in new approaches.

Developing an Interdisciplinary Standards-Based Curriculum

The multidisciplinary standards-based curriculum in Chapter 3, "Creating Multidisciplinary Programs," is a good beginning for understanding standards-based curriculum. This curriculum used a standards approach for three different subject areas. The theme of the Olympics was integrated into the subject areas. Each subject began the planning with the learning standards required for the area. Then the group brainstormed for the topics it could cover in a unit on the Olympics. The team members commented that this activity alone made it difficult to differentiate between disciplines. Two additional steps would have moved this curriculum to an interdisciplinary level rather than a multidisciplinary one. One, each team could have selected a cross-disciplinary standard all would teach. This would move the curriculum beyond content. Two, each team could create a culminating activity that demonstrates the cross-disciplinary skill and the knowledge and skills taught in each subject area. This chapter offers an interdisciplinary version of standards-based curriculum with an explanation of the thinking that accompanies it.

Key Ideas

This model represents my thinking after working with educators in both the United States and Canada trying to wrestle with standards to enhance student learning. My first attempts (Drake, 1995) began with teachers choosing cross-disciplinary skills and then assigning content. This was very confusing to teachers. It did make the point that the standards were much larger than the disciplines and that any content could be made to fit. It often felt like a forced fit, however. Now I ask teachers to consider the content first. This approach is not as abstract and allows teachers to think about standards within the context that they will be teaching.

There are two webbing activities. The first is a content web to identify possible content. This is similar to the webbed theme found in Chapter 4, "Using Interdisciplinary Approaches." The second

CROSS-DISCIPLINARY STANDARD (SKILLS):

CULMINATING ACTIVITY

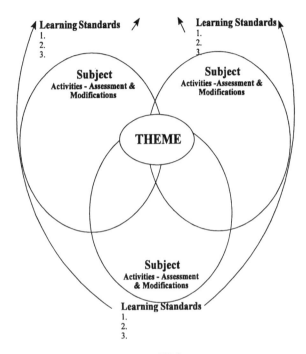

Figure 6.3. Curriculum Activities Web

activity (Figure 6.3) is the curriculum activities web. This web ties together the learning standards from the subject areas, with the cross-disciplinary skill acting as the umbrella. The learning standards selected for the subject areas should lead to the cross-disciplinary skill. This is a relatively easy thing to do, given that the content standards are related to more complex interdisciplinary skills.

Selecting activities and assessment is the last step in this model, as it is with the other models in this book. Teachers are used to thinking of activities first. This approach ensures that the activities and assessment selected are aligned with the standards and culminating activity. Multiple intelligences and Bloom's (1956) taxonomy are good guides for this selection of teaching activities.

What modifications need to made in the curriculum? Modifications are a consideration in this model. Many of the efforts at interdisciplinary approaches have evolved to address the issue of creating an inclusive classroom. Teachers need to think of the individuals in their classroom and what modifications can be made for students.

Applying the Model

This 7-step model was developed by Bruce Hemphill, Joan Sturch, and Susan Drake.

1. Choose a topic, issue, or theme that will be of interest to both you and the students (for example, environmental issues). Student input is an excellent way to check your perceptions.
2. Create a content web. This can be done by free brainstorming or directed by subject areas. Figure 6.4 illustrates the content web.
3. Decide on a cross-disciplinary outcome or standard that will be the major learning goal of the unit. What does this outcome or standard involve?

Cross-disciplinary standard: What does it know, do, be? Students will develop meaningful inquiry questions and answer them using systematic problem-solving strategies that respect the environment in the process.

> Know: Define meaningful questions; problem-solving strategies; how to respect the environment.
>
> Do: Ask meaningful questions; apply systematic problem-solving strategies; respect the environment in their solutions.
>
> Be: Respectful of the environment
>
> Create a rubric for the knowledge and skills that student will have to acquire. A sample rubric is offered in Table 6.2.

4. Develop two or three guiding questions to organize the unit. These should be complex enough that many lessons could be developed around them. For example,
   a. What are the environmental beliefs of native cultures and modern society and how do they affect us today?
   b. What can we learn from native cultures?

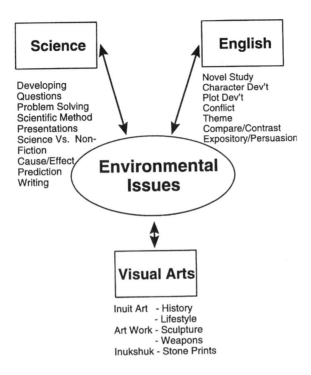

Figure 6.4. Content Web

5. Develop a culminating activity to end the unit. This activity should be fun and demonstrate to an audience that the major goal has been achieved. How will you assess this? Who will be the audience? An outcome statement should be created and given to all students so that they know the criteria for assessment.

For example, choose a modern environmental issue and, using library research, identify the problem and its causes. Develop a solution that is realistic according to your research, but would also sustain the environment in the years to come. Create a colorful, informative, and interesting triptych (three-paneled board). Illustrate your research through artwork developed in visual arts. Use the computer to process all information. Use the outside panels to describe the causes and effects. Use the inside panel to describe your solution and

TABLE 6.2 Is It a Meaningful Question?

Does the Answer Require	Yes	No
Multiple possibilities		
Library research		
Experimental research		
Expert opinion		

what you can do about it. Create an interesting way to deliver the material. Present the material to your colleagues in a way that persuades them to act in ways that honor the environment. This presentation will be in a workshop setting.

6. Develop a curriculum activities web for teaching strategies that will lead to the standards (see Figure 6.5).

For example,

a. Start with a subject area and select the learning standards that will lead you to the cross-disciplinary standard. You will find that your large cross-disciplinary standard will have many subsets of skills within it. These subsets will usually be represented in the disciplinary standards.

b. This process can be applied to each subject area.

c. Determine activities that lead to the culminating activity.

7. Decide on assessment strategies for activities. Consider, for example, scoring guides (rubrics), self-assessment, peer assessment, journals, portfolios, and conferencing. For example, using your information file, create a product for the culminating activity. This project will illustrate the relationship between the environment and lifestyle. Some examples may be a stone- cut print, an Inuksuk or a mask sculpture. Your project will be assessed for its creativity, mastery of medium, and general aesthetic craftsmanship.

English activities/assessment

Novel study—cooperative learning groups/compare-and-contrast sheets

Cross-Disciplinary Standard (Skills)

Students will ask a meaningful questions and solve it with a systematic method of problem solving (cause/effect, prediction) and respect the environment in the solution.

Culminating Activity

Create a triptych to identify the cause/effect and proposed solution of your environmental issue. Use art to enhance the presentation. Present in a workshop format to your colleagues in a way that persuades them to act in ways to help your cause.

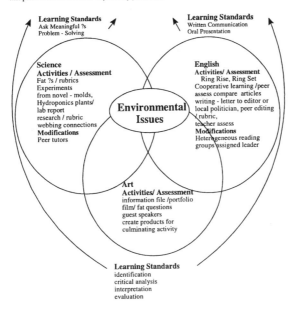

Figure 6.5. Curriculum Activities Web

Write a scenario about an issue in the novel and dramatize how the issue/script is assessed for writing style and recognition of issue

Debate/debating skills, presentation skills—peer assessment

Analyze newspaper articles/rubric for analysis, self-assessment, peer assessment

Expository writing and persuasive writing—write a newspaper article and an editorial on the same issue/quality of writing, contrast between expository and persuasive writing—read to class

Resource center research/ability to synthesize information and organize it into expository and persuasive writing

TABLE 6.3 Peer Assessment Guide

Topic	Evaluator's Name				
1. Presentation					
Eye contact	1	2	3	4	5
Voice use	1	2	3	4	5
Equal participation	1	2	3	4	5
Creativity	5	10	15	20	25
Ability to answer questions	2	4	6	8	10
2. Poster Board					
Neatness	1	2	3	4	5
Completeness	1	2	3	4	5
Interesting	1	2	3	4	5
Colorful	1	2	3	4	5
	Total score:				

Modifications: Heterogeneous groups for novel study. A strong reader is assigned as a reader for the group. All students expected to complete a compare-and-contrast sheet for each chapter. Stronger students act as mentors for weaker students.

Science activities/assessment

Fat and thin questions/rubrics

Brainstorming for science questions in novel

Science experiments generated from the novel—molds and hydroponics plant growth

Resource center research/relevance of information to question being investigated

Modifications: A senior student is assigned to the class as a peer tutor. He or she helps students who are having trouble. Stronger students are encouraged to develop more complex experiments.

Table 6.3 is a peer assessment scoring guide for the culminating activity. Note that this emphasizes the presentation. Creativity and the ability to answer questions were assigned the highest points.

The Story of Developing This Model

Developing a standards-based model is not easy at first. Once you begin to think this way, however, it becomes easy to develop curriculum that you can be confident is sound. The following description may be helpful for others who are trying to follow a standards-based path, but are confused on how to do it.

This approach evolved over 3 years of teaching with my colleague Bruce Hemphill in a grade 9 classroom. The government had mandated an integrated, outcomes-based approach to education. As well, it was mainstreaming grade 9 classrooms for the first time. We would have students with all ranges of abilities in the class. Our challenge was to find ways to engage all students in the learning. We went about this challenge by using action research to discover how students learned most effectively.

We began the year with the decision that it would be easier to work with the standards if we used one or two standards as the umbrella for our work. After much discussion and working with two other science department members (Ron Chappell and Helmut Klassen), we decided on the following standard: Students will develop meaningful inquiry questions and answer them using systematic problem-solving strategies that honor the environment in the process.

With this standard acting as the umbrella for all planning, we created four very different curriculum paths to the same outcome over four semesters. Doubtless there are many more paths, but we discovered that the trick to a more interdisciplinary approach was having only one broad-based standard to guide our planning. Too many standards is like too many cooks spoiling the broth. With one standard, there are endless subsets of skills that enable students to reach it.

Once we had massaged our cross-disciplinary standard to work for us, we were faced with new challenges. The first dilemma was coming to a common understanding of what a good question really is. Bruce and Ron were both convinced that if we could teach students how to ask a question, they would not have such a difficult time deciding on an independent study question at the higher levels of science. We discovered that most science guidelines emphasize the student as questioner or inquirer but assume that students already have this skill. As well, most suggested activities in curriculum documents have the teachers supplying the questions to the students.

It took several months before we were able to develop criteria for a meaningful question. This involved heavy discussions and trying different activities with our classes. We ended up using the concept of fat and thin questions (Fogarty & Bellanca, 1993). A fat question is a meaningful question that has a complex answer that requires multiple possibilities, library research, experimental research, and expert opinion.

We began by assuming that the systematic way of problem solving would be the scientific method. We discovered that there are many ways to solve a problem. Although we continued to use the scientific method as the core for our explorations, we added new strategies such as compare and contrast, cause and effect, and prediction skills. During our 3 years, we taught at a multidisciplinary level (integrating the sciences), interdisciplinary level (guided by one complex cross-disciplinary skill and involving other disciplines), and transdisciplinary level (the story model). We found that when we taught the story model, it was grounded in the standards-based approach.

There was much for us to learn. Through experimentation with a standards approach, our conception of what was worth knowing shifted. We began with discussions on whether or not students had to learn the parts of the microscope.

As subject specialists, we wanted science to have a prominent role in the curriculum. As we worked with this approach, what became important to know shifted. Facts were no longer so important. The parts of the microscope were not of utmost importance.

Focusing on the cross-disciplinary skill allowed us to move into the realm of concepts and generalizations. After several months, the conversations shifted to more global outcomes. Bruce commented that not all students would be scientists. For him, the most important thing was that the student turned out to be the kind of person you wanted for your next door neighbor.

Table 6.4 demonstrates some of the thoughts that we discussed on what is worth knowing. This revolves areound a collaborative science process. Clearly these are just the beginning of a new understanding of the structure of knowledge and its place in interdisciplinary curriculum.

We also needed to learn about alternative ways of assessment. We tried journals, developed rubrics, and began self-assessment and peer assessment. Presentation possibilities were opened up, and students presented their information in a wide range of formats, from skits to rap songs to computer presentations.

We learned the hard way that we always needed to teach the skills that would allow students to demonstrate their knowledge. One semester we had students do a waste audit of the school. Proud of their accomplishments, we invited parents and other teachers to the culminating activity. We had not taught presentation skills. Much to our horror, the students became mute at presentation time. They stood in the front of a large room, held up their reports, and muttered some words that no one could hear. Finally, one young woman went up with her report and a tape recorder. We were thrilled, until instead of doing something innovative, she stood there with her sign while her voice on audiotape delivered the report. We heard parents and teachers leaving the auditorium muttering that these students hadn't learned a thing. The most discouraging part was that we knew that they had learned a tremendous amount.

With the lesson learned, we began to teach all skills that students needed to achieve the standards. First we had to identify the skills, then we had to teach them. It may seem like wasted time, but it was very profitable—for it is these skills that students will need to use in a real-life context. As well, we learned the benefits of having exemplary models to show students what type of things were expected of them.

We found that when we emphasized creativity, students became very creative. They seemed to need permission to let their imaginations

TABLE 6.4 What Is Worth Knowing? A Collaborative Science Process

Do	Know Essential Ideas	Our Assumptions
Generate meaningful questions—choose one for class participation.	There are many more questions than we generally ask.	We don't know how to ask meaningful questions.
		Asking questions is a skill that improves with explicit instruction.
		Future development depends on being a good questioner.
Groups design and carry out class experiment.		Groups will not carry out experiment with equal attention to controls.
Collect observations in each group.	There are many more observations than we generally identify.	
Collate class set of data.	Collaboration facilitates greater likelihood of correct data analysis.	Observations of small group will be limited by their previous experiences.
		Discovery of differences in results leads to a careful duplication of experimentation.
Collaboratively interpret data to answer questions and generate new questions.	Generation of more questions is more important than the answer.	
	Real-life science is collaborative.	
	We can apply these principles of question generating to real-life situations.	

reign. Creativity did not really need to be defined. The assessment of creativity, from both teacher and peer assessment, was closely aligned.

Piece by piece, we were able to put together a new way of thinking about curriculum. We would try different things; if they worked, they would be added to our repertoire. We attended workshops and visited other schools implementing innovative programs. Our understanding deepened through ongoing discussions and trial-and-error experimentation that was documented through action research. During these 3 years, our beliefs about how students learned were both confirmed and challenged.

After the first year, we were able to bring together teachers from other departments who were intrigued by what we were doing. Once other disciplinary lenses were added to the discussion, we realized how much we really had in common. These commonalities emerged from the standards rather then content. For example, the science department explained the scientific method in detail to the English department. They listened carefully before revealing that they had a very similar procedure for problem solving. Finding a worthy cross-curricular standard to act as a common umbrella was not difficult.

We also discovered that we could easily find standards within our own subject areas that lead to the cross-curricular standard that we were all working toward. This meant selectively choosing the standards from our working documents. We could not cover the standards. Instead, as we focused on our cross-curricular goal, we found that many of the standards that we were expected to teach emerged naturally. Some skills students learned were computer word processing, library research, analysis, synthesis, creative thinking skills, critical thinking skills, mastery of media (materials), self-evaluation, questioning, problem-solving strategies, scientific method, debating, presentation, compare and contrast, evaluation, and writing skills—expository and persuasive.

Assessing a Curriculum Model

As educators, we need to think of how we can apply standards to our own work. The following questions can function as a guide to assess integrated curriculum models. Not all questions will apply to all efforts. Select the ones that apply to yours or, better yet, create your own.

- Are the learning standards reflected?
- Is the unit relevant to the students?
- Does the unit connect to a real-life context?
- Does the content have enough depth to sustain interest?
- Are cross-disciplinary skills included?
- Does the unit allow for different learning styles?
- Does the unit involve all levels of thinking (Bloom, 1956)?
- Are the students explicitly taught the skills that they will need to achieve standards?
- Is there a balance among whole class, group, and individual activities?
- Is the group work orchestrated?
- Are there many opportunities for active learning?
- Is there planned time for the reflections of students?
- Does the unit call on community resources?
- Are the rubrics or scoring guides simple enough to understand, but rich enough to be meaningful?
- Is there a natural fit for connections among subject areas?
- Are concepts and essential understandings made explicit?
- Are there two or three guiding questions that guide the unit?
- Is there continuous assessment?
- Are there a wide variety of assessment techniques?

Summary

This chapter has discussed how to connect standards to curriculum. It has differentiated between content, cross-disciplinary or life-long standards, and character standards. A multidisciplinary program can be connected with content standards. Cross-disciplinary standards connect at the interdisciplinary level. These standards represent complex skills that cut across all disciplines and are used in a real-life context. Finally, there are the character standards. These standards are not usually articulated, but are with us every day in our classrooms. Character standards are ones that tell us how we want students to be when they are in our schools.

The second part of this chapter presented a standards-based curriculum. A description of the process the authors of this model underwent over 3 years is offered. Finally, questions were presented for teachers to use to check the quality of their own efforts in curriculum design. As teachers, we need to use a standards-based approach to monitor and improve the quality of our own work.

7

✖✖✖✖✖✖

ALIGNING TEACHING, LEARNING, AND ASSESSMENT

✳ ✳ ✳

This chapter begins with Susan di Carlo's story:

The Village School (VS) of Great Neck is one of the oldest alternative schools in New York State (it was established in the 1960s), and it is well-known in alternative circles. We have been a member of the Coalition of Essential Schools for several years. The coalition is a nationwide organization with about 250 member schools dedicated to meaningful school and curricular reform.

The population I work with is often categorized as "at-risk." In our case, it is an umbrella term that encompasses a great deal of territory, but in general, the students who choose to attend VS (or who are encouraged to do so) have not been successful in traditional educational settings. For a variety of academic, social, and emotional reasons, their regular high school was not a good fit. Yet, they are all of average or above-average intelligence and we, miraculously, have about 80 to 90% of them going to college.

The challenge of teaching such a population is a big one! They need high-motivation material and special classroom strategies, as well as a nurturing and patient atmosphere. After working here for nearly a decade, I have found my most successful courses are interdisciplinary. Using a unifying theme or focus also helps. Consequently, I have become more of a humanities teacher—or a generalist, in coalition lingo.

The Vietnam War and the Sixties is a very successful course; it immerses the students in the time period because it looks at this time frame from a multitude of angles. Of course, we have the history of the war, which we learn from information extracted from textbooks, map reading, oral histories, and documentaries. Then there is the literature (my favorite). The Vietnam War, for all its tragedy, produced an enormous body of first-rate, extremely well-written, and moving novels, short stories, poems, and memoirs. There are also several wonderful movies that complement the literature, underscoring the grittiness and horrors of the war and the spirit (often, but not always, broken) of many of its participants. It's an easy unit to incorporate psychology into, since we take a long look at topics such as posttraumatic stress disorder and the isolation of prisoners of war. The science component involves studying the effects of Agent Orange and the long-term havoc wreaked on our environment from dioxin poisoning (with obvious follow-up comparisons to the Gulf War Syndrome, Chernobyl, etc.). A series of guest speakers from veterans organizations adds a powerful dimension to the course.

The Sixties takes a look at the culture and makes connections between the war and the protest movements of the time. We look at the music, art, fashion, literature, etc. as we study this memorable, turbulent decade in a larger historical context. I have an artifacts lesson I use and a series of interviews the students conduct with people from that generation. All in all, it's a terrific way to end this course.

By this time, the class is usually hooked and I find them more than willing to learn history because they feel so close to the events of the war and its aftermath. (S. di Carlo, personal communication, November 23, 1997)

Why did Susan's students learn in her class? They had rejected the traditional system as not meeting their needs. Embedded in her story are some principles of learning that must be the starting point for any curriculum reform. Once we know how people learn best, the rest follows. This chapter explores this concept further.

What Does Alignment Mean?

Alignment of teaching, learning, and assessment is a phrase that is currently so popular that workshops can be taken on curriculum alignment. There are a variety of reasons for this interest:

■ Underlying all aspects of curriculum reform is an embedded philosophy that is student centered and guided by certain beliefs about learning. These beliefs are often categorized under the umbrella of the constructivist approach. For new curriculum approaches to be effective, teaching activities, standards, choice of content and skills, reporting, and assessment must all be aligned to match the philosophy.

■ This same philosophy underlies much of current educational reform and is reflected in approaches to leadership, the culture of schools, and professional development (Lambert et al., 1995). Chapter 1, "What Is Integrated Curriculum and Why Is It Important?" elaborates on and contrasts this philosophy with the traditional position.

■ When all aspects of curriculum are not changed simultaneously, they will not match philosophically.

■ Success of the integrated approach that is measured by standardized test scores illustrates this philosophical discrepancy. Standardized tests measure one right answer. Teachers tend to teach to the test because they must demonstrate accountability. Teachers using integrated approaches have different goals, however, such as a deep understanding and transference of learning. Such goals cannot be demonstrated by standardized tests; they require some kind of performance.

■ Another difficulty lies in reporting. Teachers can use an integrated approach, but still be faced with a report card that requires that they assign a percentage for individual subject areas. It is difficult for the teacher to break down proportionate marks. Equally, it can be difficult for the student to recognize what he or she did to deserve a specific subject grade.

Unfortunately, we seem to be able to make sense of only one aspect of the change at a time. Districts have tended to separate the process by emphasizing only one aspect, whereas the connections have been ignored. I have been at many inservices and conferences where integration, multiple intelligences (MI), learning styles, reporting, standards, and special education needs have all been addressed in different rooms.

Teachers need to create meaning for curriculum reform through a process of trial and error, reflection, and reconstruction. As a result, fundamental change is necessarily slow. Understanding the philosophy that underlies a change helps one understand why other aspects also have to change.

What factors need to be considered to align the curriculum for purposeful educational reform? This chapter explores various techniques introduced in the classroom, where educators have tried to make curriculum more responsive to student needs and aligned with optimal ways of learning.

Constructivism

The constructivist platform originating in cognitive psychology is currently a popular way of looking at how we learn. According to the constructivist theory, we all bring mental models to any learning situation. Although there may be a "true" reality out there, we construct our own meaning to understand it. There is no shared reality (Ornstein & Hunkins, 1998). According to Heuwinkel (1996), the student constructs his or her own learning. Knowledge is subjective and continually being developed and modified by the learner. Students learn new ideas by integrating them into existing knowledge structures. The teacher's role is to create disequilibrium or to provide stimuli for students to examine, expand, and modify their existing knowledge.

Aligning teaching with constructivist principles leads to active learning, learning in a meaningful context, student choice for student autonomy, teacher as facilitator, and ongoing assessment with alternative assessment methods such as portfolios and conferences.

The constructivist perspective is echoed throughout current theories of learning and teaching. Perkins (1991) urges educators to teach for understanding or insight. *Teaching for understanding* has become an educational buzzword. According to Perkins, deep understanding can be demonstrated only when students can do something with what they know. Understanding goes beyond memorization and the information given in class.

Understanding is about making connections and being able to transfer the learning. Connections can be made within a subject area, but ultimately connecting across different subject areas and to real life leads to deeper understanding. Skills that are cross-curricular are clearly important parts of this perspective. Critical, reflective, creative, and intuitive thinking are all forms of thinking being taught for problem solving. A central concern is that we learn how we learn. This is called *metacognition;* the student understands procedural knowledge being employed to create, use, and regulate knowledge.

Using Story to Determine Teaching, Learning, and Assessment Principles

Liz tells her story of a positive learning experience when she was 16. She remembers the teacher giving the lesson and the student-teacher dialogue back and forth. Suddenly, she understood the concept that was being taught (which she has since forgotten). She was excited; a light had suddenly been turned on. After the lesson, the teacher asked if there had been a turning point during the lesson when the students felt that they had reached understanding. The light had gone on for everyone at approximately the same time. The teacher then told them that she had deliberately added the word "good" when a student contributed to the conversation at that point.

Lloyd recalls a physics teacher who performed a drama in which he played all the roles. He was teaching the difference between entropy and enthalpy. To this day, Lloyd remembers both the play and the concepts.

Daphne's teacher instructed Daphne to hem her skirt in a certain way, but she did it wrong. After ripping out her first effort, she tried again. It was still wrong. After a third botched attempt, the teacher spanked Daphne in front of the class. Daphne doesn't sew today.

From a constructivist perspective, our personal stories of learning color our implicit theories of how we learn. The above stories are about powerful lessons. Are there principles of learning embedded in these stories? Positive feedback? The power of story as a learning tool? The enduring results of public shame?

Connecting theory to our own stories of learning brings theory to life. Our stories illustrate that conventional theory is not always right. We only have to look to those who did not succeed in the traditional model of education to realize that not everyone learns in the same way or at the same rate. To go a step further, I agree with my colleague David Hunt (1988) that "good practice makes good theory." As an experienced teacher, I have come to trust my own instincts on how people learn. Other teachers also have these intuitions, but we don't always think to trust them.

In search of "experienced wisdom," I ask groups who are about to work together to tell stories about their own learning. First we exchange stories of negative learning experiences, and then we share the positive ones. Next we seek out the principles of learning that can be found in the stories. I have repeated this exercise many times with hundreds of educators to establish working principles that can be used to plan teaching activities. Regardless of the group composition, the principles tend to be identical. This approach can also be applied with younger students who are able to articulate how they learn best. Once we have made up the "list," we can compare it to the research on learning. The group now has its own data to guide it in planning how to teach and assess in ways that match learning principles.

I highly recommend that groups of teachers who work collaboratively begin by going through this process of storying. They can then develop their own learning principles and connect these with teaching and assessing practices. A list that is created from one's own experiences makes the principles more meaningful. Below are some of the principles of learning that continually appear on the lists.

- Learn by doing
- Choice
- Relevant
- Positive reinforcement
- Supportive environment
- Enjoyable
- Fun
- Challenging
- Clear expectations
- Ongoing feedback

- Reflection
- Learn by teaching others
- Modeling
- Metacognition
- Variety of strategies

These principles of learning are very much in line with the latest research. Assuming that they hold true for most learners, the next questions revolve around aligning teaching and assessing practices around these principles. This task can be done by any group that is planning curriculum. Table 7.1 presents some ideas that were generated by my latest integrated curriculum class.

Reflecting on teaching and learning strategies by beginning with learning principles is a powerful process. It allows educators to make sense of innovations and to understand the underlying beliefs behind them.

Proven Strategies to
Integrate the Curriculum

This section provides different systems that people have used to create teaching strategies aligned with how people learn.

Bloom's Taxonomy

The structure of knowledge and levels of thinking are interconnected. Moving into concepts also moves students into higher-level thinking skills (Erickson, 1995). Bloom's (1956) *Taxonomy of Educational Objectives* provides six categories of cognitive learning:

- Knowledge: Memorize previously learned material. It may involve the recall of a wide range of materials from specific facts to complete theories.
- Comprehension: Understand the meaning of the material and express meaning in one's own words.
- Application: Transfer the learning to another situation.

TABLE 7.1 Principles of Learning, Teaching, and Assessment

Learning	*Teaching*	*Assessment*
Choice	Offer choice	Choices in/with assessment
Relevant	Personally relevant	Assessment should have meaning
Positive reinforcement	Variety of positive reinforcements	Ongoing assessment should include constructive criticism and opportunity to redo
Supportive environment	Praise, learn from mistakes, taking risks, constructive criticism	
Enjoyable, fun	Fun activities	
Challenging	High standards	Assessment should not be watered down but challenging to the level of student
Clear expectations	Teach explicit criteria for expectations	Assess expectations
Ongoing feedback	Ongoing feedback	Ongoing assessment
Reflection by group and individual	Allow time for reflection	Journals, discussion, quiet time
Learn by doing	Hands-on activities	Assess the doing, performance assessment
Learn by teaching	Teach others in class, e.g., jigsaw, tutoring demonstration	Performance assessed, e.g., demonstration
Metacognition	Metacognition strategies	Assess metacognition
Variety of ways to learn	Use variety of teaching strategies	Variety of assessment
Modeling	Teacher walks the talk	Teacher self-assessment, student evaluation of teacher

- Analysis: Break down material into component parts so that its organizational structure may be understood. This may include identification of the parts, analysis of the relationship between parts, and recognition of the organizational principles involved.

- Synthesis: Put together the parts to form a different whole.

- Evaluation: Judge the value of material based on clearly defined criteria whose outcomes can be defended or validated.

Analysis, synthesis, and evaluation are considered to be higher-order skills, and each upper category subsumes the lower ones.

Most teachers are familiar with this view of knowledge although they may not use it in a conscious way. Jacobs's (1989, 1997) model in Chapter 4, "Using Interdisciplinary Approaches," uses Bloom's (1956) work as a guide for constructing activities. Figure 7.1 is a version of Bloom's ideas put into reality.

James Curry and John Samara (1990) adopt Bloom's (1956) taxonomy to create a sound basis for developing curriculum at any level from traditional to interdisciplinary. This model is interesting because it aligns teaching, learning, and assessment and simultaneously facilitates higher-order thinking skills. Figure 7.2 demonstrates this strength.

Dagget's Taxonomy

Dagget (1995) critiques Bloom's (1956) taxonomy in light of the 21st century. The world of work is fundamentally changing. In 1550, 50% of jobs were unskilled. By 1994, 33% of jobs were in this category. We are rapidly approaching the time when only 15% of jobs will be unskilled. How do subjects relate to this phenomenon? Not very well, Dagget contends. For example, we teach pure physics, not the applied physics that can be used. We teach reading, but not technical reading. Being able to read the newspaper, Shakespeare, and poetry is no longer enough to compete globally. Most other industrialized nations teach skills of application. For Dagget, Bloom's taxonomy promotes the creation of innovations and Nobel prizes. Only a small percentage of the population engages in this type of thinking. Many

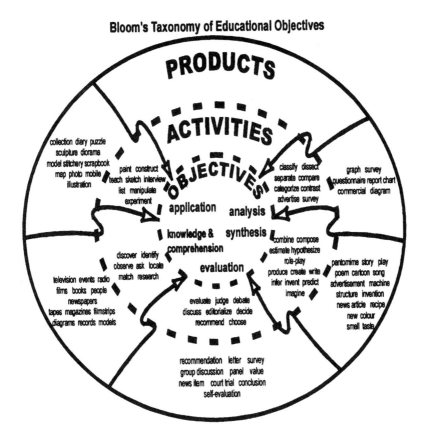

Figure 7.1. Bloom's Wheel

Adapted from Clark (1988). Reprinted with permission from the Board of Education, City of Hamilton.

people learn and use the application of knowledge, although they do not necessarily win Nobel prizes.

Dagget (1995) advocates the following taxonomy based on application:

- Apply knowledge in a discipline.
- Apply knowledge between disciplines.
- Apply knowledge to real-world predictable problems.
- Apply knowledge to real-world unpredictable problems.

Rain Forests	Basic Thinking ⟶	
	Knowledge	Comprehension

1. Characteristics
  a. locations
  b. land forms
  c. water ways
  d. layers
  e. climate
	1. Identify the absolute and relative locations of a rain forest.
	
	•world map/ bullet chart
		2. Describe the land forms found in the rain forest.
		
		•dictionary entries

2. Life in the Rain Forest
  a. plants
  b. animals
  c. humans
  d. interdependence
	7. Recall the animals and plants most commonly found in the rain forest.
	
	•word search
		8. Explain the relationship among plants, animals and humans.
		
		•cycle diagram
		•written explanation

3. Products from Rain Forests
  a. chemical
  b. medicinal
  c. wood products
  d. foods
	13. Recount chemical, medicinal, wood-based, and food products that originate in the rain forest.
	•dictionary entries
		14. Describe the phases through which any rain forest product will evolve when going to market.
		•timeline

4. Rain Forests Issues
  a. deforestation
  b. soil erosion
  c. endangered species
	19. Restate the names and locations of endangered animal species.
	
	•map puzzle
		20. Describe the cycle of soil erosion.
		
		•diagram/ oral presentation

5. Patterns...
  a. consists of repeating segments
  b. allow for prediction
  c. can be man-made or natural
	25. Identify the repeating segments of a natural cycle in the rain forest.
	
	•role play
		26. Describe man made and natural patterns in the rain forest.
		
		•class discussion/charts

INDEPENDENT STUDY	Select A Topic	Develop A Challenge

Figure 7.2. Samara's Curriculum

			Abstract Thinking
Application	**Analysis**	**Creative Thinking**	**Critical Thinking**
3. Model the floor, understudy, canopy and emergent layers of a rain forest. •class mural	4. Examine the importance of rain forest rivers. •magazine article	5. Change a rain forest's location and explain the effects on plants and animals. •descriptive essay	6. Decide which layer of the rain forest is best suited for human habitation. •illustrated poem
9. Categorize animals according to the rain forest layers in which they live. •animal puzzle	10. Compare/ contrast two kinds of animals from the same layer of the rain forest. •T-chart	11. Develop a plant, animal, or person that is suited to live in the rain forest. •videotaped documentary	12. Defend/ dispute the concept of protecting a selected plant or animal species. •debate
15. Classify various rain forest products into self-generated categories. •classification puzzle	16. Determine which rain forest products are consumed in the local community. •research presentation	17. Invent a habitat in which medicine might be produced. •labeled diagram	18. Decide on environmentally sound ways of harvesting a selected product. •letter to the editor
21. Categorize endangered species by reasons of endangerment. •information table	22. Determine how deforestation impacts habitats within the rain forest. •board game	23. Speculate how over consumption of rain forest products might be reduced. •campaign speech	24. Defend/ dispute a selected law that protects endangered species. •point of view essay
27. Categorize rain forest patterns as natural or man-made. •Venn diagram	28. Examine the patterns of two products that originate in the rain forest. •brochure	29. Generate an original natural or man-made pattern that would help the rain forest. •illustrated poem	30. Decide which natural pattern within the rain forest is impacted most by man. •persuasive speech
Develop A Plan	Gather Information	Organize Information	Present The Findings

Figure 7.2. *(continued)*

Dagget's (1995) steps move in the direction from disciplinary, multidisciplinary, and interdisciplinary to transdisciplinary. Although Bloom's (1956) taxonomy works to develop activities of substance, Dagget's taxonomy adds another important dimension. It enables us to solve ill-structured complex problems.

Multiple Intelligences

Emerging from cognitive psychology research is Gardner's (1983, 1997) concept of MI. Many exciting innovations in education today center around MI. Some of Gardner's beliefs (see also Checkley, 1997) are outlined here.

- Traditionally, schools have valued only linguistic and mathematical intelligences.
- There are at least six additional ways of knowing.
- The IQ test measures only two intelligences. The SAT reflects only students who perform well on tests, not those who are inquisitive, serious problem solvers.
- It is limiting for students when all eight intelligences are not considered. Although we each have the capacity for all intelligences, we do not have equal capability in each intelligence area, nor do we have the same combination of intelligences.
- MI encourages deeper understanding and therefore prepares people for work.
- Performance assessment supports the theory of MI.
- It is not possible to understand fully and implement the theory immediately.
- MI is not an end in itself.

Gardner's eight intelligences are presented in Table 7.2.

Gardner (1983, 1997) is considering that there may be an innate ninth intelligence—the existentialist. This intelligence asks the big questions: Who am I? What is my purpose in life? Why do we die? Where do we come from? There is not enough evidence to prove that this intelligence exists in the nervous system, however—one of the criteria for an intelligence.

TABLE 7.2 Multiple Intelligences

Linguistic	Using core operations of language	Poet, writer, speaker, orator
Mathematical	Understanding a causal system, inductive and deductive reasoning, patterns, solving complex problems	Scientist
Spatial	Perceiving the visual world accurately, recreating visual experience	Sailor, pilot, chess player, sculptor
Bodily-kinesthetic	Controlling body movements, handling objects skillfully	Athletes, performing artists
Musical	Thinking in music, hearing, recognizing, remembering, and manipulating patterns	Musician
Interpersonal	Getting along and working with others	
Intrapersonal	Having accurate knowledge of one's own strengths and weaknesses	
Naturalist	Discriminating among living things, classifying	Botanist, chef, consumer of material goods

Integrating Curricula Using MI

Gardner (1983, 1997) supports the disciplines and prefers an approach that views curriculum from several different disciplines. He also believes that curriculum should be tied to real life (Checkley, 1997). In reality, most teachers who use MI find that the curriculum becomes integrated.

The September 1997 issue of *Educational Leadership* offers many exemplary examples. There are also a number of good books that apply MI to the classroom (see Armstrong, 1993; Lazear, 1991; Marks-Tarlow, 1996). Several books align MI instruction to MI assessment (see Bellanca, Chapman, & Swartz, 1994; Lazear, 1994).

Robin Fogarty and Judy Stoehr (1995) formalize the relationship between MI and integrated curriculum models. MIs are added to previously developed models (see Fogarty, 1991). Once a teacher treads down the MI path, he or she faces a journey that becomes continually richer and richer.

Fogarty and Stoehr (1995) add a MI wheel from which to plan activities for any unit. Beverley Balch used this wheel (Figure 7.3) in planning lessons around the theme of conflict.

> Musical: Create a soundscape using orf instruments to demonstrate conflict.
>
> Visual/spatial: create a mural to encourage peaceful resolution of a conflict.
>
> Naturalist: Categorize prey and predators.
>
> Intrapersonal: Reflect in your journal on conflict resolution strategies.
>
> Interpersonal: Demonstrate conflict resolution strategies in your cooperative learning groups.
>
> Bodily-kinesthetic: Role play resolutions to issues.
>
> Logical-mathmatical: Use a priority ladder to make decisions about a local conflict.
>
> Verbal linguistic: Create an anthology of poems involving conflict.

Brain-Based Education

A great deal of attention has been paid lately to brain research and how its findings might apply to learning.

Susan Kovalic's (1994) work has influenced the field of interdisciplinary curriculum. She plans around a year-long theme with monthly components and weekly topics, all of which interconnect with each other. Ultimately, her curriculum planning schemata allows for vertical integration over several years.

Kovalic's (1994) work was based initially on Hart's (1983) brain research. This stresses the need for meaningful content, an enriched environment, trust, choices for students, time, and immediate feedback. Kovalic recommends starting with a science theme because this must come from the real world. Next, a teacher brainstorms for different content possibilities. Kovalic emphasizes that once a teacher

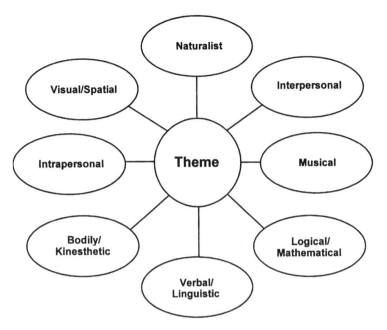

Figure 7.3. Multiple Intelligences Wheel

starts making connections through integration, there are endless connections to study. The teacher must evaluate what is worth knowing. Including state or local documents is important, but not the main emphasis of this approach. Rather, the key concepts are meaningful content and hands-on activities.

Caine and Caine (1997) consider curriculum from a brain-based approach. They begin with "brain-mind learning principles" derived from the brain research and they apply these principles to the classroom:

1. The brain is a whole system and includes physiology, emotions, imagination, and predisposition. These must all be considered as a whole.
2. Our brains develop in relationship to interactions with the environment and with others.
3. A quality of being human is the search for personal meaning.

4. We create meaning through perceiving certain patterns of understanding.
5. Our emotions are critical to the patterns we perceive.
6. Our brains process information into both parts and wholes at the same time.
7. Learning includes both focused attention and peripheral input.
8. Learning is both unconscious and conscious.
9. Information (meaningful and fragmented) is organized differently in our memory.
10. Learning is developmental.
11. The brain makes the optimal number of connections in a supportive but challenging environment; perceptions of threat inhibit leaning.
12. Every brain is unique in its organization.

Caine and Caine (1997) extend these principles to include the following applications to the classroom:

■ Learning must go beyond surface knowledge to dynamical or perceptual knowledge. This is created by generating deep meaning (connecting to the values and purposes of the students) and felt meaning (an emotional connection). Dynamical knowledge is the result of constructing our own meanings through our own perceptions.

■ Immersion in complex authentic experiences must be planned. Such experiences have a story line and are connected to real life. They include social relationships and a variety of sensory input. These variables can be tightly controlled by the teacher.

■ Experiences must be actively processed. This includes critical thinking and active questioning of ongoing ideas. The learner asks what was done, why it was done, and what was learned. The emphasis on active processing leads to a particular type of classroom environment. Students are encouraged to question everything continually throughout the assessment. The teacher models this process. The questioning leads to an enriched environment. Teachers are encouraged to connect questioning to the immediate community and the perceived needs of students.

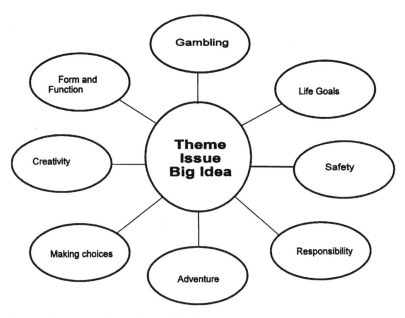

Figure 7.4. Free Association Webbing

■ Relaxed alertness is a state of mind that is enhanced by high-challenge and low-threat environments. This is the optimal state for learning.

Applying these principles, Caine and Caine (1997) experimented with approaches to integration. One approach uses a curriculum design wheel or a webbing activity that employs free association to develop the curriculum. A second way is to organize curriculum according to the passionate interests of the students. These loosely fit into the interdisciplinary and transdisciplinary models (Figures 7.4 and 7.5).

Not everyone accepts the results of recent brain research, and criticisms have been levied against both the research methodology itself and the validity of connecting the research to education (Bruer, 1997). Bruer (1997) offers cognitive psychology as a bridge between research and educational practice. It appears that the cognitive psychologists and those involved in brain research have much in common, however, and that they could learn from each other.

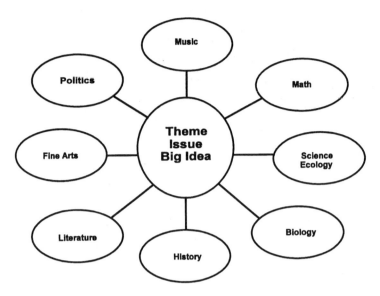

Figure 7.5. Curriculum Wheel

Learning Styles

Learning styles are grounded in personality theory. The notion that people learn differently has been around for a long time (Kolb, 1984; McCarthy, 1997). A teacher only has to reflect on classroom experiences to realize the truth of this statement. Some people learn sequentially; others make intuitive leaps. A person may learn through quiet reflection or through interaction with others. Some think in concrete ways; others think in abstract ways. Learners can be auditory, visual, or kinesthetic.

Learning styles have been categorized in different ways, but they are basically about our preferences for specific ways of thinking and approaches to learning. The styles are not fixed and can change and grow throughout life. Although learning styles make intuitive sense, there is no conclusive research to support their contribution to the enhancement of learning (Ornstein & Hunkins, 1998).

Silver, Strong, and Perini (1997) integrate learning styles with MI. They point out that learning styles emerged from theories of the personality and emphasize how individuals absorb, think about, and evaluate information. MI theory focuses on the content and products of learning, whereas learning styles consider the process. Learning-style menus have been created. These match the seven classic intelligences with the four learning styles. This produces 28 profiles. These profiles include the type of products that a combination of learning style and MI might produce. The result is a rich menu of assessment options that can open the door to a wide variety of choices for students.

Connecting Learning Styles, MI, and Brain-Based Education

How do we choose which theory to use when we want to plan curriculum? There are many overlaps among these theories, but there are distinct differences. Each looks much the same in the classroom, however. Guild (1997) points out the similarities:

- Theory is learner centered.
- Teacher and students are reflective practitioners.
- Curriculum is rigorous with both depth and quality.
- Diversity is at the heart of each theory.
- None is a panacea for education.
- Good teaching skills are essential.

Teaching Across the Curriculum

Other teaching strategies add to the curriculum and enhance learning. Some suggestions follow.

Storytelling

Using stories in classrooms is powerful. Students make meaning through stories. This can be literature. Roger Taylor (1996), for example, recommends the great books as a foundation. His work is discussed in Chapter 4, "Using Interdisciplinary Approaches." The stories can also be personal and come from the students' own lives. Or the curriculum can be integrated through the use of narrative. The use of stories in these ways is examined in Chapter 5, "Exploring Transdisciplinary Approaches."

Some activities that use the power of stories are role-playing, dramatization, telling and retelling stories, round-robin storying, writing stories based on what is being learned, creating new endings, historical narratives, mime, dance, creating a video or short movie documentary, and radio plays.

Graphic Organizers

Graphic organizers are an excellent way for students to learn to organize their thinking, and therefore read, write, and think better. Most of the diagrams in this book are graphic organizers designed to facilitate understanding of different approaches to interdisciplinary curriculum design. Hyerle (1995-1996) offers visual tools that he claims correspond to thinking processes. Examples of graphic organizers are webs, Venn diagrams, sequence chains, branching diagrams, compare-and-contrast charts, flow maps, matrix diagrams for comparing and organizing, cause-and-effect circles, and decision-making charts.

Student as Questioner/
Student as Researcher

This concept is being used more and more often. The responsibility for the specific content rests with the students. Students generate their own questions and act as researchers to find the answers. The teacher's role is to facilitate this process. To do this, students need to be taught certain skills. These are usually complex skills that can be broken down into subsets of skills.

The student as researcher has to learn many skills. Learning how to ask a good question is a part of being a researcher. Students also have to be able to process information. This skill can be broken down into the following subset of skills (Marzano et al., 1993): interpret and synthesize data; use a variety of data-gathering techniques and information resources; assess the value of the information; and recognize where and how data can be effectively used.

When students research different questions, even if the questions are all on the same topic, they learn the most about their own topic and much less about other students' topics. The crucial thing they are learning is to be an independent thinker.

Disciplinary Heuristics

In life, students will be involved in complex performances. For problem solving, students are encouraged to act and think in the roles that simulate the real-world counterpart. How would practitioners in different disciplines approach this problem? What questions would they ask? This is a disciplinary heuristic. See the narrative curriculum in Chapter 5, "Exploring Transdisciplinary Approaches," for how a disciplinary heuristic can be applied (Lauritzen & Jaeger, 1997). For example, the student may have to act as a scientist, historian, and anthropologist to solve a certain problem. Some disciplinary heuristics that Lauritzen and Jaegar (1997) suggest are artist, scientist, writer, musician, engineer, historian, psychologist, anthropologist, botanist, dancer, farmer, sociologist, and mathematician.

Metaphor

Teaching with metaphors is a powerful tool for deep understanding. Students can use metaphor to explain certain phenomenon; for example, the effect of the ozone layer, weather patterns, or comparing existing theories. This type of metaphor allows students to examine what they are supposed to learn and create a new way of explaining it.

Intuitive Thinking

The traditional model is concerned with objectivity and the right answer. The question is confined to a discipline. Now there is a recognition that there is not always one right answer, there are many possibilities and complexities in solving problems, and solutions dissolve disciplinary boundaries. Many important discoveries have been found by people who were at the edge of a discipline. They brought new ways of looking at a problem and they applied their intuitive abilities. It was through a dream that Einstein came to a realization of the theory of relativity. Valuing intuitive thinking does not mean that we throw away the time-tested models such as the scientific method. It does mean that there is room for creativity and encouraging students to move outside the boundaries that they are used to.

Reflection

Reflection is identified as a key ingredient for learning. We don't necessarily allow time for reflection, however. Some ways that reflection can be incorporated in the classroom are through journals, visualization, goal setting, and exercises for intrapersonal intelligence.

Body-Mind Connection

Learning has an emotional component. Our bodies record our emotions and respond to them. A popular expression is that our biography is our biology. There are at least two implications that are important to think about. We need to teach in ways that recognize the importance of emotions in learning. Positive emotions lead to positive learning. As well, students should be taught the importance of looking after their body, physically, mentally, and spiritually. This does not mean that religion enters the classroom, but it means we should not shirk from the big questions that spark student curiosity. What is the meaning and purpose of our lives? How can I contribute to making the world a better place?

Assessment

The shift to demonstrations of learning led to performance-based assessment tools. Now, as standards are being developed, skills are being deconstructed. Scoring guides and rubrics are being created based on these deconstructions. New assessment processes are being refined continually. The educational community is still learning how to align instruction with assessment and reporting. New technologies are being created. For example, the Association for Supervision and Curriculum Development is developing a reporting tool from which data can be accessed continuously (Betts, 1997). A school can select four to six outcomes to be measured to track student achievements on a daily or weekly basis.

Many problems with assessment are beyond the scope of this book. Including assessment is essential during the planning process, however. It should not be an afterthought, but planned along with the activities. Most important, is working with two questions that guarantee that the assessment is a part of the learning process:

- Does the assessment measure what I want to measure?
- Does the assessment match the learning principles?

Assessment Choices

Some choices for assessment are standardized tests, teacher-created tests, scoring guides or rubrics, journals, portfolios, interviews, conferences, observation, self-assessment, peer assessment, video, and performance assessment

Products

A wide variety of products can demonstrate learning. These can be used for performance assessment or combined with other measures of assessment. Some examples are shown in Figure 7.6.

Dealing With Diversity

The inclusive classroom is an issue at the top of many agendas. In Ontario, equity issues inspired the first round of curriculum reform. How can we ensure equal outcomes for all students? The classrooms in the United States and Canada are made up of very diverse populations. This diversity may be in academic ability, physical handicaps, race, ethnic background, or socioeconomic class. The most recent trend has been toward mainstreaming classrooms. This has created difficulties for many teachers because they have not necessarily been trained to deal with special needs.

Integrated curriculum has been hailed as one way to ensure an inclusive classroom. The rationale is that when we change the way we teach, we will be able to meet the needs of many more students. A relevant curriculum where students actively participate is more motivating to all students.

Books on how to teach for inclusive classrooms offer much the same picture as has been drawn in this chapter. Consider these recommendations from Cole (1995):

Objects
Collection
Costumes
Edibles
Invention
Learning center
Mask
Mazes
Mobile
Mural
Museum exhibit
Musical
 instruments
Needlework
Papier-mâché
Plaster of Paris
 model
Project cube
Prototype
Puzzle
Recipe
Sculpture
Simulation

Oral
Choral reading
Debate
Lecture
Oral defense
Oral report
Panel discussion
Peer teaching
Radio program
Seminar
Song
Sound
Telephone
 conversation

Kinesthetic
Dance
Demonstration
Drama
Game

Interview
Pantomime
Play
Press conference
Puppet show
Rock opera
Role-play
Skit
Tableau

Visual
Art gallery
Block picture story
Blueprints
Book cover
Bulletin board
Caricature
Cartoon
Chart
Collage
Comic strip
Display
Etching
Family tree
Graph
Hidden picture
Labeled diagram
Large-scale drawing
Map with legend
Matrices
Painting
Photo essay
Photographs
Picture story
Pop-up book
Postage stamp,
 commemoratives
Poster
Scrapbook
Sculpture
Timeline
Venn diagram
Webs

Media
Animated movie
Audiotape
Computer program
Database
Film
News program
Slide show
Television program
Transparencies
Video

Written
Advertisement
Anthology
Cook review
Crossword puzzle
Diary
Draft a new law
Editorial essay
Illustrated story
Journal
Letter to the editor
Manual
Myth/legend
Newspaper story
Pamphlet
Petition
Poetry
Proclamation
Quiz
Rebus story
Scenario
Science fiction
Story
Scroll
Slogan
Travel brochure

Figure 7.6. Products

- Opportunities for group work
- Reality-based learning approaches: real purposes, real audiences
- Interdisciplinary teaching
- Attention to learning styles
- Meaningful opportunities for fullest dimensions of thinking
- Multicultural teaching
- Alternative assessment
- Home-school partnerships
- Questioning strategies
- Brain-compatible instruction

The assumption is that these strategies will facilitate greater success for all students. In practice, it seems to be true. For example, I was working in a mainstreamed science class where the teacher bemoaned the lack of competence of some of the lower-ability students. The teacher commented that these students should not be in the room for safety reasons. When we shifted the instruction style and had students create their own experiments, these students did better than those deemed gifted. The teacher said this was "scary." His preconceptions of students' abilities was transformed, and now he reaches out to engage all students.

Still, we need to know how to modify the curriculum for students. Curriculum modification should be addressed in the initial planning stages as well as when necessary during implementation. Some ways of approaching differentiated instruction become obvious once the teacher starts thinking in terms of modification. The special education teacher is a fine resource. Books such as that by Tomlinson (1995) are helpful.

Summary

This chapter has offered many different lenses to view the principles of teaching, learning, and assessment. One approach may appeal to a teacher more than another. For example, a science teacher may connect with constructivist principles. A music teacher may find that MI resonates. An English teacher may find that activities developed with Bloom's (1956) taxonomy add depth and richness to the curriculum. A math teacher may find that using the big ideas or essential understandings could take the students beyond merely completing meaningless problems.

All the approaches discussed are about changing how things are taught in the classroom. They are embedded in a new philosophy of education. Once we understand that philosophy, we realize that all parts of the curriculum process must be aligned. When teachers who believe in this philosophy come together to plan curriculum, the results can be wonderful.

8

✻✻✻✻✻✻

OVERCOMING THE OBSTACLES
AND FINDING SUCCESS

✳ ✳ ✳

In 1993, I wrote *Planning for Integrated Curriculum: The Call to Adventure*, which outlined the obstacles that teachers were encountering. Five years later, the same barriers loom for novices. The good news is that many educators have confronted the hurdles and succeeded. To do so, however, they have had to challenge most of the traditional beliefs about education. As well, they have had to understand how to be a change agent. This chapter explores the obstacles and offers examples of how educators have transcended them. It also looks at being an effective change agent.

Overcoming Obstacles

Time

This is the strongest and most common recommendation in the literature. People need time not only to plan but also to make sense of new ways to deliver curriculum. Often it is difficult for a teacher to find sufficient time. For example, in Ontario, the government is planning to cut teacher preparation time while simultaneously asking teachers to adopt new methods of presentation. Cutting time is an effort to save money, but it does not allow for the absolute necessity of allowing teachers time to make subjective meaning of the changes being required.

In my own experience, I have found that much time is required to come to terms with a new philosophy of education that requires a whole new set of beliefs. This is not true for those who have already bought into the new story; however, many who are trying unfamiliar approaches are doing so with one foot in the values and assumptions of the old story, coupled with an intuitive guess that students may indeed respond well to different approaches.

When scheduling for time, one should remember the following points:

- Large blocks of planning time are needed with the people who are going to implement the curriculum.
- It is helpful to hold the first session or sessions outside the school environment, with food provided.
- Additional shorter periods of planning time will be needed for ongoing planning while teachers experiment with new ideas and make modifications.
- Common breaks in the daily schedule are immensely helpful.
- Time can be gained by adding 10 minutes a day to the schedule and then using the gained time for schoolwide planning.
- Early morning starts leave time in the afternoon for planning.

Scheduling

A second concern raised by most people is the necessity for changing the schedule. There is a need for larger blocks of time to deal with a concept in depth. This can be done in many creative ways; there is no standard formula. Here are some formulas that have worked:

- Sixty students are scheduled with two teachers for two periods.
- Thirty students are scheduled for science followed by English; another 30 are scheduled for English followed by science. Students can be placed in either separate classes or combined classes.

- Four teachers work with 90 randomly selected students in heterogeneous groups.

- Teachers work in teams for 180 minutes a day (can be divided any way).

- Team teachers have a 45-minute daily planning period together.

- All students in one high school were involved in independent studies on Wednesdays. Students could be out in the community doing research or job shadowing. They could be in the school doing remedial work or taking an interest course such as fashion design. Another school used a special timetable on Wednesdays that allowed teachers to work as an advisor with their own group of students. Both schools stressed mentorship programs (Drake, Egan, & Finlay, 1996). This model has been adopted at many schools across Ontario.

- One teacher can decide to teach a more integrated program within the existing confines of the department structure. One English teacher delivered the transdisciplinary story model to her grade 12 general-level English class for 8 weeks of the regular schedule. She found the students more motivated than usual (Drake & Basaraba, 1997).

- A science department wanted to motivate students and used a more interdisciplinary approach. The class collaborated with the English department to develop a 6-week unit for grade 9 that ended in debates on environmental issues.

- Two or three teachers can plan for an interdisciplinary program that lasts for several weeks. For example, three arts teachers planned together to deliver a short unit (Sturch, 1996). Three groups of students rotated through 5-day units of visual arts, music, and drama designed to move students toward a final dramatic production that included student-created music and sets.

- At one school, the grade 9 program consisted of four blocks of integration: math/science/technology; communications (English, geography, and French); skills for living (family studies, physical and health education, and business); and integrated arts (keyboarding, drama, visual arts, instrumental, vocal, and the like). Each cluster delivered the program differently; some groups were taught by one teacher and some had three teachers in the cluster. There were short and long periods.

- Four quadrants (a quadrant includes several subject areas) can be scheduled for all students in a grade. Each quadrant is allotted equal time. Students study two areas per semester, one quadrant in the morning and one in the afternoon. Teachers work in teams in each subject area, planning curriculum and evaluation. Special education teachers are provided. Each subject area organizes its time differently. There should be an emphasis on the importance of subject specialists working cooperatively to create curriculum that is relevant to today's student (Thurston, 1996).

- Two teachers teach 50 students math, science, history, and English at the grade 11 and 12 level, with a new unit every 4 weeks. On Monday, Tuesday, and Friday, they teach for 4 hours; on Wednesday, for 2 hours; and on Thursday, for 6 hours. This is an integrated program where students can opt to take a more traditional program offered at the same school.

The "school within a school" format is being tried in many schools. There are mixed reactions to it. The teachers who are not in the program often resent the ones who are. This happens for a variety of reasons such as the threat of the success of the new program and the extra resources that these teachers often acquire. As well, there are problems with assessment. Those in the traditional school can give grades in a traditional manner, whereas those in an integrated program find it artificial to give credit in the subject areas as they once did. Offering similar opportunities to others seems to alleviate some of this problem.

Core Subjects

One difficulty that often arises during teachers' planning sessions is distinguishing between core subjects and other subjects. Core subjects are usually English, math, science, and at least one other subject. Other subjects such as visual arts, family studies, business, and technology are usually considered noncore and therefore not given as much time in the curriculum. Interdisciplinary efforts are planned among either core or noncore subjects. Understandably, this system is not appreciated much by the teachers of subjects considered noncore. Even within these divisions, there is often a pecking order. For example, one family studies teacher complained that family studies was represented in one integrated program by the existence of a bread maker in the tech center. There are good philosophical and practical reasons for honoring all subject areas that need to be considered when this type of argument is raised:

- The inclusion of the arts is important to learning much more than the skills of a particular art. See Chapter 2, "Does Integrated Curriculum Work?" for evidence of how learning arts skills enhances other skills. For example, research suggests that math and music skills are mutually enhancing.

- The basics are being taught in every subject area in a true integrated approach. When students experience a natural enjoyment in a "frill" subject area, they are more motivated to learn the basics.

- The importance of subject areas is shifting. Technology, for example, has shifted from a subject where one learns specific skills such as drafting and electricity to broad-based technology that involves basic skills that everyone needs to know. In many schools, this is a core subject now.

- The emphasis on doing and creating as a way of demonstrating knowing rather than simply memorizing for a written test leads directly into subject areas where there is a product.

- Learning can be fun.

Resistance

Resistance can come in many forms. Some teachers claim that what they do already is interdisciplinary. Often this claim is quite true; some teachers naturally use an integrated approach because students respond well to it. For example, one teacher in our study was insulted by requests for a more integrated program, saying, "In science, math, history, and English we have been integrating for years. You can't possibly teach a subject in isolation." Insisting that a program is already integrated is often a resistance tactic, however.

Believing that one is "already doing it" can also reflect a lack of understanding. Pasting dinosaur stickers on math sheets does not make an integrated unit on dinosaurs. This tendency is a common complaint of teachers who are aware of the possible depth of integrated programs when they watch what passes for integration. We need to realize that integration, regardless of the degree to which it is being implemented, requires challenging programming and making true connections.

One of the most helpful ideas is offered by Fullan and Miles (1992). They urge us not to consider resistance as a negative thing; rather, educators do not have enough understanding of the concept that they are being asked to implement. This is the perfect situation for inservicing.

Resistance to change is a natural human emotion. Understanding that change is difficult and even painful helps facilitate the process. Allowing time for people to tell their stories is also helpful. Often their stories change as they gain insight, and this allows them to move forward.

Don't forget that there is more than one path to change. One is to change the beliefs of those who are implementing something new. Another is to ask people to implement the change even if they are not completely convinced. As people are changing, they often make new meaning of the change, and their beliefs shift as a result. In my experience, beliefs shift as we have new experiences, reflect on them, and dialogue with others to make new meaning.

Planning the Curriculum

One of the most important issues in planning the curriculum is deciding who will do the actual planning. I have seen many efforts at planning where the actual implementation team was not involved. Instead, teachers given the time off to plan were actually being rewarded for something else they had done and had no real interest in the planning. This becomes political, rather than practical. For example, many teams include an educator who is about to retire. I have not yet seen this to be helpful. Another potential obstacle is being overloaded with personnel from central office.

Rules of thumb that have been successful include the following:

- The planning takes into consideration the whole school curriculum. What is taught in what grade and in what subject area? Where is there duplication? Connections? Content that covers the same general area? This is called *horizontal integration* (across a grade) and *vertical integration* (from grades 9 to 12; Jacobs, 1989, 1997).

- The planning team includes all the people who will implement the plan.

- The teachers who have "volunteered" are the best ones to start.

- Students are worth listening to and including in the planning process.

- The nature of the subjects to be integrated is not as important as a common philosophy among participants.

- A special educator should be a team member to help with necessary modifications.

- The teacher librarian can be a helpful team member and resource.

- The central office can often facilitate planning for first timers.

- Links with local faculties of education can be helpful.

- The principal must be supportive, if not on the actual team itself.

- The first effort is the hardest.

- Teachers usually begin most successfully with short projects or units.

- There often have to be schedule changes.

Structural Barriers

Across North America, educators continue to teach as they have been taught. Efforts at innovations such as interdisciplinary studies have come and gone without a trace. This occurs in part because the organizational structure revolves around the subject disciplines, and departments place subjects in the foreground (Siskin & Little, 1995). Departments are political units that compete for control of time, budget, personnel, territory, students, and a voice in policy making (Ball & Lacey, 1995). Departments become "balkanized," with strong and enduring boundaries characterized by teachers identifying themselves as subject specialists reluctant to move outside those boundaries (Hargreaves, 1994). According to Hargreaves (1994), subject integration has the power to transform school cultures because it brings subjects and curriculum contents together. It also challenges the power and privilege invested in academic subject learning, however—and frequent resistance from universities, subject associations, and articulate middle-class parent groups.

Some ways in which schools have broken down these structural barriers include the following:

- Dissolving the role of department heads in high school
- Establishing new teams of responsibility (e.g., an assessment team) where the leader may be a staff member or a department head
- Assigning a teacher leader as the coordinator of integrated studies
- Assigning teachers from different departments to common workrooms
- Having the school identify common goals for students across subject divisions
- Establishing action research teams to investigate cross-disciplinary concerns
- Making informed decisions on the results of actual data from the school involved
- Developing a collaborative school culture where working together is the norm

Program Quality

Interdisciplinary studies, although far from being new, are not necessarily done well (Martin-Kniep, Fiege, & Soodak, 1995). Curricular integration has been defined ambiguously; thus far, the elements do not necessarily build on one another (Case, 1994). Nevertheless, researchers insist that interdisciplinary studies is the best model to cope with our rapidly changing world (Panaritis, 1995). One concern is that the curriculum may be too superficial and there will not be any depth. Certainly, this could be a charge leveled at some current attempts (Case, 1994).

Much of the current problem seems to be that educators do not have enough exemplars to guarantee sound interdisciplinary curriculum. Superficial curriculum can be developed with superficial topics, and subject areas can indeed suffer. Rigorous frameworks are available, however, that apply good curriculum principles. To guarantee a rigorous curriculum, teachers should consider strategies such as the following:

- Systematically use Bloom's (1956) taxonomy to create activities for students (Curry & Samara, 1990; Jacobs, 1989). This requires students to move through knowledge, comprehension, application, analysis, synthesis, and evaluation skills.
- Apply a sophisticated approach to learning that stimulates students to higher-order thinking skills (Erickson, 1995).
- Follow the learning principles agreed on by the planning team.
- Establish a rubric for evaluating the quality of the curriculum being developed.
- Keep a video and journal documentation of all efforts to review the process (Barrera, 1997).

The Integrity of the Disciplines

Many worry that the integrity of the disciplines will be lost in integrated curriculum. Some math teachers favor a problem-solving, real-life approach but are concerned that math will be trivialized in the process of being integrated with other subject areas such as science (Roulet, 1996). Other math teachers are creating ways that math can play a substantive role in interdisciplinary programs (Suuttamm, 1996; Warren, 1996).

Others question the necessity of preserving subject areas. Disciplines are not synonymous with subject areas (Beane, 1995). A discipline is field of inquiry about some aspect of the world that offers a specialized lens with which to view the world. Those on the leading edge of a discipline know the boundaries are fluid and often connect with other disciplines to create interdisciplinary fields and projects (Klein, 1990). Subject areas are not disciplines because they are circumscribed representations of the disciplines and do not have fluid boundaries.

Assessment Procedures

British Columbia, in its *Year 2000* document (British Columbia Ministry of Education, 1990), was one of the first jurisdictions to mandate integrated curriculum. The effort was not fully realized because the reporting procedures were not clear to the general public. The lesson here is that interdisciplinary studies must be accompanied by clear, understandable assessment and reporting procedures. Different schools are experimenting with how to do this. Some jurisdictions have responded by assessing outcomes specifically, whereas others have a section on integrated studies. Nevertheless, this is a thorny question. Outcomes are to be observable and measurable, but many complex skills such as reflection or collaboration are not easily defined, observed, or measured. They have not yet been standardized, although there are attempts at moving in this direction.

Some things to remember:

- A similar philosophy needs to underlie all aspects of curriculum building.
- Assessment and reporting must be aligned with the goals of the curriculum.
- Students need to be explicitly taught the skills that will be evaluated.
- Parents need to be educated about why shifts are being made in student assessment and reporting.
- Community members on school councils can be decision makers on these procedures.
- Policy needs to be created for how to give students credit in integrated programs.

Sequential Skills

Educators in some subjects such as math and music are resistant to interdisciplinary studies because they claim that their subject area requires teaching sequential skills. Those who believe these subject areas can be integrated with others have let go of the absolute sequential nature of the skills in their area. Others point out that the sequences are different in different jurisdictions, suggesting that the absolute necessity for a specific sequence may involve false reasoning. Still others ask why, for example, students should have to learn calculus when some will never use it for a real-life problem. "Because it will make students learn how to think" is hardly satisfactory given that there is so much else for them to learn that we can teach. To challenge these perceptions:

- Bring in teachers who have wrestled with these issues and succeeded in integration.
- Offer journal articles that illustrate that the necessity of learning certain skills sequentially is often a state of mind.

Will Students Learn the Basics?

Current critics of educational innovation fear that students will not learn the basics. Some educators look to what are being called the "new basics": the skills that will be required for students to be productive citizens of the future. Reading, writing, and arithmetic are essential, but in this complex world, students will need technological literacy and information management, problem solving, and critical thinking skills.

This transition from content to skills has resulted, in part, because there is simply too much to learn. As well, most students find that they quickly forget most of what they learn for the pencil-and-paper tests that are so prevalent in the traditional system (Hynes, 1996). We need students who can apply their skills. Dagget (1995) reminds us that if we are to compete internationally, we need students who can apply skills. Some things to remember:

- The basics are as important as ever and they can be taught in an interdisciplinary context.
- The new basics include technological skills, information management, interpersonal skills, communication skills, and managing change.

Resources

When we start integrating the curriculum, we often require new resources. Textbooks are only one source of data required today.

Schools have access to a multitude of newer information technologies, such as online databases, the Internet, electronic bulletin boards, laser disks, CD-ROMs, and multimedia (Carefoot, 1994). To stay current, most schools now have a school library information center and a school media specialist (teacher librarian). Research indicates that the size of a school's information center is the best school predictor of academic achievement; students who come from schools with large information centers tend to score higher on standardized tests regardless of economic or other factors (Wilford, 1993).

Information management or resource-based learning is a cross-disciplinary skill that is emphasized in most planning for the 21st century. It is here that a student learns to act independently, facilitating his or her development as a lifelong learner. Information literacy involves locating, selecting, recording, and using information. This requires higher-order thinking skills: understanding, analyzing, synthesizing, and evaluating. It is necessary to have skilled guides to lead students through the material and to assist them in its synthesis. This may be the teacher librarian or the teacher.

Today, large amounts of money are being spent equipping schools with computers. Computers can be a real asset or a costly diversion in the classroom. This is particularly true when teachers do not acquire computer skills or do not use computers in ways that support new models of teaching and learning. There are many innovative ways that students can use the computers, such as using e-mail, accessing the Internet to allow them to talk to others around the globe, and retrieving data on almost any subject. Some aspects to think about when considering new resources:

- Teachers must be willing to update their own computer skills and information literacy skills.

- Students need to consider technology as a tool and explore the ethics of technology.

- It is important to have educators who are skilled at guiding students through the information maze and to teach them how to judge the value of it.

- The community offers the best place for a real-world context; there will undoubtedly be experts from whom students can learn.

Public Opinion/Parents

The adult community can be wary of new programs. Adults have been to school themselves and, regardless of the quality of that experience, they know what school should look like. Parents are worried that their children are being used as guinea pigs and do not want them sacrificed to someone else's cause. It takes a valid education program for the public to understand the rationale for what we are doing in our classrooms. This means that, first, we all must understand why we are doing what we are doing. It means situating education in the context of our rapidly changing world and pointing out the basic skills that students need. Integration makes a lot more sense when we realize that subject areas do not match the real world. It is particularly helpful when parents understand how alternative assessment can both assess and be an ongoing learning tool.

Parent councils or advisory councils are becoming an important part of the school. In many areas, they are no longer simply the PTA committee that cooks hot dogs on sports days. Rather, they are collaborative decision makers who are well versed in educational policy and can make a positive difference. They can also be very helpful in promoting school policy to parents or community members who object to what is happening in the school.

As educators, we need to be proactive in promoting the positive aspects of what we do. For example, when we teach our classes using community resources, we are advertising our curriculum. We can ask the community to the "events" or rituals of the school. This includes tasks or exhibitions that demonstrate what students are learning in the classroom.

On Being a Change Agent

When I teach courses on how to integrate the curriculum, students comment that they feel they have taken two courses: the first about the actual techniques of creating such a curriculum, and the other about the change process. They agree that for successful implementation, one needs to be aware of both aspects. Creating innovative models of education values a different philosophy from that of the traditional, and it follows that all aspects of the educational environment must adapt. Following are some of the lessons of being a change agent that have worked in real life.

Sharing Stories

In my classes, we listen to each other's stories of successful change efforts to understand methods that can work, and then we compare this with current literature. In this way, the literature is not so impersonal because, as individuals, we can compare it with something from our own experience. The suggestions that follow come from real-life experiences. Most of them can also be found in the literature. It would make sense for other prospective change agents to follow the same process of exploring their own stories.

The Keystone Integrated Framework, sponsored by the Pennsylvania Department of Education (1997) and the United States Department of Education, used the concept of telling one's story to capture what happened in its 3-year project. This project involved 13 sites across the state integrating arts, civics, English, geography, and history. Each site integrated differently, and each one offers a story full of wisdom. More important, the storytelling facilitated an effective medium to share this wisdom in an accessible way. A compendium of these stories is reviewed in the resources section of this book.

Some insights discovered:

- Share war stories throughout the process. We are all kindred spirits in this venture, and sharing our personal stories allows for bonding.

- Allow time for people to share "who they are" as well as their pedagogical theories. These collaborations usually involve the heart, and there is much more understanding when we know a little about each other's personal stories.

- Be aware that there will be personal conflict during first attempts at working with each other. Stories can help one see beyond the conflicts.

- Invite others who have traveled the same territory and learn from their stories.

Leadership

For change to be successful, administrative support is essential. This support can come in many guises:

- Principals or vice-principals are part of the curriculum development team.
- Administration provides the building blocks for developing a shared vision.
- The principal gives resources and time for teams to develop the new curriculum.
- The schedule allows for block scheduling and time for teachers to plan with each other.
- The culture in the school is collaborative.
- Administration clearly supports teachers during a performance dip or the inevitable mistakes when trying new ideas, and emphasizes reflection and learning from experiences.
- Getting back on the horse is encouraged if first efforts are less than 100% satisfactory.

When the administration is not officially a part of the team, it will often assign a leader. The following characteristics of an assigned leader can determine the success of the project:

- The leader believes making school a better place for students is the top concern.
- The leader has the respect of the staff and has demonstrated being a teacher leader.
- The leader has a real understanding of the constructivist philosophy of education and has demonstrated this in his or her teaching.
- The leader develops a shared vision with all the stakeholders.
- The leader has usually had inservicing or curriculum development experience.
- The leader has a passion for the task and is curious.
- The leader is a hard worker.
- The leader will be an active participant in the implementation process.

Many of the same characteristics come into play if there is not an official leader in place. In a team that has more than two members, someone usually emerges as the leader. The concept of an emerging leader eliminates some potential conflict because the project is "owned" and cannot be seen as dictated from the top down. This way there can be shared leadership as well. In one team that I worked on, leadership shifted according to task. This evolved to suit the context because we were all committed to the project. This team felt so strongly that what it was doing was for students, it undertook changing the culture and teaching and learning practices of the whole school.

The leader needs to remember that, inevitably, a part of working together will be conflict. Conflict is inevitable among those who work on integrating the curriculum. It is helpful to remember the following stages of group process:

- Form: These are the initial stages of the group getting to know one another
- Storm: Inevitable conflict
- Norm: The group comes together to develop group norms
- Perform: The norms are established and the group can now get down to the task

The concept of moral leadership also needs to be considered. Who are our leaders? Do they have a moral purpose? Do they demonstrate a commitment to sound pedagogy as well as caring, well-being, freedom, and social justice? These are issues that both Fullan (1993) and Sergiovanni (1992) explore in great depth.

The Nature of Change

As Michael Fullan (1993) reminds us, change is a complex, continuous, and never-ending phenomenon because our universe is undergoing major change in every aspect. These changes profoundly affect our schools (Levin & Riffel, 1997). Underestimating the complexity of change is a serious error. The notion of a planned change process that will ensure that educators move through mandated change in a linear order simply does not work. The chaos model seems to be a better metaphor to operate from (Fullan, 1993; Wheatley, 1992).

In my own research (Willis, 1995), I found evidence of the operation of chaos theory. The only predictable element seemed to be that education was unpredictable. Viewing education from a larger perspective did indicate some deep structure underlying the changes, however. Bifurcation, or a sharp change in direction, was evident over and over again. Just when it seemed as if there would never be any changes, staffs that had resisted change completely would suddenly decide that they were ready to plunge in. A typical comment was uttered by a central office consultant: "Our change is very stop and go. It comes in lurches and we can't tell it's coming."

Other principles observed in our research:

- Change needs to be systemic. The organization as it exists is set up to reinforce the status quo. All parts of the system must be aligned, including teacher colleges and universities, for real change to be effected.

- When you alter one element, you must change another. For example, if you modify assessment, you need to realign the reporting methods.

- The complexity and enormity of change can be overwhelming. Educators tend to be able to assimilate and create meaning for only one chunk at a time.

- Innovation disappears after 3 years if it is not nurtured.

- A leader and staff with a common purpose are needed for long-term reform.

- It often takes a year for a school to become clear on what exactly it wants to do together and how this should be undertaken. The product is often very different from what was first envisioned.

- Until a group reaches a common purpose, there needs to be commitment to the group itself.

- Groups that begin with the question "What can we do to fulfill the needs of the students in this school?" find that resistance decreases and a common purpose is easier to define.

- Offering seed money for educators to innovate has been effective. It does not have to be a lot of money; the message that is being sent is what is important.

- When change does happen, it seems to occur unexpectedly. There seems to be a period when teachers complain until they begin to understand the innovations and then attempt to try them.

Creating a Collaborative Culture

Restructuring isn't simply about educational reform and changing the structure of schools. If change is to be authentic, a collaborative effort is necessary. Hargreaves (1995) and Fullan (1993) call this "reculturing," which means changing the values, beliefs, and attitudes of the staff in the school. They emphasize that we should be moving toward a collaborative culture, which does not mean simply that the principal tells people to work together. Hargreaves (1994) suggests that this type of administrative action may lead to contrived collaboration and actually works against building a collaborative culture.

Schools can begin the process of working collaboratively in different ways. At David and Mary Thomson Collegiate Institute in Ontario, the faculty of 60 teachers used an "off-the-wall" process (Holloway, Kennedy, & Rowan, 1997). At a staff meeting, everyone was given a few sheets of sticky paper. First they had a minute when they silently brainstormed for concerns and wrote them down. Then there was a group consensus on two or three issues. These were put down—one issue on each "sticky." The stickies were then all put up on a board at the front and, with the help of one or two facilitators, sorted into categories. These categories represented the committees that were established, such as integrated curriculum, technology, and literacy. This part of the process took about an hour. Each teacher chose to be on one "off-the-wall committee." The committees developed action plans to be implemented. The committees seemed to complement each other; for example, the technology committee decided on cross-disciplinary skills necessary for all students to acquire, such as keyboarding. The decisions of each committee were brought forward to staff meetings to be approved for implementation. These groups were not departmental; however, because they usually included members from each department, whatever issues were discussed in the committee could be taken back to individual departments. These committees worked together until they no longer seemed useful, and then new groups evolved.

Other schools create activities that encourage both a collaborative culture and a more integrated program. One high school chose common outcomes for students that all subject teachers could teach at one grade level. This is an effective means to begin interdisciplinary efforts with a staff. What outcomes does each department want for students? When these outcomes prove to be generic, as they often are, it is easier to see what the various departments have in common and how they can work together. For example, the top six outcomes voted for in one school were work habits; problem solving and critical thinking skills; interpersonal skills; information retrieval and management; use of technology; and effective communication (verbal and written).

Other schools have used Jacobs' (1997) activities for horizontal integration, beginning by exploring each teacher's material in the curriculum at each grade level. What seems to be important is that school staffs meet and agree on what they have in common, and that moves them toward making school a better place for students.

Action Research

A common factor for ensuring that change is successfully implemented is for the school to be involved in some kind of ongoing data collection. Armed with research, educators know whether or not their reforms are really having any effect and in which areas. Given the problem of standardized tests not necessarily measuring what teachers think students should learn, educators need to decide what it is they want to know and then develop measures that will accurately reflect this. Richard Sagor's (1992) work has been very helpful to teachers who are interested in knowing how to begin this process.

There are many examples of how action research itself has acted as a catalyst for continued efforts. One high school noted that there was a trend toward better standardized test efforts during an integrated program. What was really encouraging to the teachers was the fact that the students seemed to be better at problem solving and they enjoyed coming to school more. This story is echoed across many of the schools with which I have been connected.

One board mandated that all schools have action research teams. All teachers must be involved in a team, but they have a choice of teams on which they may participate. The team makes the decision regarding what it wishes to examine. Reports from teachers indicate that such teams do work; however, it often takes the entire first year for the teachers to understand what action research is and how they can apply it. Parents have been receptive to this new approach and commended data-based efforts. A problem sometimes encountered is that some teachers are resistant to being on a team and show this resistance by not participating fully. This results in an increased workload for others. An effective antidote for this is assigning students to each team; the teachers do not want to appear to be saboteurs in front of students.

Another problem revolves around measurement. Teams that choose improvement of social skills as their focus find it difficult to find a method of measuring progress quantitatively. They are currently devising new measurements to reflect what it is they actually want to measure.

Some initiatives are at the state level. The SILC School Improvement Planning Process (a collaboration among the Colorado Department of Education, the PEAK Parent Center, and the University of Colorado at Denver) established a project where action research played a central role. Teachers selected from various local schools underwent professional development during the summer. They attended workshops on different areas such as integrating the curriculum, multiple intelligences, and program modifications for students with special needs. All participants took seminars on how to conduct action research. These teachers then developed an action plan and followed through on what they had learned with action research.

The SILC School Improvement Planning Process (1997) recommends some of the following questions as a start for action research:

- How many students are absent each day?
- How many students are expelled or suspended?
- What do we know about student achievement?
- How are our students doing on the standards?
- Are the standards used to guide the content coverage in each grade?
- What kind of instructional practices are used in this school?

- How do students feel about the instructional environment?
- Are students given different options to demonstrate their learning?
- Is there a disproportionate number of students with a particular characteristic, such as disability, income level, or race, who are singled out for disciplinary action?
- What is the ethnic, income, and cultural mix of the community?
- Do teachers feel prepared to teach the current curriculum?
- Do teachers feel as if they have the resources and support they need to do their best possible job as teachers?

Summary

This chapter dealt with the seemingly formidable obstacles that one finds when first beginning to plan for integrated curriculum. Some of these barriers are internal and involve educators who are learning new methods and techniques while they are still groping for understanding. These types of issues can best be dealt with by allowing time—time for collaborative planning, inservicing, and classroom experimentation. The external barriers will fall only when there are enough people who understand the necessity of making fundamental changes in the education structure itself. These changes will involve not only the group that is implementing the innovation but the whole school, system, region, and province or state. Ultimately, it will involve all the stakeholders—we are all in this together.

Only together can we create a new story for effective education.

Resources

＊ ＊ ＊

This section offers resources for developing integrated approaches to curriculum. It includes the things that I have found helpful. Many excellent resources are available. Given the framework provided in this book, it should be relatively easy to decide what philosophy underlies the approach being presented in selected resources. From there, one can align the approach in all aspects of design.

A

Books

✳ ✳ ✳

Armstrong, T. (1993). *7 kinds of smart: Identifying and developing your many intelligences.* New York: Plume.

This is a basic primer for understanding multiple intelligences. Thomas Armstrong presents Howard Gardner's (1983, 1997) seven intelligences and offers a detailed description of each. The naturalist intelligence is missing because Gardner only recently added this to his framework. Armstrong outlines strategies to improve each intelligence. This is a practical book that sets the intelligences in the context of our everyday world.

Beane, J. (1993). *A middle school curriculum: From rhetoric to reality.* Columbus, OH: National Middle School Association.

Beane, J. (1997). *Curriculum integration: Designing the core of democratic education.* New York: Teachers College Press.

In his 1993 book, Beane describes his theory designed for middle school students. He is interested in both relevant curriculum and teaching democratic values. His conception of an integrated curriculum is dependent on student questions and concerns about themselves and their world. This is a radical but effective approach to curriculum planning. His 1997 book continues the same path. Here, he offers a much richer historical background to curriculum integration. He enlarges on his philo-

sophical stance of offering a democratic curriculum and offers
strong arguments why this approach should be the only one
considered to be integrated.

Bellanca, J., Chapman, C., & Swartz, E. (1994). *Multiple assessments for
multiple intelligences.* Palantine, IL: Skylight.
 This book defines the multiple intelligences. For each intelligence, it gives examples of teaching methods and tells the reader
how to create performance standards for the multiple intelligences.
This is an easy-to-read manual with lots of practical suggestions.

Boomer, G., Lester, N., Onore, C., & Cook, J. (Eds.). (1992). *Negotiating
the curriculum: Educating for the 21st century.* London: Falmer.
 Negotiating the curriculum is explained from many different
perspectives in this book. A theoretical framework is offered.
Stories of what actually happened in classrooms are told. All
levels of education are explored. Garth Boomer has since died,
and this is the last look at his conception of negotiation. A dense,
but very interesting, book if you want to explore this approach
in depth.

Burns, R. (1995). *Dissolving the boundaries: Planning for curriculum
integration in middle and secondary school.* Charleston, WV: Appalachian Educational Laboratory.
 Rebecca Burns facilitates groups preparing integrated approaches to curriculum. This book takes the reader through the
steps she uses. Rather than being a book about how to develop
the curriculum, it focuses more on preparing teachers to begin
the task. It covers understanding different models of integration,
assessing readiness by looking at beliefs, supports, facilitating
structures and school culture, and how to work with teams.
There is an accompanying *Facilitator's Guide.* This is a worthwhile
professional tool that groups can use to deal with the predictable
obstacles before they appear on the horizon.

Caine, R., & Caine, G. (1997). *Education on the edge of possibility.*
Alexandria, VA: Association for Supervision and Curriculum
Development.
 The Caines use a brain-based approach to education. They
begin with a vision of education for the future, describe their

work in two schools, and discuss what they have learned about brain-based learning. Although integrating the curriculum is a part of their "theory," this book is not an answer if you are looking for ideas that are easily implemented. It begins with theory and meanders through the process of shifting teachers' belief systems when they process the theory and adapt it to their classrooms. It offers interesting insights on the process of change and an alternate approach. Essentially, the Caines learned that teachers' beliefs must change at a fundamental level if they are truly to change practice. They found that if a teacher simply tries new techniques, the techniques are filtered through teacher's embedded assumptions and the practice is reduced to look like an old model. To truly restructure, educators need to make deep mind shifts.

Cole, R. (Ed.). (1995). *Educating everybody's children: Diverse teaching strategies for diverse learners.* Alexandria, VA: Association for Supervision and Curriculum Development.

Educating everybody's children means teaching all students in ways that capitalize on how we learn best. In particular, this book is concerned with reaching students of ethnic and culturally diverse backgrounds who tend to be the disadvantaged who consistently rank academically in the lower third in American schools. This is an edited book on multicultural education that speaks with one voice; this voice represents the new story in education. These chapters include strategies for teaching diverse learners and improving achievement in writing, reading, mathematics, and oral communication. Each chapter follows a similar format. A strategy is discussed and then a classroom example is given. Interdisciplinary contexts are encouraged. New standards are offered and compared with traditional ones. This is an excellent book based on sound research that covers most of the bases of teaching and learning. Although it is geared toward diverse populations, the strategies recommended are good for all students at any level.

Drake, S. M., Bebbington, J., Laksman, S., Mackie, P., Maynes, N., & Wayne, L. (1992). *Developing an integrated curriculum using the story model.* Toronto: University of Toronto Press.

The story model is the framework used in Chapter 1 of this book to describe what is happening in education today. It also serves as a curriculum model for any level of education, and is explored in Chapter 5. It is a very versatile model that explores personal, social, global, past, present, and future aspects. This book uses the example of car as the theme and develops a sample unit. Personal stories of experiences with cars are explored. The cultural and global story of cars is constructed through the knowledge component. Past and present are considered to develop a new story of the car. This new story has the values, beliefs, and assumptions that we hope will guide us in the future.

Erickson, H. L. (1995). *Stirring the head, heart, and soul: Redefining curriculum and instruction.* Thousand Oaks, CA: Corwin.

This is an excellent book for developing substantive interdisciplinary curriculum. Lynn Erickson provides a thoughtful approach to deciding what should be taught and why. Building on the structure of knowledge, curriculum developers create concepts linked to generalizations or essential understandings. The book offers the reader a rich understanding of all the components of curriculum design.

Fogarty, R. (1991). *The mindful school: How to integrate the curricula.* Palatine, IL: Skylight.

Robin Fogarty offers a continuum of 10 models of integration (see Chapter 4). For each one, she gives a description, its advantages and disadvantages, and a graphic that acts as a visual organizer. This book has been helpful for many educators to come to some understanding of what curriculum integration might look like. It is written in comic book style. This book does not offer any tools for planning curriculum.

Fogarty, R., & Stoehr, J. (1995). *Integrating curricula with multiple intelligences: Teams, themes and threads.* Palatine, IL: Skylight.

This book takes the 10 models offered in *The Mindful School* and applies the multiple intelligences to each one. Readers are walked through a step-by-step planning process. There are lots of interesting examples ranging from elementary to high school. The models are explained first and then a planning process is added. Planning with the multiple intelligences is an easy process, but at times the book can be confusing unless the reader carefully follows the differences in the models. There are many very good ideas here to provide for rich curricula, however.

Glasgow, N. A. (1997). *New curriculum for new times.* Thousand Oaks, CA: Corwin.

Problem-based learning is the focus of this book. Glasgow sets his book in the changing context of education. His examples come from the Center for Technology, Environment and Communication (C-Tec), a small school community of 250 students. It has a modified block schedule allowing for students and teachers to meet for a chunk of time every other day. The book offers detailed examples of activities that were developed for this program. Some of these nontraditional courses were the first in the state to receive accreditation from the University of California as academic courses, providing enough rigor and content for college prep classes.

Harris, D. E., & Carr, J. F. (1996). *How to use standards in the classroom.* Alexandria, VA: Association for Supervision and Curriculum Development.

This is an excellent book based on experiences in Vermont. The title accurately describes what the reader will discover in the text. It is filled with short but very instructive examples of classrooms where the learning has been streamlined to connect to standards. The book tackles how to work within a framework of national, state, and local standards. It offers a general planning process that is a sound base for developing any curriculum from a standards perspective. This is followed by chapters on aligning topics, activities, and assessment so that the learning is all focused toward selected standards.

Jacobs, H. H. (Ed.). (1989). *Interdisciplinary curriculum: Design and implementation.* Alexandria, VA: Association for Supervision and Curriculum Development.

This is the classic book on integration. Heidi Hayes Jacobs's interdisciplinary concept model is outlined in detail. Two existing interdisciplinary programs are described. A range of design options is described. David Perkins contributes a chapter on fertile themes for integrated learning.

Jacobs, H. H. (1997). *Mapping the big picture.* Alexandria, VA: Association for Supervision and Curriculum Development.

Curriculum mapping is a procedure using the school calendar as an organizer to collect information on what teachers are actually teaching in their classrooms. The information is not what should happen, but what is happening. Data are gathered districtwide from K to 12. This process allows for communication among educators and eliminates unnecessary duplication. Data are three types: content, processes, and assessment. Jacobs claims that this process leads to the "living curriculum" and that informed changes can be made quickly. This process is important if we want to ensure that interdisciplinary approaches to curriculum are accepted. For example, neither parents nor students appreciate studying the same theme for 3 years in a row.

Jones, B. F., Rasmussen, C. M., & Moffitt, M. C. (1997). *Real-life problem solving: A collaborative approach to interdisciplinary learning.* Washington, DC: American Psychological Association.

This book is written for practitioners who work together or who practice *codevelopment.* Codevelopment is the key concept of this problem-based model. It refers to the creation of materials with both groups of teachers and teachers with students. The principles of learning guide the learning/teaching process. The book is clearly written with helpful charts and graphics to guide the reader. It offers detailed descriptions of a range of interdisciplinary applications. Problem-based learning is applied to language arts and humanities, science and mathematics, interdisciplinary multicultural studies, and projects involving multiple schools. For those interested in exploring this type of learning, this is an excellent starting place.

Kovalic, S. (1993). *ITI: The model—Integrated thematic instruction* (3rd ed.). Kent, WA: Books for Educators.

Susan Kovalic has trained thousands of teachers in integrated thematic instruction (ITI). She began this approach 25 years ago in gifted education and then realized that all students should be getting this type of enriched programming. The model stresses problem solving and decision making. She uses brain research and recommends brain-compatible learning. Kovalic addresses most of the problems that might occur with integrated projects. She believes in beginning with science as the organizing center. This is a rich book that considers integrated curriculum as the program being offered through the entire school—not just a small unit.

Lauritzen, C., & Jaegar, M. (1997). *Integrating learning through story: The narrative curriculum.* Albany, NY: Delmar.
This presents an interesting approach to curriculum through story. The learning principles echo throughout this book. This approach is goal directed and uses different types of narratives (literary, historical, simulations, problem centered) as the focal point of the learning. All aspects of curriculum are considered. An excellent planning template is offered. This book is directed toward students up to intermediate level. The concepts in it could be used at any level of education, however.

Lazear, D. (1991). *Seven ways of knowing: Teaching for multiple intelligences.* Palatine, IL: Skylight.

Lazear, D. (1994). *Multiple intelligence approaches to assessment.* Tucson, AZ: Zephyr.
All of David Lazear's books are helpful for implementing multiple intelligences in the classroom. They are easy to read and chock-full of ideas that the teacher can use immediately. The book on assessment allows teachers to see how K-12 can be aligned with the teaching and learning.

Marks-Tarlow, T. (1996). *Creativity inside and out.* New York, NY: Addison-Wesley.
Enhancing creativity through the multiple intelligences is the goal of this book, designed primarily for students in grades 4 to 9. There are 24 complete lessons incorporated in 4 units. The lessons are created to stimulate learning without sacrificing rigor. The units build developmentally but can be used independently. They explore the inner world, self-expression through body, musical and social intelligences, explorations of spatial intelligences, and communication skills and finding patterns. The book also offers an index that facilitates using the exercises in a specific subject area. For example, a science teacher could reference activities of special interest to science teaching. There

are also indexes for the multiple intelligences, activities for groups or individuals, time frame, appropriate grade levels, and special populations. The book itself uses a creative approach and is crammed with ideas that are presented in a cookbook fashion.

Ozar, L. A. (1994). *Creating curriculum that works: A guide to outcomes-centered curriculum decision making*. Washington, DC: National Catholic Educational Association.

This is another book that emphasizes teaching the way that we learn. It offers a step-by-step detailed plan for working with outcomes and standards in a methodical way. The concepts covered include outcomes as the foundation of the curriculum, match the outcomes, assessments and strategies, and outcomes and assessment working together. It also addresses the being aspect of curriculum outcomes. Although this book is discipline based, it offers a sound background on how to plan using outcomes or standards.

Samara, J., & Curry, J. (Eds.). (1992). *Writing units that challenge: A guidebook for and by educators*. Portland, ME: Maine Educators of the Gifted and Talented.

This guidebook uses John Samara and James Curry's curriculum model. It has sample units for primary, intermediate, middle school, and high school. This model uses an adaptation of Bloom's (1956) taxonomy. A sample of the work of Samara and Curry is available in Chapter 6. Many different samples of their work are available from the Curriculum Project at 1-512-263-3089.

A Compendium for The Pennsylvania Keystone Integrated Framework. (1997). Harrisburg: The Pennsylvania Keystone Integrated Framework.

These are the stories of practitioners involved in a federally funded effort that integrated the arts with civics, geography, English, and history. Eleven Pennsylvania school sites each partnered with an institution of higher education. A team was established at each site that comprised five members from the school and three faculty from the partnered university or college. Intensive training was given to these team members in the summer of 1995. The programs were piloted from 1995 to 1997. The stories are very varied, and readers get a taste of what the experience was like for the participants. There are also many good ideas for curriculum. For additional information, contact Beth Cornell, Pennsylvania Department of Education, 1-717-787-5713, fax 1-717-787-7066.

Tomlinson, C. A. (1995). *How to differentiate instruction in mixed ability classrooms.* Alexandria, VA: Association for Supervision and Curriculum.

This book first points out what differentiated instruction is not. It is not individualized instruction, nor is it a way to provide homogenous groupings such as the buzzards and bluebird groups of yore. Nor is it asking harder questions of some children. Many of Tomlinson's suggestions are simply common sense. Still, for teachers faced with the challenge of inclusive classrooms, it is helpful to see so many ideas in one place. Teaching strategies are offered to manage a differentiated classroom. Tomlinson addresses both content and process issues and how to prepare both students and parents for a differentiated classroom.

Vars, G. (1993). *Interdisciplinary teaching: Why and how.* Columbus, OH: National Middle School Association.

This is an easy-to-read book that covers a lot of bases and is geared toward middle school. Different types of curriculum integration are defined. Detailed planning is described for both an interdisciplinary unit and a problem-centered unit. Vars covers scheduling, planning team dynamics, and how to include skills in the curriculum. His steps are clear and easy to follow. His personal belief that learning should be meaningful and relevant, even fun, is woven throughout the book. This is a good book for those who are starting to integrate the curriculum.

B

✳✳✳✳✳

Journals

✳ ✳ ✳

Educational Leadership. (1997). *55*(1).

This theme issue offers a variety of articles on applying the multiple intelligences (MI) in a range of settings. An interview with Howard Gardner enlightens the reader about his perceptions of the applications of his theory to the real world. The articles are rich with ideas for both MI strategies and aligned assessment. The connections among learning styles and MI are explored. The addresses of several Web sites connected to both MI and learning styles are given.

Educational Leadership.

This journal is dedicated to stories of practitioners who are offering programs aligned with learning principles. As a result, many of the articles stress some form of integration. This is an excellent resource. A subscriber to the journal becomes a member of the Association for Supervision and Curriculum Development (ASCD) and receives *Education Update* and *Curriculum Update*. These two short publications keep the practitioner up-to-date on the latest issues in education. As well, members can join a wide variety of special interest networks. For example, the Interdisciplinary and Instruction Network Curriculum has a newsletter called *Connections*. The first 1997-98 issue covers brain-based learning and current brain research. As well, there is a short article on change. Membership in ASCD is highly recommended. State and provincial affiliates are usually very active organizations.

Drake, S. (Ed.). (1996). Creating integrated curriculum: Voices in the new story of education. *Orbit, 7*(1).
Guest editor—Susan Drake.

This theme issue focuses on applications of integrated, standards-based curriculum. The stories largely come from Ontario educators who were mandated to implement this type of approach. As a result, many of the stories are also descriptions of overcoming obstacles. This is a very informative magazine written by educators for educators that offers 23 real-life scenarios of curriculum ventures that have been successful. It includes classroom stories, innovative schools, and planning formats for standards-based approaches. Phone: 416-447-8186.

C

Videos

✳ ✳ ✳

Integrating the Curriculum. (1993). Salt Lake City, UT: Video Journal of Education.

This video features Heidi Hayes Jacobs. There are actually two videos. The first deals with the nature of interdisciplinary work and offers a rationale for it. The second shows teachers developing a unit using Jacobs's interdisciplinary concept model. A workbook accompanies the video. The process comes alive when the second videotape is used. For an overview of this model, refer to Chapter 4.

Planning Integrated Units: A Concept-Based Approach. (1997). Alexandria, VA: Association for Supervision and Curriculum Development.

This video features Lynn Erickson and her concept-based approach. It is a 65-minute video that explains the theory and offers an 8-step procedure to plan integrated units. This approach is outlined in detail in Chapter 4. The video comes with a facilitator's guide. It is designed for K-12 teachers, administrators, staff developers, and curriculum specialists who want to plan lessons that will ensure higher-level thinking skills. Using the facilitator's guide, one could plan two workshops of different lengths. Activities, handouts, overhead masters, readings, and a reference list are included.

D

Newsletters

✳ ✳ ✳

The Core Teacher.
Edited by Gordon Vars, this newsletter is the best bargain around. Vars, a professor emeritus from Kent State University, has been an advocate for integrated approaches for many years through the National Association for Core Curriculum (NACC). For a yearly subscription ($10.00), the reader gets a quarterly update on what is happening in the field of integration. A typical issue reviews conferences that Vars has attended and gives details of upcoming conferences. Recent studies in curriculum integration are critiqued. Each issue offers reviews of the latest published books. Members can order NACC materials from NACC, 1100 East Summit St., Suite 5, Kent, OH 44240-4094; email: GVarsNACC@aol.com.

E

✗✗✗✗✗✗

Programs

✳ ✳ ✳

Integrated Science Program
   This program is offered by the University of Alabama's Center for Communication and Educational Technology. This is a nonprofit organization that has created a new middle science curriculum. Information is available at 1-800-477-8151.

REFERENCES

✳ ✳ ✳

Aikin, W. M. (1942). *The story of the eight year study.* New York: Harper.

Alteritz, J. (1994). Making connections in the middle school. *Schools in the Middle, 4*(1), 8-10.

Anderson, J. (1992, October 30). Music on the brain. *Chicago Tribune,* p. 2.

Arhar, J. M., Johnston, J. H., & Markle, G. C. (1989). The effects of teaming on students. *Middle School Journal, 20*(3), 24-27.

Arhar, J. M., Johnston, J. H., & Markle, G. C. (1992). In J. Lounsbury (Ed.), *Connecting the curriculum through interdisciplinary instruction.* Columbus, OH: National Middle School Association.

Armstrong, T. (1993). *7 kinds of smart: Identifying and developing your many intelligences.* New York: Plume.

Aschbacher, P. R. (1991). Humanitus: A thematic curriculum. *Education Leadership, 49*(2), 16-19.

Association for Supervision and Curriculum Development. (Producer). (1997). *Planning integrated units: A concept-based approach* (Video). Alexandria, VA: Author.

Atkin, J. M., & Black, P. (1997). Policy perils of international comparisons: The TIMSS case. *Phi Delta Kappan, 79*(1), 22-28.

Ball, S. J., & Lacey, C. (1995). Introduction. In L. Siskin & J. Little (Eds.), *The subjects in question* (pp. 1-22). New York: Teachers College Press.

Barrera, M. (1997). Instructional strategies for developing a framework for an integrated curriculum. In *A compendium for the Pennsylvania Integrated Framework* (pp. IV1-IV24). Harrisburg: Pennsylvania Keystone Framework.

Beane, J. (1993). *A middle school curriculum: From rhetoric to reality.* Columbus, OH: National Middle School Association.

Beane, J. (1995). Curriculum integration and the disciplines of knowledge. *Phi Delta Kappan, 76*(8), 616-622.

Beane, J. (1997). *Curriculum integration: Designing the core of democratic education.* New York: Teachers College Press.

Begley, S. (1996, February 19). Your child's brain. *Newsweek*, pp. 55-62.

Bellanca, J., Chapman, C., & Swartz, E. (1994). *Multiple assessments for multiple intelligences.* Palatine, IL: Skylight.

Betts, F. (1997). ASCD special report: Scoreboard for schools. *Educational Leadership, 55*(3), 70-71.

Bialo, E., & Sivin, J. (1991). Microcomputers. *Emergency Librarian, 19*(2), 57-60.

Bloom, B. S. (1956). *A taxonomy of educational objectives* (Handbook 1, Cognitive domain). New York: McKay.

Boomer, G. (1992). Negotiating the curriculum. In G. Boomer, N. Lester, C. Onore, & J. Cook (Eds.), *Negotiating the curriculum* (pp. 4-14). London: Falmer.

Boomer, G., Lester, N., Onora, C., & Cook, J. (1992). *Negotiating the curriculum.* London: Falmer.

Bracey, G. W. (1997). On the difficulty of knowing much about anything about how schools reform over time. *Phi Delta Kappan, 79*(1), 86-88.

Brady, M. (1989). *What's worth teaching? Selecting, organizing and integrating knowledge.* Albany: State University of New York Press.

Brady, M. (1993). Simple-discipline schooling. *Phi Delta Kappan, 74*(6), 438-439.

British Columbia Ministry of Education. (1990). *Year 2000: A framework for learning.* Victoria: British Columbia Ministry of Education Program Development.

Bruer, J. (1997). Education and the brain. *Educational Researcher, 26*(8), 4-16.

Budzinsky, F. K. (1995). "Chemistry on stage"—A strategy for integrating science and dramatic arts. *School Science and Mathematics, 95*(8), 406-410.

Burns, R. (1995). *Dissolving the boundaries: planning for curriculum integration in middle and secondary school.* Charleston, WV: Appalachian Educational Laboratory.

Caine, R., & Caine, G. (1997). *Education on the edge of possibility.* Alexandria, VA: Association for Supervision and Curriculum Development.

Carefoot, L. (1994, spring). Information skills: What does it mean to be literate? *School Libraries in Canada,* 11-15.

Case, R. (1991). *The anatomy of curriculum integration: Forum on curriculum integration* (Triuniversity integration project, Occasional paper 2). Burnaby, BC: Simon Fraser University.

Case, R. (1994). Our crude handling of education reforms: The case of curricular integration. *Canadian Journal of Education, 19*(1), 80-93.

Casey, J. (1994, fall). Literacy instruction in an integrated curriculum: Integrating computers in the primary classroom. *The Computing Teacher,* 33-34.

Checkley, K. (1997). The first seven . . . and the eighth. *Educational Leadership, 55*(1), 8-13.

Clark, B. (1986). *Optimizing learning.* Columbus, OH: Merrill.

Clark, B. (1988). *Growing up gifted* (3rd ed.). Toronto: Merrill.

Cole, R. (1994). Interdisciplinary learning: One school's move to improve grade 9 curriculum. *Prism, 3*(2), 37-41.

Cole, R. (Ed.). (1995). *Educating everybody's children: Diverse teaching strategies for diverse learners.* Alexandria, VA: Association for Supervision and Curriculum Development.

A Compendium for the Pennsylvania Keystone Integrated Framework. (1997). Harrisburg: The Pennsylvania Keystone Integrated Framework.

Conference Board of Canada. (1992). *Employabililty skills profile: What are employers looking for?* (Brochure E-F). Ottawa: Author.

Cooper, D. H., & Sterns H. N. (1973). Team teaching, student adjustment and achievement. *Journal of Educational Research, 66,* 323-327.

Cotton, K. (1982). *Effects of interdisciplinary team teaching: Research synthesis.* Portland, OR: Northwest Regional Lab.

Curry, J. A., & Samara, J. (1990). *Curriculum guide for the education of the gifted student 9-12.* Atlanta: Georgia Department of Education.

Dagget, W. (1995, April). *Keynote address.* OSSTF Grass Roots Conference, Toronto, ON.

Darling-Hammond, L., & Falk, B. (1997). Using standards and assessments to support student learning. *Phi Delta Kappan, 79*(3), 1990-1999.

Davies, M. A. (1992) Are interdisciplinary units worthwhile? Ask students. In J. Lounsbury (Ed.), *Connecting the curriculum through interdisciplinary instruction.* Columbus, OH: National Middle School Association.

Delors, J. (1996). Learning the treasures within. Paris: Report to UNESCO of the International Commission on Education for the Twenty-First Century.

Dewey, J. (1969). *Experience and education.* New York: Macmillan/Free Press. (Originally published in 1938)

Drake, S. M. (1993). *Planning for integrated curriculum: The call to adventure.* Alexandria, VA: Association for Supervision and Curriculum Development.

Drake, S. M. (1995). Connecting learning outcomes to integrated curriculum. *Orbit, 26*(1), 28-32.

Drake, S. M., & Basaraba, J. (1997). On coming to a definition of collaborative partnerships. In H. Christensen, L. Goulet, & C. Krenz (Eds.), *Recreating relationships: Collaboration and education reform* (pp. 209-218). Albany: State University of New York Press.

Drake, S. M., Bebbington, J., Laksman, S., Mackie, P., Maynes, N., & Wayne, L. (1992). *Developing an integrated curriculum using the story model.* Toronto: University of Toronto Press.

Drake, S. M., Egan, K., & Finlay, B. (1996). A conversation with Susan Drake, Kaye Egan, and Barry Finlay. *Orbit, 27*(1), 43-47.

Drake, S. M., Hemphill, B., & Chappell, R. (1996). A novel approach: Fiction as a springboard to environmental science experiments and discussions. *The Science Teacher, 63*(7), 36-39.

Duncan, B. (1996). *Mass media and popular culture.* New York: Harcourt Brace.

Elmore, R. F., Petersen, P. L., & McCarthey, S. J. (1996). *Restructuring in the classroom.* New York: Teachers College Press.

Erickson, H. L. (1995). *Stirring the head, heart, and soul: Redefining curriculum and instruction.* Thousand Oaks, CA: Corwin.

Erickson, H. L. (in press). *Concept-based curriculum and instruction: Teaching beyond the facts.* Thousand Oaks, CA: Corwin.

Ewy, C., with student authors. (1996-1997). Kids take on "the test." *Educational Leadership, 54*(4), 76-78.

Fogarty, R. (1991). *The mindful school: How to integrate the curricula.* Palatine, IL: Skylight.

Fogarty, R., & Bellanca, J. (1993). Patterns for thinking, patterns for transfer. Palatine, IL: Skylight.

Fogarty, R., & Stoehr, J. (1995). *Integrating curricula with multiple intelligences: Teams, themes and threads.* Palatine, IL: Skylight.

Fosnot, C. (1989). *Enquiring teachers, enquiring learners.* New York: Teachers College Press.

Fosnot, C. (1996). Constructivism: Theory, perspectives and practice. New York: Teachers College Press.

Fullan, M. (1993). *The change forces.* London: Falmer.

Fullan, M., & Miles, M. (1992). Getting reform right: What works and what doesn't. *Phi Delta Kappan, 73*(10), 744-752.

Gamsky, N. (1970). Team teaching student achievement and attitudes. *Journal of Experimental Education, 39*, 42-45.

Gardner, H. (1983). *Frames of mind: The theory of multiple intelligences.* New York: Basic Books.

Gardner, H. (1997). Multiple intelligences as a partner in school improvement. *Educational Leadership, 55*(1), 20-21.

Geoghegan, W. (1994). Re-placing the arts in education. *Phi Delta Kappan.*

George, P. S., & Oldaker, L. L. (1985) *Evidence for the middle school.* Columbus, OH: National Middle School Association.

Georgiades, W., & Bjelke, J. (1964). Experiment in flexible scheduling of team teaching. *Journal of Secondary Education, 39*, 136-143.

Georgiades, W., & Bjelke J. (1966). Evaluation of English achievement in a ninth grade period three team teaching class. *California Journal of Education Research, 17*(3), 100-112.

Glasgow, N. A. (1997). *New curriculum for new times.* Thousand Oaks, CA: Corwin.

Goleman, D. (1996). *Emotional intelligence.* New York: Bantam.

Graves, D. H. (1983). Writing: Teachers and children at work. Portsmouth, NH: Heinemann.

Greenhawk, J. (1997). Multiple intelligences meet standards. *Educational Leadership, 55*(1), 62-64.

Grimmestad, B. (1982). Dramatic play: A vehicle for prejudice reduction in the elementary school. *Journal of Educational Research, 16.*

Guild, P. (1997). Where do the learning theories overlap? *Educational Leadership, 54*(6), 46-51.

Hancock, L. (1996, February 19) Why do schools flunk biology? *Newsweek,* pp. 58-59.

Hargreaves, A. (1994). *Changing teachers, changing times.* Toronto: OISE.

Hargreaves, A. (1995). Renewal in the age of paradox. *Education Leadership, 5*(52), 14-19.

Hargreaves, A., Earl, L., & Ryan, J. (1996). *Schooling for change: Reinventing education for early adolescents.* London: Falmer.

Hargreaves, A., & Macmillan, R. (1994). The balkanization of secondary school teaching. In L. Siskin & J. Little (Eds.), *The subjects in question* (pp. 141-171). New York: Teachers College Press

Harris, D. E., & Carr, J. F. (1996). *How to use standards in the classroom.* Alexandria, VA: Association of Supervision and Curriculum Development.

Hart, L. (1983). *Human brain, human learning.* New York: Basic Books.

Heuwinkel, M. (1996, fall). New ways of teaching = new ways of learning. *Childhood Education,* 27-31.

Hoerr, T. R. (1997). Frog ballets and musical infractions. *Educational Leadership, 55*(1), 43-46.

Holloway, M., Kennedy, F., & Rowan, S. (1997). Off the wall successes. *Orbit, 28*(2), 14-16.

Horwood, B. (1992, June). *Integration and experience in the secondary curriculum.* Paper presented to the annual conference of the Canadian Society for Studies in Education, Charlottetown, P.E.I.

Hunt, D. (1988). *Beginning with myself.* Toronto, ON: OISE.

Hyde, S. (1992). Negotiating mathematics. In Boomer, G., Lester, N., Onore, C., & Cook, J. (Eds.), *Negotiating the curriculum* (pp. 53-66). London: Falmer.

Hyerle, D. (1995-1996). Thinking maps: Seeing is understanding. *Educational Leadership, 53*(4), 85-89.

Hynes, W. (1996, August 31). Kudos to our classrooms. *Globe and Mail,* Toronto, Ontario, Canada, pp. D1, D3.

Jacobs, H. H. (1989). *Interdisciplinary curriculum: Design and implementation.* Alexandria, VA: Association of Supervision and Curriculum Development.

Jacobs, H. H. (1997). *Mapping the big picture: Integrating curriculum and assessment.* Alexandria, VA: Association of Supervision and Curriculum Development.

Jones, B. F., Rasmussen, C. M., & Moffitt, M. C. (1997). *Real life problem solving: A collaborative approach to interdisciplinary learning.* Washington, DC: American Psychological Association.

Kahne, J. (1995). Revisiting the eight-year study and rethinking the focus of educational policy analysis. *Educational Policy, 9*(1), 4-23.

Kaufman, D. M., & Mann, K. V. (1996). Comparing student attitudes in a problem-based curriculum. *Academic Medicine, 71*(10), 1096-1099.

Klein, J. T. (1990). *Interdisciplinarity: History, theory and practice.* Detroit, MI: Wayne State University.

Kohn, A. (1993). Choices for children: Why and how to let students decide. *Phi Delta Kappan, 75*(1), 8-19.

Kolb, D. A. (1984). *Experiential learning.* Englewood Cliffs, NJ: Prentice Hall.

Kovalic, S. (1994). *ITI: The model—Integrated thematic instruction* (3rd ed.). Kent, WA: Books for Educators.

Lambert, L., Walker, D., Zimmerman, D., Cooper, J., Lambert, M. D., Gardner, M. E., & Ford-Slack, P. J. (1995). *The constructivist leader.* New York: Teachers College Press.

Latham, A. (1997). Quantifying MI's gains. *Educational Leadership, 55*(1), 84-85.

Lauritzen, C., & Jaeger, M. (1997). *Integrating learning through story: The narrative curriculum.* Albany, NY: Delmar.

Lazear, D. (1991). *Seven ways of knowing: Teaching for the multiple intelligences.* Palatine, IL: Skylight.

Lazear, D. (1994). *Multiple intelligence approaches to assessment.* Tucson, AZ: Zephyr.

Lester, N. (1992). All reforms are not created equal: Cooperative learning is not negotiating the curriculum. In G. Boomer, N. Lester, C. Onore, & J. Cook (Eds.), *Negotiating the curriculum* (pp. 198-215). London: Falmer.

Levin, B., & Riffel, J. A. (1997). *Schools and the changing world: Struggling toward the future.* London: Falmer.

Levin, T., Nevo, Y., & Luttzatti, S. (1996, July). *Exposing teachers to the transdisciplinary curriculum: A channel for facilitating curricular thinking.* Paper presented at the second International Conference on Teacher Education, Tel Aviv, Israel.

Macrorie, K. (1988) *The I-search paper.* Portsmouth, NH: Heinemann.

Marks-Tarlow, T. (1996). *Creativity inside and out: Learning through the multiple intelligences.* New York: Addison-Wesley.

Martin, L. (1994, February). Computers and process writing in an integrated curriculum. *The Computing Teacher*, 36-37.

Martin-Kniep, G. O., Fiege, D. M., & Soodak, L. C. (1995). Curriculum integration: An expanded idea of an abused idea. *Journal of Curriculum and Supervision, 10*(3), 227-249.

Marzano, R. J., Pickering, D., & McTighe, J. (1993) *Assessing student outcomes*. Alexandria, VA: Association for Supervision and Curriculum Development.

McCarthy, B. (1997). A tale of four learners: 4MAT's learning styles. *Educational Leadership, 54*(6), 46-51.

Meagher, M. (1995). Learning English on the Internet. *Educational Leadership, 53*(2), 88-90.

Means, B., & Knapp, M. S. (1997). Cognitive approaches to teaching advanced skills to educationally disadvantaged students. *Phi Delta Kappan, 73*(4), 282-289.

Miller, J. P., Cassie, B., & Drake, S. M. (1990). *Holistic learning: A teacher's guide to integrated studies*. Toronto, ON: OISE.

Miller, J. P., Drake, S. M., Molinaro, V. , & Harris, B. (1997). *Negotiating new model of education in changing times* (Final SSSHRC report). St. Catharines, ON: OISE Center.

Noto, R. E. (1972). *A comparison between traditional teaching and interdisciplinary team teaching at the seventh grade level*. Unpublished doctoral dissertation, St. Louis University.

Numbers, P. (1996). Old Crow or bust: An exterior and interior journey. *Orbit, 27*(1), 33-35.

Oakland Public Schools. (1964). *Report of evaluation of special instructional programs at Madison Junior High School for years 1962-63 and 1963-64*. Oakland, CA: Author.

Oddeleifson, E. (1989). *Music education as a gateway to improved academic performance in reading, math and science*. Hingham, MA: South Shore Conservatory.

O'Neill, J. (1996). On surfing and steering the Net: A conversation with Crawford Killian. *Educational Leadership, 54*(3), 14-17.

Ontario Ministry of Education and Training. (1995). *The Common Curriculum*. Toronto: Author

Ornstein, A., & Hunkins, F. (1998). *Curriculum: Foundations, principles, and issues* (3rd ed.). Toronto, ON: Allyn & Bacon.

Ozar, L. (1994). *Creating a curriculum that works: A guide to outcomes-centered curriculum decision-making*. Washington, DC: National Catholic Educational Association.

Panaritis, P. (1995). Beyond brainstorming: Planning a successful interdisciplinary curriculum. *Phi Delta Kappan, 76*(8), 623-628.

Perkins, D. (1989). Selecting fertile theses for integrated learning. In H. H. Jacobs (Ed.), *Interdisciplinary curriculum: Design and implementation* (pp. 67-76). Alexandria, VA: Association for Supervision and Curriculum Development.

Perkins, D. (1991). Educating for insight. *Education Leadership, 49*(2), 4-8.

Petrie, H. G. (1992). Interdisciplinary education: Are we faced with insurmountable opportunities? *Review of Research in Education, 18,* 299-333.

Pirie, D., & Opuni, K. (1992). *Students through arts reaching success: Personal interviews with participating teachers.* Houston, TX: University of Houston.

Pring, R. (1973). Curriculum integration. In R. S. Peters (Ed.), *The philosophy of change* (pp. 123-149). London: Oxford University Press.

Rasmussen, K. (1997, summer). Using real-life problems to make real-world connections. *Curriculum Update,* 4-5.

Ravitch, D. (1995). *National standards in American education.* Washington, DC: Brookings Institute Press.

Reid, A. (1996). Negotiating curriculum with young adolescents. *Orbit, 27*(1), 7-9.

Reid, C., & Romanoff, B. (1997). Using multiple intelligence theory to identify gifted children. *Educational Leadership, 55*(1), 71-74.

Richards, B. F., Ober, K. P., Cariaga-Lo, L., Camp, M. G., Philip, J., Macfarlane, M., Rupp, R., & Zaccaro, D. J. (1996). Ratings of student performances in third-year internal medicine clerkship: A comparison between problem-based and lecture-based curricula. *Academic Medicine, 71*(6), 658-663.

Ross, J., & Hogaboam-Gray, A. (in press). Integrating mathematics, science and technology: Effects on students. *International Journal of Science Education.*

Roth, K. (1994, spring). Second thoughts about interdisciplinary education. *American Educator,* 44-48.

Roulet, G. (1996). Subject integration and mathematics teachers' practical knowledge. *Teachers and teaching: Theory and practice, 2*(1), 87-103.

Royal Conservatory of Music. (1994). *Community arts & education partnership: Towards a comprehensive arts and education program for metropolitan Toronto through community partnerships: Assessment and recommendations.* Toronto: Author.

Sadowski, M. (1995). Moving beyond traditional subjects requires teachers to abandon their "comfort zones." *The Harvard Education Letter, 11*(2), 1-6.

Sagor, R. (1992). *How to conduct collaborative action research.* Alexandria, VA: Association for Supervision and Curriculum Development.

Samara, J., & Curry, J. (Eds.). (1992). *Writing units that challenge: A guidebook for and by educators.* Portland, ME: Maine Educators of the Gifted and Talented.

Schmidt, H. G., Machiels-Bongaerts, M., Hermans, H., ten Cate, T. J., Vanekamp, R., & Boshuizen, H. P. A. (1996). The development of diagnostic competence: Comparison of a problem based, an integrated, and a conventional medical curriculum. *Academic Medicine, 71*(6), 658-663.

Scroth, G., Dunbar, B., Vaughan J., & Seaborg M. B. (1994). Do you really know what you are getting into with interdisciplinary instruction? *Middle School Journal, 25*(4), 32-34.

Seixas, P. (1994). A discipline adrift in an "integrated" curriculum: History in British Columbia schools. *Canadian Journal of Education, 19*(1), 99-107.

Sergiovanni, T. (1992). *Moral leadership.* San Francisco: Jossey-Bass.

The SILC School Improvement Planning Process. (1997). Denver: University of Colorado at Denver.

Sherlock, P. M. (1954). *Anansi the spider man: Jamaican folk tales.* New York: Crowell.

Silver, H., Strong, R., & Perini, M. (1997). Integrating learning styles and multiple intelligences. *Educational Leadership, 55*(1), 22-27.

Siskin, L., & Little, J. (1995). Introduction. In L. Siskin & J. Little (Eds.), *The subjects in question* (pp. 1-22). New York: Teachers College Press.

Smith, J. L., & Johnson, H. (1993). Bringing it together: Literature in an integrative unit. *Middle School Journal, 25*(1), 3-7.

Smith, K. (1993). Becoming the "guide on the side." *Educational Leadership, 51*(2), 35-37.

Sparks, D. (1998). Improving student learning requires deep change. *Results, 2,* 6.

Sternberg, R. J. (1996). IQ counts but really counts is successful intelligence. *NASSP Bulletin, 8*(583), 18-23.

Sternberg, R. J. (1997). What does it mean to be smart? *Educational Leadership, 54*(6), 20-24.

Sterns, H. N. (1969). *Student adjustment and achievement in a team teaching organization.* Unpublished doctoral dissertation, University of Michigan.

Sturch, J. (1996). The arts quest: Integrating drama, music and visual arts. *Orbit, 27*(1), 36-37.

Summary report of the Integrated Science Student Impact Study. (1997). Birmingham: University of Alabama Center for Communication and Educational Technology.

Suuttamm, C. (1996). Enhancing the richness of mathematics: Creating links with other disciplines. *Orbit, 27*(1), 47-48.

Sylwester, R. (1995). *A celebration of neurons: An educator's guide to the human brain.* Alexandria, VA: Association for Supervision and Curriculum Development.

Taylor, R. (1996, January). *Analyzing human activities.* Presentation at the fourth annual Conference on Curriculum Integration, Scottsdale, AZ.

The Ontario Curriculum, Grades 1-8, Mathematics. (1997). Toronto: Ministry of Education and Training.

The Ontario Curriculum, Grades 1-8, Language. (1997). Toronto: Ministry of Education and Training.

Thurston, K. (1996). Muskoka's initiative in integrated programming. *Orbit, 27*(1), 18-20.

Tobin, B. W. (1997). Nutrition in the basic medical sciences curriculum: An introduction to generalist physician training through problem-based learning. *Nutrition Today, 32*(2), 54-62.

Tomlinson, C. (1995). *How to differentiate instruction in a mixed ability classroom.* Alexandria, VA: Association for Supervision and Curriculum Development.

Top ten: The U.S. Department of Education's "new American high schools." (1996, September). *Techniques,* 32-33.

Trjillo, L. (1981). *Enhancement of self-concept and academic achievement through ethnic dance.* Boulder: Colorado University Center for Multicultural Research and Service.

U.S. Department of Labor, The Secretary's Commission on Achieving Necessary Skills. (1991). *What work requires of school: A SCANS report for America 2000.* Washington, DC: Author.

Vaille, W. (1997). Multiple intelligence in multiple settings. *Educational Leadership, 55*(1), 65-69.

Vars, G. (1993). *Interdisciplinary teaching: Why and how.* Columbus, OH: National Middle School Association.

Vars, G. (1995). Effective interdisciplinary curriculum and instruction. In *Annual review of research for the middle and high school leaders.* Reston, VA: National Association of Secondary School Principals.

Vars, G. (1996, January). *Curriculum integration: An untested fad?* Presentation at the fourth annual National Conference on Curriculum Integration, Scottsdale, AZ.

Vars, G. (1997). New AIS directory shows growth in college interdisciplinary programs. *The Core Teacher, 47*(1), 3-4.

The Video Journal Curriculum. (Producer). (1997). *Planning integrated units: A concept-based approach.* Alexandria, VA: Association for Supervision and Curriculum Development.

Video Journal of Education. (Producer) (1993). *Integrating the curriculum.* Salt Lake City, UT: Author.

Warren, M. (1996). Integration through the eyes of a mathematician. *Orbit, 7*(1), 10-12.

Wheatley, M. (1992). *Leadership and the new science.* San Francisco: Berrett-Koehler.

Wiggins, G. (1989). Teaching to the authentic test. *Educational Leadership, 46*(7), 41-47.

Wiggins, G. (1993). *Assessing student performance: Exploring the purpose and limits of testing.* San Francisco: Jossey-Bass.

Wiggins, G. (1996-1997). Designing authentic assessment. *Educational Leadership, 54*(4), 18-25.

Wilford, V. J. (1993, November). Technology is not enough. *School Library Journal,* 32-35.

Williams, P., Williams, M., Guray, C., Bertram, A., Brenton, R., & McCormack, A. (1994). Perceived barriers to implementing a new integrated curriculum. *Curriculum Perspectives, 14*(1), 17-23.

Willis, S. (1995, March). Making integrated curriculum a reality. *Educational Update,* 4.

Wright, D. (1997). Integrated curriculum by Livengood. *Curriculum Report,* 1-2, 4-6.

Zimmerman, W. A. (1962). *Departmental and unified seventh grade programs in English and social studies: A study of changes in subject matter achievement and personal adjustment.* Unpublished doctoral dissertation, Syracuse University.

INDEX

✻ ✻ ✻

Accountability, 7
  assessment and, 3
ACT, 38
Action research, 195-197
Action research teams, 196
Advisory councils, 189
Aikin, W. M., 29
Alignment:
  definition, 152-153
  interest in, 152
Alteritz, J., 40
Alternative schools, 150
American Association for the
    Advancement of Science, 46
Anderson, J., 36
Appalachian Educational
    Laboratories, 41
Arhar, J. M., 33, 39
Armstrong, A., 106, 164
Armstrong, T., 164
Arts education, 36-37
Aschbacher, P. R., 34
Assessment, 172-173
  accountability and, 3
  alternative, 8, 27, 133, 145, 153
  choices, 173

constructivism, 153
  integrated curriculum model,
    147-148
  learning process, 173
  ongoing, 8
  performance-based, 172
  procedures, 186
  standards and 133-134
  traditional, 133
  See also specific types of assessment
    procedures
Association for Supervision and
    Curriculum Development, 172
Atkin, J. M., 5
Authentic assessment, 125
Authentic change, 194

"Back to basics," 2, 7
Ball, S. J., 183
Ballanca, J., 144
Barrera, M., 185
Basaraba, J., 179
Basics:
  importance of, 187
  new, 10, 187

Beane, J., xiv, 19, 23, 28, 39, 117, 118, 120, 123, 134, 185
Bebbington, J., xiii, 4, 22, 100
Beckles, J., 51
Begley, S., 14
Bellanca, J., 164
Bell curve, 6
Bertram, A., 27
Betts, F., 172
Bialo, E., 39
Binder, M., 164
Bjelke, J., 34
Black, P., 5
Bloom, B. S., xiii, xv, 69, 71, 76, 81, 137, 148, 156, 158, 162, 176, 185
Bloom's taxonomy, 176, 185
  Bloom's Wheel, 159
  cognitive learning categories, 156, 158
  critiqued by Dagget, 158
  curriculum integration strategies, 156, 158
  Jacobs' concepts/essential questions model, 71, 76
  standards-based curriculum model, interdisciplinary, 137
  Taylor's human connections model, 69
Boomer, G., xiv, 113
Boshuizen, H. P. A., 31
Bracey, G. W., 3
Brady, M., xiv, 22, 120, 123
Brain-based education, 164-169
  brain-mind learning principles, 165-166
  classroom application of learning principles, 166-167
  criticism of, 167
  curriculum wheel, 168
  free association webbing, 167
Brenton, R., 27
British Columbia Ministry of Education, 186
Bruer, J., 167
Budget cuts, 3
Budzinsky, F. K., 39
Bulli, P., 97

Burns, R., 18

Caine, G., xv, 15, 35, 165, 166, 167
Caine, R., xv, 15, 35, 165, 166, 167
California Achievement Test (CAT), 34
Camp, M. G., 31
Canadian Achievement Tests, 35
Carefoot, L., 188
Cariaga-Lo, L., 31
Carr, J. F., xii, 19, 50
Case, R., 19, 32, 184
Case's typology of integration:
  dimensions, 19
  forms, 19
  modes/types, 19
  purposes, 19
Casey, J., 38
CD-ROMs, 188
Center for Technology and Communication (CA), 96
Center for the Arts in the Basic Curriculum, 36
Change, nature of, 192-194
  chaos model, 192-193
  principals, 193-194
Chapman, C., 164
Chappell, R., 25, 143
Character standards, 131-133, 148
  assessment, 134
Checkley, K., 162, 164
Clark, B., 16, 38, 159
Classroom setup, 6
Coalition of Essential Schools, 150
Coghlan, M., 65
Cole, R., 39, 173
Collaborative culture, creating, 194-195
Collaborative learning, 8
Collaborative planning process, 116-120, 123
  application, 119-120
  brainstorming, 118
  core curriculum, 117
  key ideas, 117-119
  progressive education, 117

questions, 117
student skills needed, 118
themes, 118
Competencies, 20, 124. *See also*
Standards
Computers, 188
uses, 13
Conference Board of Canada, 12,
127
Conferencing, 140, 153, 173
Constructivism, 152, 153-154, 175
active learning, 153
aligning teaching with, 153
metacognition, 154
ongoing alternative assessment,
153
student choice, 153
teacher as facilitator, 153
teaching for understanding,
153-154
Content standards, 128-129, 148
assessment, 133
declarative knowledge, 129
multidisciplinary program, 148
procedural knowledge, 129
typical, 129-130
Cooper, D. H., 34
Cooper, J., 152
Core subjects, 180-181
versus arts, 180-181
Cotton, K., 34
Cross-disciplinary approaches, 8
Cross-disciplinary topics, 13
Curriculum building, 19
assessment, 8
content selection, 7
instructional strategies, 8
reporting, 8
standards, 8, 19
Curriculum integration, 1-2, 9, 24
importance of, 2-11
using MI, 164
variety of forms, 9
See also Integrated curriculum;
Curriculum integration
strategies

Curriculum integration strategies,
156-162
Bloom's taxonomy, 156, 158
Dagget's taxonomy, 158-159, 162
Curriculum planning, 182-183
horizontal integration, 183, 195
student involvement, 183
vertical integration, 183
volunteers, 183
Curriculum standards, 129
Curry, J. A., xv, 158, 160-162, 185

Dagget, W., 12, 28, 46, 158, 159,
162, 187
Dagget's taxonomy, 158-159, 162
application-based, 159
complex problem solving, 162
Darling-Hammond, L., 124
Davies, M. A., 40
Declarative knowledge:
content standards, 129
DECtalk, 35
Delors, J., 13
Desert Sky Middle School (AZ), 40
Dewey, J., 27
di Carlo, S., 150
Dietz, G., 26-27
Disadvantaged students, 17
Disciplines, integrity of, 185
Drake, S., 138
Drake, S. M., xiii, 4, 13, 19, 22, 25,
39, 40, 41, 42, 100, 136, 179
Dunbar, B., 32
Duncan, B., 13
Durnford, M., 51

Earl, L., 14, 19
Educational reform, 2-3
underlying philosophy, 152
Egan, K., 179
8-Year Study, 27, 28-30, 117
influence of, 29-30
major principles, 29
Electronic bulletin boards, 188
Elmore, R. F., 41

Elster, A., 37
E-mail, 188
Emotional intelligence, 16
Employability Skills Profile, 127
Erickson, H. L., xiii, 17, 18, 61, 76,
    79, 81, 83, 156, 185
Erickson's concepts/essential
    understandings model, 61,
    76-91
  activities, 86-91
  application, 83-91
  brainstorm, 83
  complex performances, 81
  concepts, 82
  content, 81-82
  content assessment, 82
  create web, 83
  develop culminating
      performance, , 85
  develop unit outcome, 85
  essential understandings, 82
  evaluation rubric, 88-90
  generalizations, 82
  identify universal concept, 83
  key ideas, 79-83
  list complex performances/key
      skills, 85
  process, 82-83
  select topic, 83
  topics, 82
  write guiding questions, 84-85
Ewy, C., 97
Expectations, 20, 124
  clear, 8
  See also Standards

Falk, B., 124
Fiege, D. M., 11, 32, 184
Finlay, B., 179
Fleece, R., 114
Flockhart, K., 72
Fogarty, R., xii, xv, 18, 61, 62, 63,
    64, 65, 71, 144, 164
Fogarty's theme approach, 61-67
  application of web model, 65-67
  assessment, 66

brainstorm for themes, 65-66, 67
curriculum continuum, 61
expand activities using web, 66
fertile themes, 65, 66
interdisciplinary models, 63
intrinsic models, 64
key ideas of webbed model, 61,
    65
manipulate theme to question, 66
multidisciplinary models, 62
select goals, 66
skills emphasized, 65
topics/concepts/issues, 66
Ford-Slack, P. J., 152
Fosnot, C., 14, 30
Foster, A., 72
Fullan, M., 182, 192, 193, 194
Fusion curriculum approach, 20,
    44-46
  application, 44-46
  artist educator, 44
  example, 44

Gagliardi, M., 51
Galt Collegiate Institute (ON), 96
Gamsky, N., 34
Gardner, H., 16, 162, 163, 164
Gardner, M. E., 152
Geoghegan, W., 40
George, P. S., 34
Georgiades, W., 34
Glasgow, N. A., 96
Goleman, D., 16
Graham, J., 65
Graves, D., 110
Gravesande, S., 51, 115-116
Greenhawk, J., 34
Grimmestad, B., 37
Guild, P., 169
Guray, C., 27

Halkett-Rischke, N., 16
Hancock, L., 15, 37
Harbreaves, A., 14, 19, 184, 194
Harris, B., 39, 40, 41, 42

Harris, D. E., xii, 19, 50
Hart, L., 164
Hemphill, B., 25, 138, 143
Hermans, H., 31
Heuwinkel, M., 153
Hoerr, T. R., 26, 34
Hogaboam-Gray, A., 37
Holloway, M., 194
Hopkins, S., 83
Horwood, B., 37
Hunkins, F., 153, 168
Hunt, D., 155
Hyde, S., 114
Hyerle, D., 170
Hynes, W., 187

Illinois Goal Assessment Program, 97
In-between stories, 7
Inclusive classrooms, 173, 175
  integrated curriculum, 173
  teaching strategies, 175
  See also Mainstreaming
Information processing, 131
Integrated curriculum, 23, 42
  academic gains, 33-36
  and other curriculum reforms, 11
  and purpose of school, 12-13
  Beane's definition, 19, 23
  Burns' definition of, 18
  Case's definition, 19
  continuum, 20-21
  Drake's definition, 19, 22
  Erickson's definition of, 18
  inclusive classroom, 173
  Jacob's definition, 19
  knowledge explosion and, 11
  nonacademic benefits, 39-40
  overcoming obstacles to achieving, 177-189, 197
  rationale for, 11-18
  reducing duplication, 11
  resistance to, 181-182
  structural barriers, 183-184
  student benefits, 17-18, 33-40
  teacher benefits, 18, 40-42

what is worth knowing, 13-14
workplace preparation, 12
See also Curriculum integration; Integrated studies; Interdisciplinary studies; Learning
Integrated science (IS) programs, 35-36, 46-47, 56, 212
  3-year overview, 48-49
Integrated studies
  background of, 27-28
  unsuccessful examples of, 32-33
  See also Curriculum integration; Integrated curriculum; Interdisciplinary studies
Interdisciplinary curriculum, 11, 18, 20, 21, 22, 91
  characteristics, 60
  Erickson's concepts/essential understandings model, 61, 76-91
  Fogarty's theme approach, 61-67
  gifted students, 38
  higher-level thinking, 17
  Jacobs' concepts/essential questions model, 61, 71-76
  Taylor's human connections model, 61, 68-70
  See also specific models; Interdisciplinary studies
Interdisciplinary programs. *See* Interdisciplinary curriculum; Interdisciplinary studies
Interdisciplinary studies, 27-28
  criteria, 32-33
  global interest, 27
  in Australia, 27
  in Canada, 28
  in Israel, 27-28, 41-42
  in United States, 28
  postsecondary destinations and, 30-32
  program quality, 184-185
  See also Integrated studies; Interdisciplinary curriculum
Interdisciplinary team teaching:

and middle school students,
34-36
International High (Queens, NYC),
25
Internet, 11, 188
Interviews, 27, 173
Iowa Test of Basic Skills, 34

Jacobs, H. H., xiii, 18, 19, 61, 62, 63,
64, 71, 72, 76, 80, 98, 158, 183,
185, 195
Jacobs' concepts/essential
questions model, 61, 71-76
application, 72-76
Bloom's taxonomy, 71, 76
brainstorming, 71, 74
data box, 71
guiding questions, 74
higher order thinking skills
(HOTS), 71
key ideas, 71-72
organizing center, 72
planning activities, 74, 76
Jaeger, M., xiii, 98, 99, 101, 171
Johnson, H., 39
Johnston, J. H., 33, 39
Jones, B. F., 94
Journals, 140, 145, 173

Kahne, J., 30
Kaufman, D. M., 31
Kennedy, F., 194
Klassen, H., 143
Klein, J. T., 185
Knapp, M. S., 16, 17
Kohn, A., 23
Kolb, D. A., 168
Kovalic, S., 164

Lacey, C., 183
Laksman, S., xiii, 4, 22, 100
Lambert, L., 152
Lambert, M. D., 152
Laser disks, 188

Latham, A., 26, 35
Lauritzen, C., xiii, 98, 99, 101, 171
Lazear, D., 164
Leader:
assigned, 191
emerging, 192
Leadership, moral, 192
Leadership, successful change and,
191-197
block scheduling, 191
collaborative school culture, 191
principals, 191
vice-principles, 191
Learning, 14-17
brain research, 14-16, 164-169
conceptions of intelligence, 16
physical exercise and, 15
principles, 155-156
products, 173, 174
relevant curriculum, 14
sequential skills, 16-17
understanding and, 17-18
See also Emotional intelligence;
Multiple intelligences (MI)
Learning principles, cognitive
psychology and, 17
Learning styles, 168-169
personality theory, 168
with MI, 168
Lester, N., 113
Levin, B., 192
Levin, T., 28, 42
Lifelong learning standards, 129, 148
interdisciplinary program, 148
Life skills, 8
teaching, 9
Little, J., 183
Los Angeles Unified School
District, Humanitas Program,
34
Luttzatti, S., 28, 42

Macfarlane, M., 31
Machiels-Bongaerts, M., 31
Mackie, P., xiii, 4, 22, 100
Macrorie, K., 69

Mainstreaming, 2, 173
Malone, T., 164
Mann, K. V., 31
Markle, G. C., 33, 39
Martin, J. H., 38
Martin, L., 39
Martin-Kniep, G. O., 11, 32, 184
Maryland School Performance
    Assessment Program, 34
Marzano, R. J., 129, 131, 170
Maynes, N., xiii, 4, 22, 100
McCarthey, S. J., 41
McCarthy, B., 168
McCormack, A., 27
McKelvey, R., 96
McTighe, J., 129, 131, 170
Meagher, M., 38
Means, B., 16, 17
Media literacy, 13
Merritton High School (St.
    Catherines, ON), 25
Metacognition, 154
Miles, M., 182
Miller, J. P., 39, 40, 41, 42
MI profile forms, 26
Moffitt, M. C., 94
Molinaro, V., 39, 40, 41, 42
Multidisciplinary curriculum
    approach, 18, 20-21
  application, 51-59
  key ideas, 51
  standards-based, 50-59, 58
  steps for one subject area, 50
  See also Multidisciplinary
    program
Multidisciplinary programs:
  arts unit example, 48-50
  fusion, 44-46
  integrating subdisciplines, 46-47
  main criteria, 43
  versus parallel disciplines, 47-50
Multimedia, 188
Multiple intelligences (MI), 26, 34,
    162-164, 175
  bodily-kinesthetic, 16, 163
  curriculum integration, 164
  existentialist, 163-169

integrating curricula using, 164
interpersonal, 17, 163
intrapersonal, 17, 163
learning styles and, 168
linguistic, 17, 163
mathematical-logical, 17, 163
musical, 17, 163
naturalist, 17, 163
New City School, 34
spatial, 17, 163
standards-based
    interdisciplinary curriculum
    model, 137
Taylor's human connections
    model, 69
Multiple intelligences wheel, 165
Music education, higher-order
    thinking and, 37

Narrative curriculum model, 97,
    98-100, 123
  application, 100, 101
  assumptions, 97-98
  key ideas, 98-99
  planning template, 101
National Association for Core
    Curriculum, 27
National Council of Teachers in
    Mathematics, 28
National Science Teachers
    Association, 46
Negotiating the curriculum
    approach, 22-23, 113-116, 123
  application, 114-116
  cooperative learning, 113
  intent, 113
  key ideas, 113-114
  values, 134
Nevo, Y., 28, 42
New American High School
    Conference, 28
New City School, 26
  MI and, 34
New story of education, 23
  assumptions, 8
  creating, 11

curriculum integration in, 11-18
modification, 9
practices, 8
reflection, 9
North York Board of Education, 44
Norviel, K., 95
Noto, R. E., 34
Numbers, P., 97

Oakland Public Schools, 34
Ober, K. P., 31
Observation, 173
Oddeleifson, E., 36
Oldaker, L. L., 34
Old story of education, 5-6, 10-11
assumptions, 6
challenging, 6
factory method, 23
practices, 6
O'Neill, J., 16
Online databases, 188
Ontario Ministry of Education and
Training, 70
Opportunity-to-learn standards,
129
Opuni, K., 37
Ornstein, A., 153, 168
Outcomes, 20, 124. *See also*
Standards

Panaritis, P., 184
Parallel disciplines:
versus multidisciplinary
disciplines, 47-50
Parent councils, 189
Peer assessment, 27, 140, 145, 173
guide, 142, 143
Pencil-and-paper measurements, 6
Performance assessment, 27, 173
Performance indicators/criteria,
importance of, 9
Performance standards, 129
Perini, M., 168
Perkins, D., 65, 153
Petersen, P. L., 41

Petty, J., 95
Philip, J., 31
Pickering, D., 129, 131, 170
Pirie, D., 37
Portfolios, 26, 27, 140, 153, 173
Port Townsend High School (WA),
26
Pring, R., 20
Problem-based learning (PBL), 31,
93-97, 123
application, 95-97
case studies, 31
history of, 93
key ideas, 94-95
learning tools, 31
problems with, 95
sample classroom situations,
95-97
scientific method, 93
self-learning, 31
skills learned, 93
student-centered, 21
students' role, 31
teachers as facilitators, 93
topic-oriented, 31
viability of , 31
See also Problem based learning
as co-development (PBL-CD)
model
Problem-based learning as
co-development (PBL-CD)
model, 94
elements, 95
thinking processes, 94
See also Problem-based learning
Procedural knowledge, content
standards and, 129
Progressive Education Association,
28
Progress reports, 26
Project method, 22
Public opinion/parents, 189

Questions:
criteria for meaningful, 140, 144
fat, 144

thin, 144

Radnor Middle School (PA), 38
Rasmussen, C. M., 94
Rasmussen, K., 95, 96
Ravitch, D., 128
Reculturing, 194
Reid, A., 119, 120
Reid, C., 38
Resource-based learning, 188
Resources, student, 187-188. *See
also specific types of educational
resources*
Resources for integrated
curriculum programs:
books, 199-207
journals, 208-209
newsletters, 211
programs, 212
videos, 210
Richards, B. F., 31
Riddell, C., 83
Riffel, J. A., 192
Riley, R. W., 28
Romanoff, B., 38
Ross, J., 37
Roth, K., 32
Roulet, G., 185
Rowan, S., 194
Royal Conservatory of Music
(Toronto), 36, 44
Learning through the Arts
program, 37, 44
Rubrics, 9, 27, 140, 145, 172, 173
for story model assessment, 111
Rupp, R., 31
Rust, H., 51
Ryan, J., 14, 19

Sadowski, M., 25, 28, 38
Sagor, R., 195
Samara, J., xv, 158, 160-162, 185
SAT, 36, 38
Scheduling, 178-180
changing, 178

Schmidt, H. G., 31
School, purpose of, 12-13
School library information center,
188
School media specialist, 188
School-to-work program, 28
lifelong learning standards, 129
School within a school, 180
Scoring guide. *See* Rubrics
Scroth, G., 32
Seaborg, M. B., 32
Secretary's Commission on
Achievement of Necessary
Skills (SCANS), 127
Seixas, P., 32
Self-assessment, 27, 140, 145, 173
Sequential skills, 186-187
Sergiovanni, T., 192
SILC School Improvement
Planning Process, 196
action research questions,
196-197
Silver, H., 168
Siskin, L., 183
Sivin, J., 39
Skills teaching, 9
Smith, J. L., 39
Smith, K., 114
Smith, S., 164
Soodak, L. C., 11, 32, 184
Southeastern Regional Vision for
Education (SERVE), 35
Sparks, D., 40
Special education teacher, 175
Speed, B., 106
Staats, J., 65
Standardized tests/testing, 6, 7, 26,
27, 173
and open teaching approach, 97
integrated approach and, 152
preparation time, 97
Standards, 20, 126-127
assessment, 124
catalyst for reform, 125-126
curriculum content, 124
defining, 128-143
general purpose, 124

generic, 10
problems, 128
reporting, 124, 152
teaching strategies, 124
understanding use of, 9
See also Character standards;
  Competencies; Content
  standards; Curriculum
  standards; Expectations;
  Lifelong learning standards;
  Opportunity-to-learn
  standards; Outcomes;
  Performance standards
Standards-based approach, 125, 127
  skills and curriculum, 134
  See also Standards-based
  curriculum model,
  interdisciplinary
Standards-based curriculum
  model, interdisciplinary, 149
  application, 138-143
  Bloom's taxonomy and, 137
  developing, 136
  key ideas, 136-138
  MI and, 137
  modifications, 138
  steps, 138-143
  story of developing, 143-147, 149
  webbing activities, 136-137, 139,
  141
Stanford Achievement Test, 36
Standards pyramid, 131-132
Status quo, maintaining, 6
Sternberg, R. J., 16
Sterns, H. N., 34
Stevens, D., 72
Stoehr, J., xv, 61, 62, 63, 64, 65, 164
"Storying," 4
Story model, 4-5, 22, 97, 100, 102,
  123
  action stage, 111
  application, 106-17
  assessment, 125
  assumptions, 97-98, 100
  brainstorming, 103
  cultural story, 5, 102
  evaluation strategies, 111-113

global story, 5, 102
key elements, 100
key ideas, 102-104
major objectives, 100, 104
new story, 110
old story, 109-110
personal story, 4-5, 102, 154-156
planned activities, 103
present story, 107-109
real-world web, 103-104, 107-
  108
rubric for assessment, 111
standards-based approach, 144
steps, 104-105
transdisciplinary approach, 4
understanding process of, 7-11
universal story, 5, 102
values, 134
Strong, R., 168
Student-centered approach, 7
Students:
  disadvantaged, 17
  gifted, 38
  middle school students, 34-36
  passive learners, 6
Sturch, J., 48, 138, 179
Subdisciplines, integrating, 46-47
  application, 46-47
"Success for all," 13
Sullivan, L. A., 65
Supradisciplinary approach,
  120-122, 123
  application, 122
  concepts, 122
  conceptual components, 120, 121
  example, 122
Suuttamm, C., 185
Swartz, E., 164
Sylwester, R., 15

Taba, H., 30
Taylor, R., xii, 61, 68, 70, 169
Taylor's human connections
  model, 68-70
  AHA planning chart, 70
  application, 69-70

Bloom's taxonomy, 69
books and arts, 69
character-ethics education, 69
cooperative learning, 69
creative problem solving, 69
creativity, 68
focus, 68
analyzing human activities
    (AHA), 68
higher-order thinking skills
    (HOTS), 68, 69
inclusion, 69
I-search research, 69
key ideas, 68-69
mastery learning, 69
MI, 69
morality, 68
portfolio-authentic assessment,
    69
rich curriculum, 68
synectics, 69
universal theme, 68
Teacher librarian, 188
Teachers:
as change agents, 189-190
as leaders-learners, 41-42
attitudes, 32
changing roles, 2-3, 41
collaboration, 41
computer skills, 188
facilitators, 8
feeling undervalued, 3
lecturers, 8
personal stories, 9
professional development, 42
sharing stories with each other,
    190
working collaboratively, 18
Teaching:
brain research concepts and,
    15-16, 164-169
to the test, 26, 97
See also Teachers; Teaching
    strategies
Teaching strategies, 169-172
body-mind connection, 172
disciplinary heuristics, 171

graphic organizers, 170
inclusive classrooms, 175
intuitive thinking, 171
metaphor, 171
reflection, 172
storytelling, 169-170
student questioner/researcher,
    170
Technological literacy, 13
ten Cate, T. J., 31
Tests, teacher-created, 173
Textbooks, 187
Thematic units, 33
Thurston, K., 180
Time:
cutting, 177-178
for delivering curriculum, 177
for planning curriculum, 177
Tobin, B. W., 31
Tomlinson, C., 175
Traditional curriculum approach,
    20
Transdisciplinary curriculum
    approaches, 21, 123
characteristics, 92-93
examples, 21-23
See also Collaborative planning
    process; Narrative curriculum;
    Negotiating the curriculum;
    Problem-based learning; Story
    model; Supradisciplinary
    approach
Trjillo, L., 37
Tyler, R., 30

U.S. Department of Labor, 12, 127
UNESCO, 13
Universities:
admissions requirements, 28
Brock University, 31
Colorado College, 30
David and Mary Thomson
    Collegiate Institute, 194
funding cuts, 31
interdisciplinary medical
    education, 31

interdisciplinary studies, 30-32
McMaster University Medical
   School, 93
University of Alabama, 35, 46
University of Guelph, 30
University of Texas at Arlington,
   30

Vaille, W., 27, 38
Values, teaching, 132
   assessment, 134
   curriculum planning, 132-133
Vanekamp, R., 31
Vars, G., 30, 33, 42, 94
Vaughan, J., 32
Video, 173
Video Journal Curriculum, 79
Video Journal Education, 71
Village School (VS) of Great Neck
   (NY), 150
Virgilio, J., 72

Walker, D., 152

Warren, M., 35, 185
Waterloo Board of Education (ON),
   132
Wayne, L., xiii, 4, 22, 100
Wheatley, M., 193
Wiggins, G., 125, 128
Wilford, V. J., 188
Williams, M., 27
Williams, P., 27
Willis, S., 193
Within one subject curriculum
   approach, 20
Work-related skills, 8, 12
   teaching, 9
Wright, D., 37
Writing to Read (WTR) program,
   38-39

Year 2000 document, 186

Zaccaro, D. J., 31
Zimmerman, D., 152
Zimmerman, W. A., 34